THE REASON
LINCOLN
HAD TO DIE

D1598714

Don Thomas

PUMPHOUSE PUBLISHERS
CHESTERFIELD, VIRGINIA

Dedication

This book is dedicated to the framers
of the United States Constitution.

This investigation into Abraham Lincoln's assassination is an
effort to defend the supreme law of the first modern democratic
republic against its domestic enemies.

PUMPHOUSE PUBLISHERS
Chesterfield, Virginia, United States

WWW.REASONLINCOLN.COM
Visit the web site above for the latest information about this and
upcoming books by Don Thomas and Pumphouse Publishers,
along with related articles and links.

SECOND ENGLISH EDITION

Nonfiction
1. American History   2. Unsolved Crimes
3. Assassinations   4. Abraham Lincoln

ISBN: 978-0-9894225-2-9

Large Print and e-Book Editions also available.

TABLE OF CONTENTS

INTRODUCTION 1

1 THE CONDEMNED 7
    The Mysterious Samuel Thomas 14
    The Executions 14

2 TWO CONSPIRACIES 17
    January, 1865 18
    Booth's Plot to Kidnap President Lincoln 19
    Nowhere to Go 20
    MOTIVE: Negotiating Peace 22
    ABILITY: Lincoln's Rivals 23
    The European Assassination Plot against Seward 27
    Who Did Booth Work For? 27

3 CAUSE FOR ALARM 29
    Inform the President! 33

4 DESPERATION 35
    The Celebration 36
    The Despondent Victor 37
    Lincoln's Last Chance 39
    Stanton Undermines Lincon's Vulnerable Peace 41

5 LAST CHANCE 45

6 AGENTS & SECRETS 50

7 A BAND OF IDIOTS 59

8 WEAPON & MOTIVE 70
    Tracing the Weapon 73
    Establishing Motive 74

9 REASSURANCE 76

10 "I SAW JOHN WILKES BOOTH!" 80

11 THE CHAMBER MAID 87

12 OBSTRUCTION OF JUSTICE 92

13 LIE OR DIE! 98
    Get Weichmann! 99
    Arresting Mary 101
    Arresting Arnold & O'Laughlen 103
    Arresting Atzerodt 104
    Fabrications 107

14 FOLLOWING THE SCRIPT 112

15 ONE MAN 121
    The Diary 124

16 MEANS OF ESCAPE 130

17 THE STACKED DECK 135
    Stanton's Man Baker 136
    Stanton the Puppetmaster 140
    Stanton's Man Holt 142

18 TESTIMONY VS. EVIDENCE 144

19 "HOW IMPOTENT IS JUSTICE!" 152

EPILOGUE 159
    Mary & Robert Lincoln 159
    The Killing of Mary Surratt 160
    Jefferson Davis 160
    The Demise of Lafayette Baker 163
    Gone Missing: Sarah Antoinette Slater 163
    What Happened to George Emerson? 164

BIBLIOGRAPHY 167

AUTHOR'S NOTES 175

APPENDIX A: BOOTH'S 1864 MANIFESTO 208

APPENDIX B: BOOTH'S DIARY 213

APPENDIX C: ATZERODT'S CONFESSION 216

APPENDIX D: ARNOLD'S CONFESSION 221

APPENDIX E: THE RADICALS IN MISSOURI 226

INDEX 230

ACKNOWLEDGMENTS

I never would have lived long enough to finish this book without the help from a very special few.

I want to take this opportunity to thank my favorite uncle and aunt who answered my plea for help. Looking beyond my inadequacies they listened to my ravings with unswerving belief that I would one day write this story. My agony in writing this book was much relieved by their help, support and faith.

I owe a special tribute to my dear friend, John Kerr, who shares with me a passion for history, and who was able to help me turn my thoughts into words. Using the patience that only an experienced educator has, he painstakingly transformed my feeble first ten attempts at writing a manuscript into a comprehendible text. I attribute a good portion of my documentation to John's uncompromising standards for accuracy. Being a gifted teacher, he never tried to tell me what I should write, only how it should be written.

John graduated from the State University of New York College at Fredonia and completed his studies at the University of Buffalo, New York. After 34 years of teaching history in the Buffalo area, John retired to Powhatan, Virginia, and lived behind my parents' home, where we first met. John helped me look after my father during a difficult transition in my dad's life, and for that alone I will be forever grateful. Mr. Kerr was the president of the Powhatan County Historical Society, and he has written a book about Powhatan County history. He currently lives in Glen Allen, Virginia, with his wife Laura, also a professional educator.

I wish to express my gratitude to the illustrator, Mary Firestone Foore. Even though thousands of books have been written about Abraham Lincoln and his assassination, many with illustrations of scenarios and key characters, there are a few crucial facts and faces that have never in history been made visual. Thanks to Mrs. Foore's efforts, this book offers the opportunity to behold for the very first time the attire John Wilkes Booth wore when he murdered the President (which helps to reveal how the assassination was possible). For the earliest edition of this book she also provided an artist's sketch of the man who persuaded Booth to commit the crime, composed from the descriptions of two of the assassin's associates (since then a photograph of the man has been discovered). Mrs. Foore was also most helpful in aiding our efforts with final edits and test readers.

The quality and high standards of this publication are the direct result of Ian Wesley's experience as an editor and designer. He has worked in book and periodical publishing since the 1980s, and currently lives near my home in Chesterfield County, Virginia. Not only has Ian joined with me as an agent and promoter for this book, but he also shares my commitment to working to advance a new era of realization. The partnership we have forged over the past year to expose this story comes from an equal determination to replace myths and fables with accurate and logical interpretations of recorded history. We both share a deep belief that this book must be published regardless of personal sacrifice. Ian's contribution has made this story coherent to anyone who has the objectivity to compare this critical history to the fabricated propaganda that has been promoted by our predecessors. His organizational, editing and design skills transformed my volumes of research into a streamlined and logical narrative, and an attractive publication as well.

Despite our different backgrounds and personalities, Ian Wesley has become a close friend whom I sincerely appreciate. He has unselfishly sacrificed his time to this project and dedicated himself to helping me produce the high quality book I had so long hoped to see.

THE REASON
LINCOLN
HAD TO DIE

Introduction

After spending over four years researching the conspiracy behind Abraham Lincoln's assassination, I not only found out the true motive for his death, I also discovered why the men who plotted his murder had remained an unsolved mystery.

When Lincoln was shot he was sitting in a theater in the heart of Washington, D.C., surrounded by 1,600 people, many of whom were military and police officers, yet the assassin was still able to escape. Today, everyone is in agreement that John Wilkes Booth shot Lincoln, but, unlike Lee Harvey Oswald (the assassin of John F. Kennedy), Booth was never suspected as being a lone gunman, and he was definitely part of a conspiracy. Mainstream history claims that the identities of the actual masterminds behind John Wilkes Booth can never be known. But I not only found out who these conspirators were, I learned how and why they persuaded Booth to kill Lincoln.

Many history writers still imply that John Wilkes Booth was a Confederate agent assigned by Jefferson Davis to assassinate Lincoln. However, early in my research I discovered that Jefferson Davis was proven to have played no role in the assassination. I naturally wondered (as anyone researching this story would) why anyone with that knowledge would want to leave the false impression that Booth was working as a Confederate agent.

My documented evidence will prove that John Wilkes Booth was persuaded by the United States Secretary of War, Edwin Stanton, and not by anyone from the former Confederacy, to assassinate President Abraham Lincoln. Using a double agent, Secretary Stanton employed Booth and his associate, Lewis Powell, to kill both Lincoln and Secretary of State William Seward. James Donaldson was Stanton's double agent who had previously infiltrated Booth's conspiracy to kidnap the President, and there is a paper trail linking him to both Booth and Stanton. And for me, the biggest mystery about the entire conspiracy was: "why has James Donaldson remained in complete obscurity throughout all of mainstream history?"

Sometime during the day of the assassination, Booth was assured that he would be provided unrestricted access to Lincoln, and it was also guaranteed that he would be allowed to escape from Washington. Only conspirators within the Federal government could have arranged such a guarantee. Booth believed that after he killed Lincoln, the President's political rivals would then be free to assume power. He was convinced that he would be brought back to Washington as a hero. Booth had always held Lincoln responsible for all the atrocities committed during the Civil War, and he was led to believe that Donaldson was an agent working for the Peace Democrats. This was a movement within the Democratic Party called "Copperheads," which had always opposed the President, and had been calling for an armistice to stop the fighting throughout Lincoln's first term.

By April, 1865, the Civil War had ended, but even after the war had been won, Lincoln was still in a years-long battle against a different group of political rivals over an issue as great as the war itself—the reunification of the states. These rivals were not the Democratic Copperheads, but a coalition within his own party. The faction most opposed to Lincoln's second term plan for bringing the Southern states back into the Union was a coalition referred to as "the Radicals," even by members of their own party. The politically moderate remainder of the party, who supported Lincoln, was called "conservatives." The fact we know today (but Booth never understood) is that if Lincoln had not been assassinated, his second term agenda would have been even more lenient for the Southern states than that of the disastrous administration of his successor, the Southern Democrat Andrew Johnson.

The Radicals' impeachment attack on President Johnson shared the same motive as their attacks on Lincoln and Seward. These same Radicals who plotted Lincoln's death turned their attack on Johnson to prevent him from implementing the same amnesty plans for the Southern states that Lincoln would have carried out, had he not been killed.

The true purpose for killing Lincoln was to prevent his reconstruction policy for a post-Civil War America, which would have diminished the Congressional power of the Radicals. Lincoln's assassination was plotted because of an argument over America's future, and not because of the phony alibi about revenge for America's past. On the day Lincoln was killed, April 14, 1865, the dispute between the states that resulted in a civil war had been finalized, but the remaining dispute about the fate of the Southern states (specifically their political and economic resources) was only between Lincoln and his rivals.

The Radicals were elected to protect the economic and political powers in the industrial sector of the Northeastern states. This coalition of political rivals against the President also included many vengeful Union generals who wanted the United States government to hang the surviving Confederate leaders, not grant them amnesty. Furthermore, many wealthy Northeastern industrialists realized they would lose their congressional majority if the Southern state representatives returned to Congress. The assassination was certainly not the end result of a dispute between Lincoln and the desperate leftovers from an extinguished Confederacy. The defeated Confederate leaders were counting on Lincoln's protection from the Radical Congressmen who were campaigning to have them all executed.

It was Lincoln's plan to grant amnesty and restore political equity to the South. Several key industrialists would have preferred to render the Confederate states subjugated territories without Congressional authority, and without a say in the course of the expanding nation. Lincoln had been under a four-year political attack by this large coalition within his own party, and when the war ended their time was running out to prevail over the President. The coalition's political purpose was to take away the President's Executive powers. These Radicals were led by Supreme Court Justice Salmon Chase, Congressmen Charles Sumner and Thaddeus Stevens, and Secretary of War Edwin Stanton.

During the war, Stanton had used the military's presence in key states to intimidate voters and influence elections for Congressional Radicals.[1] He and the Radicals were working to build a House majority to see that Lincoln's re-unification plan would never be implemented. After the war suddenly ended, Stanton not only needed to remove Lincoln from office fast, he also had to conceal his crime by framing the assassination on Confederate agents and Southern sympathizers. Stanton's War Department spies had a ready-made list of zealot sympathizers in the capital city. John Wilkes Booth, who had previously plotted to kidnap Lincoln, would be the perfect executioner. Stanton could conceal his own involvement by sending to Booth his double agent James Donaldson, posing as a Southern Copperhead.

The idealistic Booth did not understand the political infighting within Lincoln's administration, and he was led to believe that a new Democrat administration under Johnson would welcome him back a hero after they assumed control from Lincoln. That explains why Booth made no arrangements to escape the country, nor bothered to find some safe sanctuary, or even pack a bag with clothes and ample money. Neither Booth nor any of his convicted accomplices had any getaway plans for after the assassination. Booth was then tracked down by a select military detachment, organized by Stanton's chief investigator, to assassinate him (far from Washington) so that his true accomplices would never be revealed.

The Radicals responsible for Lincoln's murder had emerged victorious from the chaos of a government at war with itself, and after the President was gone they gained complete control over the investigation of his murder and the conspiracy trial that followed. Today those men are portrayed as American icons, and the public has grown very complacent with the allegation that secessionists were responsible for Lincoln's death, even though it was discovered two years later by a Congressional committee that they were not.[2]

If the Confederate government was not responsible for plotting the successful killing of Lincoln, then the only other plausible suspects would have to be from a conspiracy within the United States government. Censorship and control over mainstream history has become the only way to conceal this shameful realization.

To prove my point that this history has been tampered with, I challenge the notion that everything there is to be told about the assassination has already been broadcasted or written. After years of researching this subject, I found there are many *discernible* people and events missing from this history, and to understand the reason they have been omitted became my resolve. It is my conviction that our histories are not completely free from censorship, and continue to be sanitized.

To give just one example of this incomplete story, I used common logic to question how the most popular assassination theories assume that John Wilkes Booth preplanned to kill both Lincoln and General Grant in a crowded theater in the heart of Washington, D.C., using only a muzzle-loading, single shot Derringer, good only at very close range. After his first shot, what did Booth think would happen while he rammed more powder and another ball down the muzzle of his little gun? Did he expect General Grant (had he been there) to just sit patiently, waiting to be shot in the back of the head as well? And how did Booth plan to escape the theater, not to mention the Capital city, full of police and soldiers, with only a knife as a defensive weapon? If he did preplan an escape, never to be caught, why did he not make prior arrangements to leave the country? Booth ran from Washington with little money and neither a change of clothes nor even a hat on his head. The only arrangements he made on the morning prior to his attack on the President was, allegedly, to send some field glasses to Surrattsville Tavern to be picked up on his run to nowhere. I realized there had to be something more to this story, but it must have been (for some deceitful reason) left out.

The popular historical accounts about John Wilkes Booth and the assassination plot are nothing more than poorly constructed conspiracy theories. Despite evidence that tells a different story, so many facts are left out of this history, and so many events that could not have happened are presented as truth, and done so in scores of widely marketed movies, books and documentaries.

In the most popular version of Lincoln's assassination, the public is asked to believe that some unknown Confederate agents were the ones who plotted the assassination with John Wilkes Booth. In that same breath it is also said that during the Civil War, the use of spies and counterespionage was so undeveloped that the Secretary of War, Edwin Stanton, was completely unaware of a possible threat to Lincoln's life. This impression is suggested without regard or respect for the abundance of published books that detail the extensive spying and espionage that took place during the entire Civil War.

The Confederate capital city, as well as Washington, D.C., was full of spies and double agents. There are hordes of books and documents exposing the elaborate undercover war that was being waged throughout every state in both the North and South, including also Canada and Europe. One of the most noted spies during the Civil War was Elizabeth Van Lew, who reported straight from the Confederate White House to the War Department in Washington. She was even given assistance from several servants employed in the home of Jefferson Davis. Timothy Webster, F. W. E. Lohmann, John C. Babcock, Virginia B. Lomax, Pryce Lewis and John Scully are just a few well-known Union spies who reported to Washington from in or around Richmond. However, you will not read about those spies in this book. My purpose is not to repeat proven facts, but to reveal the spies that have been curiously edited from history.

This book presents a verifiable and obvious motive to kill Lincoln, told with painstaking notes and credits. More than just the 19 chapters, it is the Author's Notes section that exposes the in-depth story that cannot be falsified or altered. What the readers can learn from information in this book is only limited by their curiosity. The Notes and Appendices are a road map to as much of this history as one is interested and willing to discover.

I am a history purist, and I have put this book together without political affiliation or one-sided, biased opinion about the subject, and defend only the Constitution.

Abraham Lincoln has been given saintly status in American ideology. We have carved his likeness on a mountaintop, and erected a colossal Greek temple in our national capital in his honor. Isn't it time we showed him the respect he truly deserves by holding the true conspirators behind his murder accountable for their crimes against him?

Due to the immense volume of events and characters surrounding Lincoln's assassination, it is impossible to tell the complete story in a single book. The story told for the past century and a half omits key events and characters, claiming the conspiracy to kill Lincoln will always remain a mystery. The prevailing assassination theories are just that—*theories*—ignoring the fact that Lincoln was at odds with the most powerful men in his party over the fate of post-Civil War America. It is time to put speculation aside and finally examine the hidden evidence, the ignored players, and *The Reason Lincoln Had to Die.*

1

The Condemned

On June 29, 1865, eight prisoners were convicted of conspiracy to kill the President.

1 SAMUEL ARNOLD was the first accomplice to be recruited into Booth's kidnapping plot. However, Arnold had dropped out of the plan to kidnap the President a full two weeks before the assassination.[1, 2, 3] Despite that fact Samuel Arnold was sentenced to life in prison for his role in the conspiracy to kill the President.

2 MICHAEL O'LAUGHLEN was recruited as a kidnapping accomplice the same day as Samuel Arnold. O'Laughlen had known Booth all his life, worked with him on several business ventures, and helped to plot Lincoln's capture. However, during his conspiracy trial the prosecution made no distinction between Booth's telegrams dealing with business ventures, and his messages to Michael pertaining to kidnapping.[4] Michael O'Laughlen was also given life in prison despite the prosecution's disputed testimonies, and he died of yellow fever two years after he began serving his sentence.

3 DAVID HEROLD was captured along with Booth in the Virginia tobacco barn at Garrett's farm. He was also a member in Booth's gang, but he had no assigned role in the kidnapping plot because of his childish mind.[5, 6, 7, 8, 9] His father sent him to no less than four different schools to help mature him, but David never received a diploma, only a certificate for pharmacy employment. He eventually obtained work at a druggist's, but was never trusted with any sensitive tasks. Multiple people who knew him for most or all of his life testified that he had the mind of a child, that he was too immature to trust with any responsibility, and that he never held any political views. David could most often be found playing with children, and he was one of four conspirators sentenced to death by hanging.

4 **George Atzerodt** was a homeless German immigrant who spoke broken English with a thick accent. George was a wagon painter by trade, and his duty to Booth was to work with David Herold, taking care of the horses and doing menial jobs. George Atzerodt revealed the complete story about Booth and all his gang members in a recorded confession (*see* Appendix C), but it was never introduced as evidence during the conspiracy trial. Secretary of War Stanton intended for the confession to be destroyed forever. Atzerodt's confession was not found until 1977, and few historians, if any, have elucidated its relevance. The confession agrees with evidence and furthermore names and describes Stanton's agents who infiltrated Booth's gang. George Atzerodt was the third conspirator executed by hanging.

5 **Lewis Powell** was Booth's only accomplice in the conspiracy to assassinate President Lincoln and Secretary of State William Seward.[10] Powell was a true Confederate spy who worked with John Surratt, Jr., who was also a Confederate spy in Booth's gang. Both spies were couriers for the Confederate Signal Corps, delivering orders to the generals in the field from the Confederate high command. Powell had previously been a captured Confederate soldier, and transferred to a prison in Baltimore. He escaped and served over a year with John Mosby, the flamboyant Confederate cavalry commander. Lewis Powell left the Mosby Rangers and returned to Baltimore around January, 1865, and began relaying secret messages for the Confederate Secret Service. Both Powell and Surratt plotted with Booth to capture Lincoln, however Lewis Powell was only known in Washington by his alias, James Wood, or by his nickname "Mosby," the last name of his former commanding officer. Powell, at the age of twenty, was the only truly guilty person executed for assassination conspiracy.

6 **DR. SAMUEL MUDD** was convicted of aiding and abetting in the escape of John Wilkes Booth, and given a sentence of life in prison. The prosecution solicited damning testimony from his neighbor, Daniel Thomas, along with testimony from several of Dr. Mudd's former slaves.

Daniel Thomas was a prosecuting witness against Mudd. Thomas held a commission as a secret civilian detective, issued by Col. John C. Holland, the Provost Marshal for the fifth District of Maryland. Some of Washington's secret service detectives for the National Police Chief, Lafayette Baker, told Daniel Thomas that he was entitled to a reward if Dr. Mudd was convicted.[11] A great majority of Mudd's defense involved challenging the credibility of Daniel Thomas. Six of Thomas's neighbors and life-long associates testified that they considered him deceitful and untrustworthy, and declared they would not believe his account.[12]

Another prosecuting witness was William A. Evans, a minister who also held a secret commission as an independent detective, reporting to the War Department. He too gave damning testimony against Dr. Mudd, but his testimony was later disputed after cross-examination.[13]

The testimony by Dr. Mudd's former slaves, Milo Simms, Melvina Washington, Elzee Eglent, and Mary Simms, were all proven to be contrived and unreliable after the defense testimonies disputed their claims.[14, 15, 16, 17] Several other former slaves as well as neighbors in the community where Dr. Samuel Mudd lived challenged the testimonies against him.

At the time of the trial, former slaves in Maryland had not been freed by federal law, but by an amendment to the Maryland state constitution. Few today realize the Emancipation Proclamation applied only to slaves held in the *Confederate* localities, and did not apply to any slaves states loyal to the national government. The Proclamation specifically stated that rebel territories under Union occupation were exempt, which included the states of Virginia, Louisiana and later Tennessee. The Proclamation was an executive order, not a law, effectively abolishing slavery *only* in the Confederacy as of January 1, 1863. Before the Constitution was amended, slavery remained legal in the *Union* states where it had previously existed. Essentially the Emancipation Proclamation was an ultimatum, saying to the Confederate states, *if you want to keep slavery, you have to return to the Union within 100 days.*

Throughout the war there were no Confederate state representatives in the U.S. Congress. Nonetheless, even as the war had ended and Lincoln lay dead, Congress had not abolished slavery throughout the Union, and would not do so until ratifying the 13th Amendment on December 6, 1865—*eight months* after the war's end. Until that time slavery was *never* illegal by Federal law. The decision to make abolition national law was entirely up to Union Congressmen, and was never argued between the U.S. and Confederate governments. Before the 13th Amendment, states had the Constitutional right to choose or abolish the institution of slavery independent of the national authority.

A determined coalition within the United States government had for many years been pushing to abolish slavery in every state, but without majority support from Congress. More than a year before the war had ended, the Confederate states Arkansas and Louisiana abolished slavery within their state constitutions. In contrast, representatives of Union states New Jersey, Kentucky and Delaware had rejected the 13th Amendment when presented in early 1865. As Dr. Mudd stood trial, his state, Maryland, had only outlawed slavery months before (November 1, 1864, and the first Union state to do so), but slavery in the Union was still legal by Federal law.

Dr. Mudd's trial had nothing to do with conspiracy, but was actually exploiting his association with slavery. The military prosecution was attacking Dr. Mudd's character and reputation by portraying him as a disloyal citizen because he had (legally) owned slaves. The prosecution accused Dr. Mudd of disloyalty to the Union because some of his former slaves alleged that he once threatened to send a fellow slave (who still lived with Mudd) south to help build the Confederate defenses around Richmond.

Jeremiah Dyer was called as a defense witness to explain the situation that led to this accusation against Dr. Mudd. He too had been a slave owner whose slaves now lived without servitude to him, and he disputed the claim that Dr. Mudd was disloyal to the Union. Dyer testified:

> I then heard that some thirty or forty of the hands had left, and I went down to hire other hands to secure the crop. I heard that a man by the name of Turner ... was going to catch all the negroes in that neighborhood and send them away. I never heard Dr. Mudd say any thing about sending off his hands to Richmond.[18]

The prosecution was trying to portray all of Booth's accomplices as being Confederate agents, and they used the political issue of slavery as a means to identify Lincoln's assassins as disloyal Confederates. The prosecution failed to prove that Dr. Mudd was a disloyal citizen, while the defense showed that the prosecution's witness, the civilian informant Daniel Thomas, had previously been of questionable loyalty, and that he could not be trusted with telling the truth.

The prosecution then had to focus Dr. Mudd's trial on exactly how well he knew John Wilkes Booth, and why Booth was offering to buy his farm. But the evidence strongly suggested that Booth was looking to buy land in lower Maryland for its potential oil reserves. The nature of Dr. Mudd's acquaintance with John Wilkes Booth was established using the testimony from another civilian informant, Louis Weichmann, employed by Baker's National Police. Weichmann was reporting to the War Department about Booth and his associates, John Surratt and Lewis Powell, long before the assassination.

Dr. Mudd's conviction came after his unconvincing story about not recognizing John Wilkes Booth the night he set Booth's broken leg, contrasted with the presentation of the boot, stamped with Booth's name, which Dr. Mudd had to cut with a knife to remove. The boot was innocently found by his wife and voluntarily offered to the detectives. The overlooked logic is that if Booth had prearranged to use Dr. Mudd in his escape plan he would have also had to pre-plan his broken leg, because that was the only reason he stopped at Dr. Mudd's home on his run from Washington.

Dr. Mudd was sentenced to life in prison, but he was given a presidential pardon four years later for his humanitarian efforts to care for his fellow prisoners suffering from yellow fever.[19]

 *7* MARY SURRATT has long ago been proven to be not guilty of the crime she was charged with. The most shameful fact about Mary's trial is that the judges who sentenced her to death knowingly withheld the evidence that would prove she was not involved in the assassination. That evidence was deceitfully excluded from the trial, and the weak and flimsy case against her was questioned right up to the moment of her execution.

Her son, John Surratt, Jr., was Booth's closest kidnapping conspirator and a Confederate spy, but he escaped the country after the assassination. John Surratt knew nothing of the assassination until the day after Lincoln was shot. John was extradited back to stand trial in a United States civilian court, where he was found in 1867 to be uninvolved in the assassination. His mother, Mary Surratt, was not legally executed, but murdered in order to conceal the reason Lincoln had to die.

8 ED SPANGLER was given six years in prison for aiding and abetting the escape of John Wilkes Booth after the testimonies from several prosecution witnesses, such as Jacob "Jake" Ritterspaugh.

On May 30, 1865, during the conspiracy trial, Jake was called as a witness for the prosecution because he claimed to be the first person to chase behind John Wilkes Booth as he escaped across the stage and out the theater's back door.

Jake testified:

> I saw a man that had no hat on running toward the back door. I made for him, and he struck at me with the knife, and I jumped back, then. He then ran out and slammed the door shut. [...] I could not get it open. In a moment afterward I opened the door [...] the man was [riding] down the alley. [...] I came back on the stage where I had left Edward Spangler, and he hit me [...] and said, "Don't say which way he went." [...] I told it to nobody but [James] Gifford, the boss.[20]

Jake and Ed Spangler boarded together at the home of a Mrs. Scott, on the corner of 7th and G Streets in Washington. Spangler did not have a room, but only took his meals there. He slept at the theater while keeping only a bag of belongings, but no clothes, at the Scott house.

Spangler and Jake were both stagehands for Ford's Theater. John T. Ford, the theater's owner, testified that it was absolutely necessary that Spangler was present for every play, from moment the curtain rises until it falls. Jake's duties were to help shift the stage wings and fetch things from the cellar.

On June 2, Jake was recalled to the witness stand, and by then his story had somewhat changed. During cross examination he said that the next day after the assassination he also told Mr. James Lamb (the artist and scene-painter) about Spangler slapping him and saying, "Shut up, don't say which way he went." Jake also said he told another theater employee, Louis J. Carland, the same story. During the cross examination of James Lamb and Louis J. Carland, they both denied Jake ever told them that Spangler said, "Don't say which way he went." Both men agreed that Jake told them Spangler said, "Hush up, be quiet, what do you know about it?" and "You don't know who it is; it may be Mr. Booth, or it may be someone else."[21, 22]

A second prosecuting witness, Joseph B. Stewart also testified that he too followed after John Wilkes Booth as he was escaping the theater. He gave a similar testimony as Jake about Booth slamming the door shut, and after Stewart got the door opened he testified that he heard someone say, "He's getting on a horse." Then, Stewart claimed, "As soon as the words reached my ears I heard the trampling of a horse." Stewart went on to give a rambling account of his struggle to stop the man on the horse, overlooking the fact that he had just testified that Booth was already riding away after he finally got the door opened.

Anyone who could have possibly been connected with the assassination was arrested, except for Baker's secret informers and Secretary Stanton's double agents. Jake was held in custody at the Carroll Prison, and on the day of his release testified that one of Baker's detectives (whose name he did not know) came to his boarding house to talk with him about what had happened during Booth's escape. Jake described Baker's detective as a man weighing about 140 pounds, with a moustache and black whiskers.

Other witnesses who saw Booth escape said there was a man (assumed to be Ed Spangler) who aided Booth with opening and closing the stage door. However, the man they described also had dark whiskers and a mustache just like Baker's detective. Ed Spangler had red hair, and no one ever saw him with a mustache. Later that same evening a stranger weighing about 140 pounds with dark whiskers and a mustache checked into the Pennsylvania House, and spent the night in the same room with George Atzerodt, a member of Booth's kidnapping gang.

The Mysterious Samuel Thomas

John Greenawalt was the clerk at the Pennsylvania House where the black-whiskered stranger, Samuel Thomas, stayed on the night of the assassination with George Atzerodt. Greenawalt testified:

> I had an uneasiness about the thing myself; thought there was something wrong. ... This man Thomas, I noticed, kept a close eye on me as I came in. It was Thomas who asked for the room. Atzerodt asked for his old room [no. 51]; I told him [it] was occupied, and he would have to go with this man [to room 53]. The name he gave was Samuel Thomas. He got up about 5 o'clock [the morning after the assassination] and left the house. ... [He] was about five foot seven or eight inches high, and ... about 140 pounds, I should judge. Thomas had the appearance of a laboring man. ... I judge that his clothes were worn as a disguise. He was poorly dressed, in dark clothes. His hair, moustache and whiskers were black.[23]

Detectives were looking for the man whom witnesses described as having dark whiskers and a moustache, about 140 pounds, dressed in shabby clothing—the man who held the Theatre's back door for Booth. Samuel Thomas, who fit this description perfectly, was arrested and held, only to be released.[24] He wasn't even called to be a witness, even though he spent the night of the murder with one of the accused conspirators! In spite of the conflicting testimony and circumstantial evidence, Ed Spangler was still convicted by Stanton's hand-picked military judges during their closed-door deliberations.

The Executions

On July 7, 1865, four civilian prisoners were executed by the United States military under the supreme authority of Edwin Stanton, the Secretary of War. They were convicted of plotting to assassinate Lincoln, and their sentence was to hang by the neck until dead.

A few minutes after 1:30 PM that afternoon, the gallows floor dropped these four convicted criminals into midair. As the hot July sun beat down on the crowd, they celebrated the execution with lemonade and cake. Meanwhile

the four criminals remained hanging for a full 30 minutes to be certain of their deaths.

Hanging on the far right of the gallows, the homeless bum, George Atzerodt, heaved his stomach flat in a violent attempt to catch a breath. The cloth bindings tied around his hands, arms and legs prevented him from accomplishing anything other than to gasp in a pointless effort to prolong his condemned life.

Next to Atzerodt was the dimwitted, young David Herold, pulling his cloth-bound legs up to his chest as if to relieve his body weight from the rope that was stretching his neck and choking out his life. His twisting and turning did nothing to lessen the pressure as the rope slowly strangled the air from his frantic body.

A large support post separated Atzerodt and Herold from the next prisoner, who took the longest to die. Lewis Powell had a thick, muscular neck, and for him the strangulation process was most severe. It was estimated that Powell struggled and jerked for over eight minutes before he became the last condemned prisoner to finally hang motionless.

The last criminal to be hanged for being a conspirator to have Lincoln removed from office was America's first executed woman. Mary Surratt had possibly passed out, or her neck had broken in the fall, as she made little noticeable attempt to resist the noose that had been the only support for the weight of her falling body. In the minutes before the trap floor was released, as the canvas sack was placed over her head, the rope draped around her neck, and the cloth bindings were being attached to her limbs, she could only mutter in a state of horrified denial; "Don't let me fall," repeating "*Please* don't let me fall."

As executioners prepared Mary to be strangled to death, the canvas sack, knotted noose and cloth bindings were also being adjusted around the big body of Lewis Powell. Unlike Mary Surratt, who had gone almost insane from fright and disbelief, Lewis Powell kept the same cavalier demeanor that he had maintained throughout his trial and conviction.

In complete contrast to Powell's seemingly unconcerned attitude about the certainty of his last agonizing moments on earth, David Herold was fully alert to what was about to take place for him. Before that day his childish mind had never comprehended the consequences from following along with his admired, older friends. Herold had only trusted and believed that whatever they were doing must be the right thing. Despite being unable to make his own choices before he was convicted of aiding in Lincoln's murder, he could easily comprehend how he was about to die. Scared and hysterical, he could only cry and beg to be set free.

The criminal, George Atzerodt, met his end after he lost his case that had been defended by an Army Captain serving under the direction of the Secretary of War. The evidence that could prove him not guilty of conspiracy to commit murder was asked by his own counsel to be excluded. His attorney instead issued a defense plea of being a "constitutional coward," a strategy that sidestepped the use of his last confession, which would have accounted for all the evidence and charges against him.

The last words that came from the gallows just before they all fell to their tortured execution was from the convicted coward, George Atzerodt. Reporters covering the exhibition heard Atzerodt say as he turned to his condemned neighbors just before the trap was released, "May we all meet in another world!"[25] A moment later this constitutional coward dropped to his slow but certain death.

2

Two Conspiracies

I would save the Union. I would save it the shortest way under the Constitution. The sooner the national authority can be restored; the nearer the Union will be "the Union as it was."

—Abraham Lincoln
Letter to Horace Greeley
August 22, 1862

The conspirators' trial ended with a deliberate miscarriage of justice, and beckons a reexamination of the assassination. The burning questions yet to be resolved are: who could have been the people behind the assassin, and what would have motivated them to remove Lincoln from office? The investigation, hearing and judgments have long since concluded with eight prisoners convicted, but the conspiracy has remained an unresolved mystery. In a legitimate investigation and trial, the three key elements in identifying the guilty party are a suspect's *motive, opportunity* and *ability* to commit the crime.

A review of the trial transcripts does not establish who provided Booth with the ability and opportunity to murder the President. Only one of the eight convicted was guilty of being complicit in Lincoln's assassination, but all eight were convicted without establishing motive, opportunity and ability. A deeper study of the trial (including its withheld evidence) shows that the true conspirators got away with murder.

A careful examination of the 1860s political landscape in Washington, D.C., utilizing all the resources presently available, exposes what Lincoln's death meant to those in power—who would profit, and who would lose. The real conspiracy to assassinate Lincoln was not merely to kill the man, but to destroy his vision for a post-Civil War America. Even a casual investigation into just motive alone can reveal those who would most desire Mr. Lincoln's second term policies restructured.

War is politics without law, and during the Civil War Federal policy over the states was enforced through the authority of military might. By the day Lincoln was shot, Washington, D.C., had already celebrated the end of the Civil War, and there was no Confederate government left to contest the national authority of the Union. Lincoln's policy for his second administration was to again have the *states* resolve their issues and enforce their resolutions through Constitutional means. Four months into his second term Lincoln was restored as President of all the states.

This restored union was still a patchwork of industrial states, agricultural states, new states, territories and disputed frontiers. A daunting challenge facing the Federal government was the many regional issues of this changing and expanding republic. Lincoln's vision was to allow the states, jointly and severally, to decide their own solutions to these regional concerns. However, many in Lincoln's party opposed restoring Congressional authority to former Confederate states, and advocated rendering these states as territories under martial law. This coalition was desperate to change the President's reconstruction policy. They had the means and the will, if necessary, to destroy him.

January, 1865

During his tenure in office, Lincoln was constantly surrounded by many people, but he was not always sure he could distinguish friend from foe. The President begrudgingly tolerated around the clock bodyguards, and occasional military escorts when he traveled outside the city of Washington. He was heavily dependent upon a young staff to arrange his daily appointments and correspondence, with John Hay and John Nicolay being his two closest aides. Their first daily duty was to sort through the presidential mail bags, which contained a noticeable increase in hate letters after the hotly-contested November 1864 election, making their usual routine a bit more taxing than it had been during Mr. Lincoln's previous term.

On a seemingly uneventful January morning, both secretaries quickly sorted through the pile of mail to pick a good letter for Mr. Lincoln to see first. Lighthearted news was hard to find, but Hay spotted one from General Van Alen of New York, and he knew that the President always enjoyed hearing from a loyal friend.

The screening of the mail was not intended to hide any real threat to the President, but to topically categorize the heavy volume of letters. One would think that Lincoln's secretaries would have been instructed to divert any hate letters before they reached the President, but, according to the chronicles written by John Nicolay:

> [T]hreats came in every form. … Most of these communications received no notice. In cases where there seemed a ground for inquiry, it was made. … The President was too intelligent not to know he was in some danger. … [Mr. Lincoln] would sometimes laughingly say, "our friends on the other side would make nothing by exchanging me for Hamlin."[1] (Hannibal Hamlin was the Radical Vice President during Lincoln's first term, replaced in 1864 with Andrew Johnson.)

However, the most dangerous and threatening letter of them all was written, but never mailed. The man who would kill Abraham Lincoln after all the fighting had ended addressed his political manifesto to himself and sealed it in a thick, heavy envelope.[2] John Wilkes Booth left that letter in Philadelphia with his sister for safekeeping, and it was only after Lincoln's death that the letter would be opened and read for the first time. The manifesto was regarding a kidnapping plot to exchange the President for Confederate prisoners.

Booth's Plot to Kidnap President Lincoln

Booth never had a plot to kill Lincoln until the day of the assassination. Prior to that time the only plans Booth had were to abduct the President. Booth wrote his manifesto in November, 1864, explaining to "whom it may concern" his motivation for kidnapping Lincoln, in which he admitted the plan was solely his own, without help from anybody in the South. He declared:

> The South has never bestowed upon me one kind word; a place now where I have no friends, except beneath the sod.[3]

Just after the assassination Booth's brother-in-law, John Sleeper Clarke, opened the sealed envelope and read the manifesto. Immediately he turned this letter over to U.S. Marshal William Milward, also in Philadelphia, who in turn shared the contents with *The Philadelphia Inquirer,* which printed the

Confederate prisoners awaiting transfer at the sprawling Belle Plain Union supply depot near Fredericksburg, Virginia, on the Potomac River. In the distance are camps and campfires of the workers and soldiers who resided there.

manifesto only two days after Lincoln died.[4] The military police confiscated the letter, arrested John Clarke and transferred him to Washington, holding him for a month in the Old Capitol Prison. The letter had been published more than a week before Booth had been captured, and while the investigation into Lincoln's assassination had only just begun. This telling letter should have been used as evidence in the conspiracy trial, but only the readers of one newspaper in the city of Philadelphia ever read it. The letter provided evidence that John Wilkes Booth was not working for the Confederacy, and the War Department needed to suppress the manifesto in order to implicate the South.

That one single document by itself destroyed the theory that the Confederate government was originally involved in Booth's plan to kidnap the President. The letter was an outpouring of his deepest thoughts and feelings behind his motives to abduct Lincoln. Booth left this letter with his sister, along with a second letter, oil stock certificates, and U.S. bonds.

Nowhere to Go

Apart from relying on historical evidence, common logic can deduce that, even if Booth were able to pull off his impossible plot to capture Lincoln, he would have had *nowhere* to take him. After January, 1865, the whole of eastern Virginia was under siege by the Union Army. Richmond was a twenty-hour

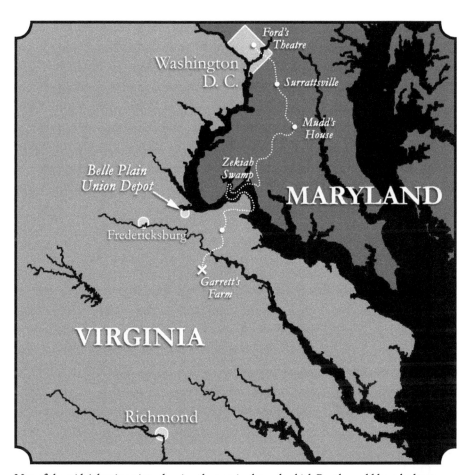

Map of the mid-Atlantic region, showing the terrain through which Booth would have had to transport his captive in early 1865.

journey from Washington that Booth would have to successfully make, while carrying the shackled U.S. President, without being intercepted. Every primary and secondary road in Virginia was being traveled by Union forces, and all traffic on the Potomac River en route to Richmond was controlled by Belle Plain, a Union depot just northeast of Fredericksburg, halfway between Washington and Richmond. The depot housed a large garrison of Union troops and gunboats that were there to receive and distribute weapons and supplies, along with the conveyance of captured Confederate prisoners. If Booth had planned to deliver the President to Richmond, he would first have to get out of Washington, cross the Potomac, then get past the garrison at the Belle Plain Union Depot.

If Booth was in fact working for the Confederate government to kidnap Lincoln, the question is, *where and how could he have delivered Lincoln to the Confederate government when all of eastern Virginia, between Washington and North Carolina, was under tight Union control?* After January no kidnappers carrying the captured President could get south of Washington without the many Union checkpoints allowing their access. Any claim that the Confederate government was involved with Booth's plan to kidnap Lincoln is an allegation with complete disregard for the chronology and geography of proven historical events. By late March Lincoln could not have been kidnapped and carried to Virginia because he was already in Virginia.[5]

Negotiating Peace

Beginning around the first of January the war was very close to ending, and all of eastern Virginia was locked in battle; and by February it was under Federal control. The siege of Richmond was imminent. By mid-January, Lincoln was making plans to talk peace with Confederate President Jefferson Davis.[6] Undaunted by numerous dangers, including rumors about assassination threats, Lincoln continued to travel outside of Washington, refusing to give in to intimidation. He made several trips to Virginia in early 1865, beginning with the proposed peace conference, which convened at Hampton Roads in early February.

On January 18, Lincoln offered his arrangements to Jefferson Davis for the peace conference. On January 21, Davis agreed to Lincoln's proposed meeting to negotiate bringing the war to an amicable end. There Lincoln and Seward met with the Confederate commission, consisting of Davis' Vice President Alexander H. Stephens, Judge John A. Campbell, and congressman Robert M. T. Hunter. The President left the negotiations with a promise to propose his concessions to his Cabinet. But, upon his return to Washington, the President's Cabinet unanimously rejected Lincoln's deal.

During this time the Confederate government would not have been planning to kidnap Lincoln as a bargaining chip. Jefferson Davis was making arrangements to send a peace commission to negotiate a deal for ending the fighting. He would not simultaneously plan to abduct Lincoln because the Confederate Vice President and two representatives would be in the custody of the United States military. How could Jefferson Davis have a plot to capture Lincoln and negotiate peace?

SECRETARY OF WAR
EDWIN STANTON

CHIEF TELEGRAPH OFFICER
MAJOR THOMAS ECKERT

Richmond knew that after January no kidnappers carrying the captured President could get south of Washington without the Union army allowing their access. And by late March Lincoln could not have been kidnapped and carried to Virginia because he was already there at City Point. By April 4, ten days before Lincoln's assassination, he was in Richmond and sitting behind the desk of Jefferson Davis in the Confederate White House. Meanwhile, Jefferson Davis and the bulk of his administration were on the run from General Sherman's army. The Confederate president was trying to avoid capture and possibly being hanged, and he was pursued all the way down into Georgia before being apprehended in early May.

The myth of Booth working for the Confederate government began as a fabricated allegation by Lincoln's rivals who were determined to frame the Confederates for the conspiracy to kill Lincoln.

Lincoln's Rivals

The Secretary of War, Edwin Stanton, was responsible for assigning an escort messenger for the Confederate peace commissioners, and he chose Major Thomas Eckert for the duty. Eckert was not only the Chief Telegraph Officer for the War Department, he was Stanton's first officer in his exclusive intelligence gathering division.[7] Stanton formed his own secret division that reported all their findings directly to him, and to no one else. Eckert's devotion to Stanton earned him a senior position over the War Department's affairs and policies.

On February 1, Secretary of State Seward arrived at Fort Monroe, Virginia, to prepare for the peace negotiations. Two days later Lincoln entered to lay out his terms for surrender. The three Confederate commissioners sat down together with Lincoln and Seward to work out a deal for ending the fighting. No agreement was reached, but the Confederate commission found Lincoln willing to make an amicable concession to end the war.

Lincoln's negotiations with the Confederate commission caused quite a concern with his Radical rivals. The two most powerful Radical leaders in Congress, Massachusetts Senator Charles Sumner and Pennsylvania Representative Thaddeus Stevens, called on Secretary Stanton to discover firsthand exactly what Lincoln was willing to give away to their enemy during this planned conference in Virginia.[8] Stanton appointed Major Eckert to find out for the Radicals all that he could about Lincoln's meeting, then immediately report back whatever deals Lincoln had offered to secure peace between the states.

The President's rivals relied on Stanton's War Department to help them pressure the administration into using the war as a means to restructure the governments of Southern states. The Radicals feared that the war would end before they could be assured that the former Confederate Congressmen would be prevented from returning to Congress. Major Eckert was unable to uncover any details because the parties agreed that the conference would be informal, with no written records. Without a way to monitor Lincoln's negotiations, Sumner and Stevens called on their majority-controlled Congress to force the President to report any offers he had made.[9]

On February 8, the Speaker of the House, Schuyler Colfax, Jr., wrote Lincoln:

> The Senate have been hastening for two days about Mr. Sumner's resolution asking for information as to the recent conference at Hampton Roads. I stated to Mr. [Thaddeus] Stevens this morning that I understood from you that you had no objection to communicating the information, and a resolution has been passed unanimously asking for it.[10]

And so on February 10, a week after the negotiations with the Confederate commission in Hampton Roads, Virginia, Lincoln submitted a very detailed report explaining the conference to the House of Representatives.

News about the peace negotiations reached the rebel blockade runners working under cover in Europe, but with curious inaccuracies. They were led to believe that Seward was the reason the Cabinet rejected Lincoln's proposed concessions to the South.[11] In mid-March, Lincoln returned to Virginia, during which time assassins from France were sent to Washington to kill William Seward in order to keep him from interfering with Lincoln's lenient and generous peace proposals.[12] The mission of these assassins demonstrates that after the conference the Confederacy would not have wanted Lincoln captured or dead, but alive and well to negotiate his intended concessions for peace. This European assassination plot has been left out from histories written by the proponents of the Confederate conspiracy, because it, too, is further evidence that the South *needed* Lincoln in order to achieve an acceptable end to their hopeless cause.

After Lincoln won his second election, many who were closest to him expressed their fears that he may be killed. One such concern came in a letter from Lincoln's personal friend General James H. Van Alen, who had always supported Lincoln's policy of reunion throughout his first administration, and gave his political and military recommendations to the President more as a friend than as an advisor. In Van Alen's last letter to Lincoln, he urged the President:

> … for the sake of your friends and the nation, guard your life and not expose it to assassination by going to Richmond.[13]

Lincoln always wanted to convey in his responses to his friends and allies a show of appreciation for their concern about his safety. He often wrote about the comfort he enjoyed from having so many people who supported his efforts to restore the Union and bind the nation's wounds. His last note to Van Alen ended with:

> … to use your language, a Union of hearts and hands as well as of states.[14]

By the latter part of March the President and Mrs. Lincoln were both in City Point, Virginia, just east of Petersburg, confident of complete security under the protection provided by the United States military. At the beginning of April, Lincoln was able to stand on the deck of the River Queen steamboat, anchored at the City Point dock, where he witnessed the dark evening sky flash bright as mid-afternoon while the city of Petersburg was being bombarded by a deafening barrage of Union cannon and mortar shells.[15]

By April 4, Virginia was so secure that Lincoln was able to walk openly through the city streets of Richmond, where he entered the Confederate White House and sat in the chair behind the desk of Jefferson Davis. He propped his feet victoriously on the desktop and looked around the ransacked office that once belonged to the President of the Confederacy. Surely he must have sensed the rise and fall of conflicting emotions. On the one hand, it was sweet victory for the Union, but as that wave reached its crest, the fall exposed the job yet to be done. Order and authority had to be reestablished, and economic stability restored. Reassuring to the President was the fact that not a single incident of any kind disrupted his visit to Virginia, even during his stay in the city of Richmond.

What Lincoln did not realize was that in Washington, D.C., his assassination was being plotted. It would be in the very heart of Washington, not in Richmond, where he would soon meet his violent end, while under the protection of Stanton's War Department and Washington's metropolitan police force.

By April 3, Union forces had already captured the city of Richmond, ending any chance that Lincoln could be held there as a hostage. On April 5, Lincoln again met with John Campbell, the peace conference commissioner, and by then the only concession Lincoln could promise was to save the Confederate leaders from being hanged.[16] This was nine days before Lincoln's assassination, so why would anyone among the Confederate high command want to kill the only person in Washington willing and able to save them from execution?

After the negotiations in February, it was clear to the Confederate leaders that Lincoln was resolved to reunite the seceded states back into the Union as they had been before the Civil War. They knew full well that if Lincoln were to fall, the fate of the South would be determined by those with far greater malice and much less mercy.[17]

The European Assassination Plot against Seward

Throughout the war the Confederacy received armaments and financing from various covert factions within Europe. The State Department had spies operating overseas to gather intelligence on the rebel blockade runners and their European suppliers. These spies reported their surveillances directly to Secretary of State William Seward (not to the Secretary of War, Edwin Stanton). On April 5, 1865, while Lincoln was in Richmond, Seward showed Stanton[18] three letters he received from his agents in Europe, which warned of two rebel assassins on their way to Washington from France to kill Seward and General Sherman.[19]

Seward immediately made ready to travel to Richmond to meet in person with the President to show him these letters.[20] However, before he could depart from Washington, he was almost killed in a carriage accident, which left him in a coma, with a broken shoulder and jaw. When Stanton telegraphed Lincoln about Seward's injuries, he did not reveal the news about assassins sent from France,[21] nor did he mention them to Lincoln even a week after his return to Washington. Lincoln was left to find out about the assassins on his own, and only hours before his own fatal attack.

On the last day of Lincoln's life, he confronted Stanton about the European assassins, but Stanton reassured the President, insisting the plot was just another baseless rumor. Hours later at Ford's Theatre (a perfect location for Booth), Lincoln was left unprotected by men serving under Stanton's War Department, a situation and setting that only Stanton could have arranged. No Confederate agents had the ability to arrange Lincoln's location and security.

The President had many political enemies in Washington, namely the Radicals, who did not share the sentiment of "hearts and hands." They didn't wish to welcome back the former rebel states as equals, but instead demanded they be *disfranchised*—stripped of political autonomy. After four years of bitter war, the Confederate leaders were hated, held responsible for the bloodshed of loyal Americans. The idea of reinstating Congressional authority to their former enemies was nothing short of detestable.

Who Did Booth Work For?

After Lincoln was assassinated in Washington a theory was alleged and circulated that John Wilkes Booth had been some type of Confederate agent, assigned by Jefferson Davis to kidnap Lincoln, and the plan was modified later to kill Lincoln. But it was proven two years after Lincoln's death that Jefferson Davis was completely uninvolved with Lincoln's murder. The masterminds of Lincoln's assassination plot knew the President's schedule, personal security, and the security surrounding Ford's Theater that specific day. Whoever plotted Lincoln's assassination has remained an unresolved mystery, while the Confederate conspiracy theory has continued to circulate, in spite of being proven false. The claim that Booth and Jefferson Davis conspired together to assassinate Lincoln originated as Stanton's allegation that the deed was an act of war, thus putting the investigation and trial under his authority.

Nine days before his assassination in Washington, Lincoln had walked openly through the streets of the Confederate capital, looming head and shoulders above the crowds. Had there been any advantage to the South in killing Lincoln, the Confederate government could have left assassins hidden in the ruins of Richmond.

3

Cause for Alarm

*A*fter the Hampton Roads peace conference failed to end the war, the rebel agents in France held William Seward responsible for not reaching acceptable surrender terms with Lincoln. The unsettled issue between Lincoln and the Confederate commission was not the total emancipation of slavery, but the restoration of the national authority throughout all the states.[1]

The Confederates were holding out for independence, and they offered to abolish slavery in the South if the Union would recognize them as an independent nation. Lincoln explained that his surrender terms were contingent upon the reunion of the states, not total emancipation. The President then pointed out that there was no longer any debate about emancipation in every state because it had just been proposed in the House of Representatives only three days before. Lincoln told the commission that, if the rebel states pledged their loyalty to the Union, he would petition Congress to partially reimburse the enormous $2 billion deficit emancipation would leave in the economy of both the Union and Confederate slave states. He told the Confederate commission that he thought Congress would agree to $400 million in compensation for emancipation, roughly the same amount it would cost the government to continue the war for two more months.[2] However, Lincoln's proposal never got past his Cabinet, and rebel spies in Europe held William Seward responsible for killing the offer.

The war drudged on, and after a heated debate the Confederate Congress voted to arm the slaves and enlist them in the Southern Army. During this time both the President and William Seward were back in Virginia (Lincoln at City Point and Seward at Fort Monroe) to assess the war's progress. After a short stay Seward left to travel back to Washington. His first order of business was a large stack of mail which had accumulated on his desk during his absence. Shuffling through the hefty pile, he spotted a letter from his secret agent in Europe, and being intrigued he decided to open it first. The letter—a true cause for alarm—revealed an assassination plot coming out of France.

A syndicate within the nations of France, England, Germany and Spain were working closely with the Confederate government to supply war materials to help the South break Lincoln's naval blockade. The fighting between the states was of great importance to the consortium in Europe, whose purpose for aiding the Confederacy was solely to keep the United States weakened by perpetuating its division. In March, 1865, with the South completely bankrupt, economically ruined, and with no hope of winning independence, there could be no other reason for any entity to supply the Confederacy with costly war materials. While working to crush this smuggling ring, Secretary of State Seward had the unenviable task of spying on this syndicate, while at the same time maintaining diplomacy. This required having many agents with special skills.

Seward had assigned agent Freeman Harlow Morse to head his Consulate in London, and from there he could also direct the European counterespionage division, headquartered in England. Agent Morse had previously expressed his concerns during the summer of 1864 about assassination plots and conspiracies, but Secretary Seward remained very confident that no such tactics would be employed by players within the American political system. His only interest in the information from agent Morse at that time was about the contraband being smuggled to the South from Europe.

Seward's perception about assassination being contradictory to American politics[3] was an odd impression considering the nation's history. Even though no president had yet been killed, in 1835 a would-be assassin, Richard Lawrence, suspected of being sponsored by European factions, failed in his attempt to kill President Andrew Jackson only because both of his pistols misfired.

During his second term, Jackson replaced his Vice President, John C. Calhoun over domestic disputes regarding trade and tax legislation, appointing his Secretary of State, Martin Van Buren (who went on to become the next President). While Van Buren presided over the Senate, he carried with him two loaded pistols because of persistent and credible rumors about assassination plots to remove him from office.

In July of 1864, Secretary Seward responded to agent Morse's warnings about assassination rumors with great skepticism, writing that there was "no ground for anxiety." He scoffed at the idea, insisting assassination could not become part of the American political system. In this same encrypted telegraph, Seward revealed to agent Morse that the President often traveled "to and from ... the Old Soldiers' Home ... two or three miles from the city ...

on horseback night and morning unguarded," and that he himself did the same, also without regard to any danger.[4] Just weeks after Seward leaked this sensitive information about Lincoln's habits, John Wilkes Booth had a plan to kidnap Lincoln during his trips to and from the Old Soldiers' Home.

The April letter Seward received from Morris reported that a Federal agent in France, John Bigelow, had uncovered an assassination plot against Secretary of State William Seward and General W. T. Sherman. Agent Bigelow's foreign assignment was to report on war supplies being smuggled from Europe and through the Union Navy's stranglehold on Southern ports. During his investigation of blockade running he discovered the plot to kill Seward and Sherman. Bigelow was working undercover in France when he learned of the plot, and he in turn alerted his boss, F. H. Morse, about two rebel assassins heading for the United States. Morse received two letters from Bigelow with details about war shipments along with information about the two assassins.

The first letter from Bigelow was sent from Paris and received in London on Sunday, March 12, 1865, stating, "two desperate characters have just left here," via steamer, named Clark and Johnston, heading for the United States. Bigelow knew Clark but he had never met Johnston. Bigelow learned that all their expenses had been paid, and that they would each receive $5,000 after the successful assassinations of Seward and Sherman. Bigelow stated that the party who divulged the plot would not have said such a thing to him if it were not true. Because Bigelow had never met Johnston, he could not describe him, making it difficult to arrest him once he reached Washington, however he could describe Clark.

Two days later, Bigelow reported again, responding to a request from Morse in London for a full description of Clark, and the particulars concerning the shipment of war supplies sent to the South. In the second letter, Bigelow suggested other rebel agents were eager for the same assassination mission. He reported that the operatives in Europe wanted Seward dead because "he does as he pleases," and without him they thought Lincoln would have made an amicable arrangement to secure peace with the South. The rebels wanted General Sherman dead because they felt no other Yankee could fill his place.[5] They hated Sherman and felt he needed to be stopped because he had committed atrocities against the South during his "march to the sea," and would continue to do so. Bigelow's second letter confirmed that the rebels did not want Lincoln assassinated nor did they have any plans to assassinate

General Grant (those allegations were fabricated by the War Department after Lincoln's assassination).

Bigelow described Clark as having been born in Texas, about 5'-9", rather thin, with high cheekbones, a low forehead, dark, sunken eyes, and his hair much darker than his large brown mustache and long goatee. His demeanor was described as very quiet; he seldom spoke in company unless first spoken to. In both letters Bigelow revealed his source of information was a rebel business agent named Cooper, who was traveling throughout France, directing the purchase and shipment of war materials to the South. Agent Bigelow had traveled with Cooper often in France, pretending to be a rebel, and believed the disclosure of a plot to assassinate Seward and Sherman was well founded. He explained that Cooper was his only source of information, and there were no other means for him to learn anything more.

Bigelow indicated that once the assassins entered the United States, Clark was to make his own way south into Sherman's camp as a private and assassinate the General during a battle. Johnston was to go north to Washington and assassinate Secretary Seward at his first opportunity. Bigelow warned that these men would stop at nothing to accomplish their goal, and "it's war to the teeth with them." Bigelow ended his message asking Morse to see that his name would not be not used in Washington. Such a revelation "might prove fatal" for him.

Agent Morse in London originally felt that the plot was improbable because sending assassins from Europe would take much more time and expense than using local operatives already in the United States. Also, any assailants sent from Europe would be sure to forfeit their own lives during an attempt to kill any American officials. With that assumption in mind, and being aware of Secretary Seward's conviction that assassination was not probable, Morse hesitated before he decided to pass this information on to Seward.[6] Morse personally assumed in his warning that if the assassins did openly attack political and military leaders they might also include Lincoln and Grant in their vengeance if such opportunities arose. However, that was not the rebel plan, only an assumption made by agent Morse. Morse's letter to Seward included the two letters from his agent "B" [Bigelow].

Nine days before Lincoln was assassinated, the President had traveled northwest from City Point, into the captured city of Richmond. On that same day,s Seward anxiously telegraphed Lincoln to tell him that he wished to meet with him in person. Seward wired the President: "are you coming up or shall I go down?"

Lincoln answered: "I think there is no probability of my remaining here more than two days longer. If that is too long come down."

Seward's impatience to see Lincoln right away was about more than just "several government matters" as his telegram from the War Department indicated—such things could have easily waited for Lincoln's return to Washington. Seward's urgency was about giving Lincoln the letters from agent Morse concerning this Confederate assassination plot coming out of Europe. It had always been Seward who was the most skeptical, and did not believe anyone would actually attempt an assassination. But the letter he held in his hand not only identified and described assassins, but named *him* as the target for assassination, not Lincoln.

Inform the President![7]

With the three letters shoved down into his coat pocket, Seward rushed to the War Department to find Secretary of War Stanton but all he found was an empty office. As he turned to leave, a corporal carrying a stack of papers brushed past Seward to place the papers down on Stanton's desk. Seward excitedly asked him where he could find Secretary Stanton, and the soldier snapped to attention saying, "Sir, Secretary Stanton can be found in the telegraph office with Major Eckert."

Seward rushed to Eckert's office finding Stanton with his back to the door barking out commands at his telegraph officer: "Wire [the assistant Secretary] Charles Dana in Richmond a communiqué stating that he *must* find out as quickly as he can what the President is promising to Judge Campbell and the enemy legislators. Tell him I must be informed of any concessions the President has promised at the *earliest* possible moment."

Seward anxiously interrupted Stanton, "Mr. Secretary I have a matter of utmost importance to discuss with you, if I may please borrow but a moment of your time." Seward showed Stanton his letters about the two assassins heading for the United States, and the Secretary of War responded with complete surprise.

Stanton then escorted Seward back to the privacy of his office. With convincingly sincere tones Stanton expressed concern and compassion for Seward, Sherman, and possibly even the President. "Yes, yes of course, our

Commander *must* see these letters. God forbid if anything should happen to either of you, especially after all we have accomplished, and with so much left to be done. Let's get you to Richmond right away, and earnestly convince Mr. Lincoln to avoid all public gatherings or any needless exposure to possible assault."[8]

Major Eckert slipped softly into Stanton's office and in a low voice asked, "Please excuse this interruption, Secretary Seward." Turning to Stanton, Eckert handed his boss a telegram from Richmond, and reminded him that he had demanded to see Dana's message as soon as it arrived.

Stanton scanned the dispatch and a flush of red color welled up from his collar and his complexion began to glow like a hot ember. Tiny beads of perspiration dotted his forehead and grew, until some descended his face in tiny streams that disappeared into his scraggly, foot-long beard. An eerie transformation came over him, revealing to Seward the manifestation of a deep-seated, yet long hidden, psychopathic personality. Slamming his fist on the table, Stanton bellowed, "We have our iron heels resting on the throats of these guilty murderers who have been warring upon the existence of our country, and Mr. Lincoln is going to let them up! They now pray to God for mercy but I will see that these rebel criminals pray to us!"

After witnessing that disturbing outbreak of rage Seward left the War Department and quickly made arrangements to leave for Richmond to meet with the President in person. But only two hours later, he was nearly killed in a carriage accident before he could leave Washington.

Stanton immediately sent a wire to Lincoln in Richmond to inform him about Seward's near-death accident. Lincoln returned to Washington two days later, while Secretary Seward remained in a coma. Mysteriously, Stanton never told the President about the rebel assassins sent to Washington from France, even though he and Seward had agreed that Lincoln should know about the threat right away.

4

Desperation

At 6:00 PM on April 5, Stanton telegraphed Lincoln in Richmond to let him know about Seward's accident. The next day Lincoln returned to City Point and prepared to board a steamer back to Washington. Stanton again telegraphed the President early that next morning to tell him that Mrs. Lincoln had already left Washington the previous day to join him in Virginia. He added that she had left with friends hours before Seward's accident. Lincoln decided to wait for his wife's party to arrive at City Point so they could return to Washington together. It would not be until April 7 that Mr. and Mrs. Lincoln finally boarded the River Queen and steamed back to Washington.

While the President was waiting for Mrs. Lincoln to reach City Point, he sent a telegraph to General Grant telling him about Seward's accident, and also to inform the General about his Richmond meeting with Judge John Campbell.[1] Jefferson Davis and his administration had boarded a train south to avoid being captured, and John Campbell was the only Confederate administrator left to negotiate with Lincoln. The President informed Grant that he gave his Major General in charge of Richmond, Godfrey Weitzel, a private letter instructing him to allow the acting Virginia state legislators to meet if they would agree to cease all hostility against the United States. At that point Virginia was under Union control, and Grant had trapped Lee's army. All that remained for Grant to end the war was Lee's signature on the surrender papers.

Meanwhile Lincoln was in Richmond trying to persuade the Virginia legislature to convince Lee's army they must stand down. On April 5, Lincoln told Judge Campbell, "As to peace I have said before [referring to the Hampton Roads peace conference], and now repeat that three things are indispensable:

1. The restoration of the national authority throughout all states.

2. No receding on the Executive of the United States on the slavery question, from the position assumed thereon, in the late Annual

Message to Congress, and in preceding documents.

3. No cessation of hostilities short of an end of the war, and the disbanding of all forces hostile to the government."[2]

Over the next two days Lincoln sent a series of telegrams from Virginia to
Stanton informing him about Grant's final campaign to force General Lee
into submission. Grant had cut off Lee's southern retreat, forcing him to turn
his starving army west.

The Assistant Secretary of War, Charles A. Dana, had been assigned to
follow Lincoln to Richmond to promptly report back to Stanton whatever
concessions the President had offered Judge Campbell to secure peace. Dana
telegraphed Stanton on April 5th at 4:00 PM, telling him that Lincoln had an
interview with John Campbell that morning. He telegraphed Stanton that all
Campbell had asked for was amnesty and a military convention to cover appearances. Slavery, they admitted, was defunct. The President did not promise
the amnesty, but told Campbell he had the pardoning power, and he would
save any repentant sinner from hanging. Campbell was sure if amnesty could
be offered the rebel army would dissolve and all the states would return.

Dana telegraphed Stanton again on April 7, and told him that the President said that "Sheridan seemed to be getting the Virginia soldiers out of the
war faster than this legislature could think."[3]

On April 7, at 11:00 AM Lincoln wired Grant from City Point: "Gen.
Sheridan says 'if the thing is pressed he thinks Lee will surrender.' Let the
thing be pressed! A. Lincoln"[4]

On April 9, 1865, General Lee surrendered the Army of Northern Virginia to General Grant at Appomattox Courthouse, and even though there
were still Confederate forces in the field, the Confederacy was essentially defeated.

The Celebration[5]

On the morning after Lee's surrender, Tad Lincoln (the younger of Mr. Lincoln's two surviving sons) was awakened by the sound of another heavy April
rain beating against his bedroom window. The spring of 1865 was turning
out to be a wet and muddy end to four years of Civil War. And from the
White House the 12-year-old Tad had spent the majority of his young life

with a front row seat to witness firsthand the start of the Civil War, and now its finish.

News about Lee's surrender inspired immense numbers of people to gather in the sporadic spring showers and muddy streets to celebrate an end to the agonizing, past four years.

The sounds from an approaching army of celebrators heading towards the White House brought Tad to the window, and once again he had the exclusive front row seat to see it all unfold. From his vantage point he could see a legion of people swaying towards him, and he could hear their shouts over the band music, and he could hear the cannons belching out thunderous euphoria instead of anger and death.

Captain Tompkins' Quartermaster Regiment band melted together with the Fourteenth Regiment band to follow a procession of over 3,000 people sloshing up the muddy Pennsylvania Avenue towards the White House. Their first stop was the front of the War Department, and the cheering masses called for their hero, the Secretary of War Edwin Stanton, to come out, greet the crowd, and give a speech. Getting no response from Stanton the great army turned and advanced toward the White House. They filled the portico, the carriageway and spilled out onto the pavement on either side. The rest of the crowd was left to stand in ankle-deep mud, and they all were calling for Mr. Lincoln to come out and speak. There was no leaving until Lincoln appeared, and after several loud cheers their Chief Magistrate joined his son Tad at the window to address the crowd.

The President requested that they give three cheers for Grant and three for the Navy. Lincoln only spoke briefly, but said lightheartedly that they had fairly captured one of the South's best tunes, and one of the best he ever heard. He added that the Attorney General had given his legal opinion that the tune was now their lawful prize. Then Lincoln requested the band play "Dixie." After that tune was played it was followed by "Yankee Doodle." Lincoln was cautious not to make a statement that had not been well rehearsed, realizing his every word would go directly into print. He gave the crowd a short farewell until tomorrow, then disappeared from the window.

The Despondent Victor

The frenzied mob marched back to the War Department for a second time, and tried again to rouse their hero Secretary Stanton. But Stanton was in no mood to celebrate. The dejected Secretary of War stayed out of public slight. He felt there was no way left for him to stop Lincoln's policy for reunification, and he wrote his resignation to give to the President the next day.

While the Washington celebration continued, Lincoln's other political enemies—the Radical coalition led by Charles Sumner, Thaddeus Stevens and Salmon Chase—who had worked hard to prevent his 1864 nomination, had not yet given up. They had met secretly to find a way to stop Lincoln's reconstruction plan, which would allow the Southern states to rejoin the Union and share equal rights and privileges with the other states.

The motive of Lincoln's political enemies for fighting the Civil War had been the exact opposite of the President's. Lincoln was fighting to restore the Union by defeating the eleven Southern states that had claimed independence. However, the Radical faction didn't want "the Union as it was" before; they wanted a *new* balance of authority, with control over the defeated Southern territories, exploiting them for the benefit of their constituents who put them in office. The Radicals were from the industrial northeastern states, and they had been elected to represent and promote the economic interests of powerful industries. These legislators were predominantly backed by financial contributions and media support from northeastern industrialists, in particular the executives who had formed the Union Pacific and the Central Pacific railroad companies. These capitalists had the power and wealth to get Lincoln elected, but, to their frustration, they were unable to direct his administration.

The ultimate goal of the Radicals was to completely and forever annihilate their southern agricultural competitors through legislation. Congressional votes controlled the nation's land use, regulations, trade routes, government spending and taxation. If they could prevail in the legislative branch of this expanding nation, they could direct the nation's wealth. Every major Congressional resolution from the day the Constitution was ratified by the states in 1788, until the Civil War ended 77 years later, had been over the issue of a majority of votes in Congress controlling the fates of the states. If the Southern states were allowed to return to Congress restored to their antebellum status, their legislators would vote in concert with the northern Democrats and Congressmen from the northwestern agricultural states, overwhelming the Radicals. This would reclaim the United States' agriculture-based economy, similar to the Jeffersonian and Jacksonian periods. Author and historian Hans L. Trefousse surmised the Radicals' "achievements might still be annulled in the very hour of victory."[6]

By April the Civil War was over, but the desperate northern industrialists were facing the truth that they were on the verge of losing their congressional majority if the Southern representatives were allowed to return to government. Such was precisely the plan of the moderate President, whose influence and popularity were now augmented by the Union victory. There was now virtually nothing to stop Lincoln from implementing his reunification agenda.

Lincoln's Last Chance[7]

During the entire secret meeting to bring Lincoln back under control, the two Radical Congressman, Sumner and Stevens, never sat down and could only pace back and forth, while Salmon Chase (Lincoln's former Treasury Secretary, whom he dismissed from his Cabinet the previous year) sat behind his huge, opulent oak desk, with eyes fixed on the floor, and in deep thought.

Sumner growled out, more to himself than to his colleagues, "Four years of war and Mr. Lincoln in one day has destroyed all we have accomplished."

Chase added, "I think we still have a chance, but we must act with determination equal in degree to the consequences Mr. Lincoln's policy will leave upon us. If we stand together there is a chance, if we don't pull as one all will be lost."

Stevens circled to the front of the massive desk and placed his hands down on the polished oak, looking at Chase eye-to-eye and said, "I would suppose you have formulated some plan that can now at this late hour reverse Mr. Lincoln's direction—a direction we as a single-minded body with equal determination have not been able to change for the past fifteen months."

The pudgy-faced Chase looked up at Stevens' wrinkled, snarling gaze and said, "We must each attack upon every point of the Executive. We must persuade Mr. Lincoln that his second term will be one of no political tolerance for his policy to reinstate those rebel murderers back into Congress."

Sumner angrily chimed in, "Our past resolutions over the Executive took every persuasion and called in every favor just to hold the line that has only brought us to this desperate point. Without a voter base in the South to stem the tide of our opposition we have no chance under Mr. Lincoln's policy. He has become unstoppable."

Chase calmly reminded Sumner that they still had leverage if everyone pulled from the same direction. "Stanton can break up the cozy relationship Mr. Lincoln has been enjoying between the Virginians and General Weitzel.

CHIEF JUSTICE SALMON P. CHASE

REPRESENTATIVE THADDEUS STEVENS

SENATOR CHARLES SUMNER

I called on Stanton last Thursday to assign his Assistant Secretary Charles Dana to Richmond so he could assess Mr. Lincoln's situation with Campbell and the Virginia legislature. It looks as though Richmond will unconditionally accept Mr. Lincoln's terms, but with a little pressure from Stanton on Weitzel, Judge Campbell and Mr. Lincoln may not remain so willing to congeal their differences. Meanwhile I will lay before Mr. Lincoln a clear picture of the dark consequences he will face from returning Southern congressmen to vote against our republic.

"More than just barring former rebels from returning to Congress, we must take control of the state elections in the South by way of colored suffrage. Lincoln's restoration of the Union by just changing the slave states into Union free states does nothing but worsen our legislative position. Without mandating voting rights to the Negro population in the South all their representation in Congress will only help to further strengthen a new rebel majority. Without a colored voter base in the South we will be outnumbered in Congress by an insurmountable margin."

Sumner snapped back at Chase, "You're given *one* chance to turn Mr. Lincoln, but if there is no change, other processes of which you are aware are already in place that will not fail to save our hard-won republic." Chase was still sitting with his shoulders pushed forward towards the desk, but pulled his head back to look up at the 6'-4" Sumner standing there in front of his desk next to the equally distraught and growling Stevens.

Chase tried to console his colleagues, saying, "I will talk with Stanton today and assure him that all is not yet lost. He has expressed to me that after Seward's accident, another accident—to Lincoln—might not be seen as anything other than deliberate."

Sumner approached closer to Chase and spoke low, but determined, "Anything less than deliberate would be a foolish waste of effort. Call on Stanton. If Mr. Lincoln will not heed our last warning there will be few among our ranks who would not agree there is no way left but a deliberate way. Stanton can make the arrangements, and after Mr. Lincoln is removed from office there will be no one who can facilitate an objection."[8] With cold resolve the meeting adjourned, and Stanton and Chase were left to begin their attack from both ends to change Mr. Lincoln's mind—or else.

Stanton Undermines Lincoln's Vulnerable Peace

Stanton's job was to break up the cordial relationship between General Weitzel and Judge Campbell, and he chose to attack using the deeply personal subject of prayer. Campbell had made a request to General Weitzel to allow the Episcopal churches in Richmond to assemble on Sunday.

All that was left for the citizens in the smoldering, burnt-out city of Richmond was the church. All else had gone, homes were ashes, there was no economy, no government, and their future hopes resting in the next generation where dead, wounded or starving. Their faith in God and their hope that a better day would come was all that was left to them in their lowest moment of defeat and despair.

On April 9th, the day of Lee's surrender, Stanton's spy in Richmond, Assistant Secretary of War Charles Dana, telegraphed Stanton at 9:00 AM to tell him that Weitzel had allowed the ministers to open the churches on the condition that no disloyalty should be uttered, and that they were required to read a prayer for the President.[9] Judge Campbell felt that requiring the devastated Richmonders to pray for Lincoln was too much to ask, and he asked Weitzel to drop that one requirement. Weitzel agreed and sent the Military Governor of Virginia, George F. Shepley, to Charles Dana to request that the order might be relaxed so that the clergy would only be required not to pray for Jefferson Davis.[10] This was Stanton's opportunity to drive a wedge between

Weitzel and Campbell. He would use the church to break up their reconciliation by ordering complete allegiance from the defeated southern population.
Stanton wired Major General Weitzel:

> It has just been reported to this Department that you have, at the
> instance of Mr. Campbell, consented that service should be per-
> formed in the Episcopal churches of Richmond to-day without
> [the prayer] for the President … and that you have even agreed
> to waive that condition. If such has been your action it is strongly
> condemned by this Department. …[11]

Weitzel protested, explaining that he had three interviews with Campbell,
two of which were in the presence of the President, and no orders were given
as to what would be prayed for, only what would not be permitted. At neither
interview was there any discussion about prayers.[12]

But Stanton wired General Weitzel, further expanding the order: "all denominations are required to pray for the President [only], with no less respect
than they had shown toward the rebel chief before he was driven from the
capital."[13]

Weitzel conveyed his order from Stanton to Judge Campbell, and Campbell in turn expressed his concerns about such a pointless and rigid execution
of force. Campbell felt this would impair his efforts to persuade the Virginia
legislators to meet to call off all hostility against the United States government.

The day after Judge Campbell's meeting with Lincoln, he wrote to General Weitzel that all the powers of negotiation are in the hands of the President.
"I have made a statement to the practical difficulties that exist in order to
encourage you to persevere in the course of patience, moderation, forbearance
and conciliation that has marked your conduct since you entered Richmond.
Many of the difficulties will be removed or lessened by such a course, and I
do not know of any that will not be aggravated by the adoption of the opposite."[14]

Weitzel sympathized with Campbell's point and he telegraphed Lincoln
at 3:00 PM on April 12, to protest Stanton's decree saying, "You spoke of not
pressing little points. You said you would not order me, but if you were in
my place you would not press them. The passports [for crossing Union check-
points] have gone out for the Virginia legislature, and it is common talk that
they will come together."[15]

The condition of Richmond, Virginia, while Stanton was ordering its inhabitants to offer prayers for Abraham Lincoln in their churches the following Sunday. This act, unknown to the President, was a deliberate ploy to derail the disarmament of the Confederacy. Stanton would never have to answer for this abuse of authority because Lincoln would be dead by Saturday.

Stanton alone was demanding that all denominations in Richmond must profess that God was on the side of the army responsible for their city's condition. The President, however, had previously faced this same issue of the military using the churches to influence public opinion. Two years earlier, during a division in Missouri's loyalist regime, a debate raged about government and religious freedom. Lincoln summed up his position between the government's duty to the public good versus the liberty of free speech. He wrote to the military head of Missouri, Major General Samuel R. Curtis, that the General "on the spot" is left to determine how best to protect the public interest, but specified:

> ... the U.S. government must not, as by this order, undertake to run the churches. When an individual, in a church or out of it, becomes dangerous to the public interest, he must be checked; but let the churches, as such take care of themselves. It will not do for the U.S. to appoint Trustees, Supervisors, or other agents for the churches."[16]

Lincoln sent General Weitzel a telegram revealing he had no knowledge of the demands Stanton had issued regarding prayer.[17] Unaware of that conflict, Lincoln then issued a second telegram dismissing the Virginia legislature, as he did not consider them a legitimate governing body, and General Grant had since accomplished the disarmament of Virginia by capturing their armies. "Their withdrawal is no longer applicable. ... Do not allow them to assemble; but if any have come, allow them safe return to their homes."[18]

Stanton's plan to antagonize Campbell and the Virginia legislature worked, and the sense of reconciliation among the Southern opposition was replaced with renewed passions against Northern aggression.

5

Last Chance

*I*n-between the alternating sunshine and sudden soaking showers, Mr. Lincoln decided to take a short trip down his well-beaten path to the War Department. His heavily-used trail stretched between an overhanging canopy of trees that separated the two buildings. Stomping the mud off the bottom of his boots before going into the building, the President was unaware of the solemn mood that awaited him on the other side of the building's large back door.

During the days leading up to Lee's surrender, Secretary Stanton had been full of excitement about the captured rebel flags and the arrangements for the Fort Sumter ceremonies that officially reclaimed the Charleston Harbor as Federal property. Mr. Lincoln was caught more than a little off-guard when he met a sullen Stanton coming out of his office holding the resignation that he had only just finished writing.

"What is this?" the surprised Commander-in-Chief asked in a sober tone.

Stanton didn't speak, but only extended the document out for the President to receive.

Looking down, Mr. Lincoln quickly scanned the paper then shifted his eyes back to meet Stanton's blank expression. "You cannot go!"

There was a long pause without a word as each warrior tried to stare down the other. Lincoln was first to break the standoff, saying, "You understand the situation better than anybody else, and it is my wish and the country's that you remain. You have been our main reliance. You must stay on. Reconstruction will be the most difficult and dangerous part, even more so than the war."[1]

Power and authority were what Stanton had always lived for, and to have the last word was his purpose in life. Ambition and bile fueled his unbridled will to be the supreme authority, and it was authority that defined his sense of allegiance. His loyalty was to power, not to some foolish ideal of, "by the people, for the people." Before the war began, Edwin Stanton was the Attorney General for President James Buchanan, and during the 1860 presidential elections, he supported Buchanan's Vice President, the Democrat nominee

John Breckenridge. In the early part of the war, Stanton elaborated to Democrats about the advantages a divided Union would bring, but he wisely kept
his options open, and talked loyalty with the loyalists.[2]

John Breckenridge was Edwin Stanton's presidential choice over Lincoln;
however Breckenridge lost that election, but went on to become the Confederate Secretary of War. Stanton chose to side with the loyalists, and became the
counterpart to Breckenridge. Only days after the northern victory, the U.S.
Secretary of War was peering up into the eyes of the man who destroyed his
incentive for siding with the Union. It was Mr. Lincoln who had won, and
nothing short of reversing the President's course could restore Stanton's lost
dream of complete triumph over the losing side. Stanton had played his old
game well, giving lip service to the President, while scheming and plotting
with his backdoor comrade, Salmon P. Chase.[3]

During Chase's bid to keep Lincoln from serving a second term, Stanton helped Chase by deliberately pulling General Butler away from taking
Petersburg in order to prolong the war.[4] If Petersburg were taken in early
May of 1864, the war's end would have quickly followed, and Lincoln would
have emerged a hero, assured of the nomination just before the Republican
National Convention in June. Neither Chase nor Frémont, the two Radical
contenders for Lincoln's Job, would have had a chance of beating Lincoln for
the nomination, and time would run out for the plan by Sumner and Stevens
to completely destroy the social, political and economic infrastructure of the
South. They also needed Stanton to continue the war long enough for Sherman's "march to the sea" to fulfill Sumner's congressional supremacy thesis,
calling for reducing Southern states to territories. Lincoln's strongest supporter
in his Cabinet, Montgomery Blair, pleaded in a long letter to the President
that Sumner, Stevens and Chase wanted the whole rebel region made a *tabula
rasa* (clean slate).[5] Blair became the first Lincoln conservative to be driven out
of the cabinet by political pressure from the Radicals.

Lincoln said "no more" to Stanton, handed the resignation back to him,
and gave a look that could only mean there will be no debate. "You must stay
on."

Stanton was consumed with mental anguish from his natural desire to
stay on and to immerse himself in the unrestrained, authoritarian domination
he could finally, and so justly inflict upon his demoralized enemy—but not
with Lincoln at the helm. For Stanton it was agonizing to be that close—to

reach this place of destiny, only to find the President ready to "bind up the nation's wounds" and allow the captured enemy to go free.

In Stanton's dream, Salmon Chase was to be the one, not Lincoln. And with Chase as president he would appoint Stanton as his new Secretary of State. There was no way that Stanton could be a part of Lincoln's restored Union, it was not even an option he could choose. No part of his being would allow him to give quarter to an enemy who was now on their knees.

Without another word spoken, Mr. Lincoln quietly turned and walked away, leaving Stanton standing as he found him, still holding his resignation. In the corridor Stanton lingered, conflicted and frustrated, staring at the tiles on the floor until he was interrupted by a voice from a young assistant, "Mr. Secretary, you have a message." A plain envelope reading, "Attention Mr. Stanton," was handed to the Secretary. The note he read was the light of dawn that follows the darkest hour of night. It read, "Hold your position. I have spoken with Sumner and Stevens, and they have assured me we still have a chance. Present the details of our reconstruction policy to the Cabinet when they next meet." It was signed "SP Chase."

A surge of electricity pulsated through Stanton's body as if struck by a bolt of lightning. He realized that his goal could still be achieved, to still prevail with Sumner, Stevens and Chase at the helm. Through clenched teeth he inaudibly muttered, "Those rebel criminals will pay!" With the valor of a reborn Christian soldier, Stanton almost ran back to his desk, tossing his resignation into the waste paper basket. Anxious and excited, Stanton began his draft for the presentation for the Radical reconstruction policy for the defeated states—the same punishing agenda Lincoln had fought so long and hard to reject.[6]

While Stanton was launching his antagonistic attack against Lincoln's reconciliation with Virginia, Chase painted a clear picture for the President of the dark consequences he would face by snubbing the Radical post-war agenda. On the morning of April 11, Salmon Chase began his part to pressure the President into conceding to Congress his executive authority regarding confiscated Southern property, which Lincoln wished to return to the rightful owners. He also argued that Congressional representation for the rebellious states should be denied. Chase again strongly advised the President he should also mandate voting rights to the Negro population in the South.

Chase wrote Lincoln at length about his objections to the President's reconstruction plan. He explained to Mr. Lincoln that he was very anxious about the future, especially about which principles (his or Lincoln's) were to govern reconstruction. His main point was to emphasize securing suffrage to colored loyalists in the rebel states, arguing that the rebel states are "not likely ... to be either wise or just, until taught both wisdom and justice by new calamities."[7] His reference to *new calamities* meant the use of rigid and excessive force against any in the South who defied their new, imposed government.

Chase argued to Lincoln that:

> ... many of our best men [the Radicals] in and out of Congress had become thoroughly convinced of the ... injustice from allowing representation in Congress to the states which had been in rebellion and they were not yet prepared to concede equal political rights [...]. They felt that if such representation should be allowed & such states reinstated in all their former rights as loyal members of the Union, the colored population would be practically abandoned to the disposition of the white population, with every probability against them.[8]

This was Chase's rationale to pressure Lincoln into creating a pro-Northeastern (pro-industrial) voter base in the Southern states. The elected regional administrators representing their individual districts in the Southern states would be all replaced with Northern carpetbaggers under the Radical reconstruction plan. These new government officials would descend on the devastated southern economy to rebuild with a new, politically-controlled voter base for electing representatives. This was the chief issue that could only be changed by Lincoln's consent, or by his death, and this issue was argued to Lincoln *only* by the Radicals. If he withheld his consent they would plot his assassination to achieve their goal of selecting their own Southern Congressional representatives.

The President was defending the right of the defeated states to have equal representation in Congress. The President was trying to bring the country back together as an undivided union of states, while the Northeastern Radicals were fighting Lincoln to prevent a return of the agricultural power base in Congress.

Later that day, after reading Chase's letter, Lincoln gave his last public address. In it he made compromises toward the arguments that the Radical coalition had against his reconstruction plan. Lincoln altered his position on black suffrage by conferring voting rights for the most intelligent African-Americans and those who served as Union soldiers.[9] But even this compromise fell far short of assuring the Radicals that they could maintain their majority in Congress. Establishing a pro-Northeastern voter base in the South and preventing Southern representatives from returning to Congress were the only sure ways to protect the economic power of the New England industrial region. The decision to keep Lincoln from serving another full term was confirmed by his Radical antagonists. Assassination was now the only option left to prevent the President's reconstruction plan from being enacted.

For the Radicals, Lee's surrender had pushed the issue to remove Lincoln to a critical and desperate situation. Every minute Lincoln stayed in office, the more damage he would cause until there would be no way left to reverse his policies for reconciliation with the former secessionist states.

Two days before Lincoln's assassination, Salmon Chase again wrote the President, and for the last time. Chase reminded Lincoln about his long-held position on voting rights for the colored loyalists in the Southern states. He all but admitted that controlling votes in Congress was the whole purpose for the Civil War.[10] Legislation could regulate the distribution of the Nation's wealth through a majority of Congressional votes. Their opportunity had come to lay claim to all the wealth that the United States had, and all its untapped wealth yet to come. If Lincoln threw away the sacrifice the Union had given to secure the Northeastern voting power in Congress, then (to the Radical coalition) the President's assassination would be as justified as any blood spilled in the name of loyalty. The dirty deed would be left to the Secretary of War—to finish what they had started so many years before. And no man was more capable to end the Civil War with a *total* victory for the Northeastern industrialists than Edwin M. Stanton.

6

Agents & Secrets

*B*y the second week of April, 1865, President Abraham Lincoln had made many deadly political enemies in Washington. On the west side of the White House were Lincoln's enemies under Stanton's War Department, and on the east side was the Treasury Department, both of which served the interests of the Radical coalition, and both employed the military to help them steal everything they could get their corrupt hands around. And throughout the city of Washington there were Lincoln's angry civilian enemies.

John Wilkes Booth was one such angry civilian, who knew the President only from the media or other second-hand sources. Even though Booth was well known for his vocal opposition to Lincoln's political policies, without help from an insider such as Stanton he posed no credible threat. The months-old plan that John Wilkes Booth had made to capture Lincoln and smuggle him south had become pointless.

Even before Lincoln won the November election, both the Radicals and Booth independently devised separate plans to keep Lincoln from serving another term as president. In May, 1864, Stanton was plotting with Salmon Chase to help Chase win the Republican nomination for the next presidential term. In November, Booth wrote a manifesto to justify the act he was setting out to commit: "to make for her [the South] a prisoner of this man [Lincoln]."[1] He began his letter by professing, "I have loved peace more than life" and "the Union beyond expression." He blamed Lincoln for the war, and although he was not a Southerner nor had any connection to slavery, he viewed the slave institution as "one of the greatest blessings (for both themselves and us) that God ever bestowed upon a favored nation."[2]

Booth never knew the real Lincoln because he only knew him through what he had read in the newspapers or what he had been told by others. Booth never learned or understood the truth about the President's reasons for the war. Without reading the full text of Booth's manifesto, no one can understand the truth about why he plotted to kidnap Lincoln. Booth's political reason for wanting to do something decisive was much different from what most historians claim. Quotations from his manifesto have been suspiciously published out of their proper context, misconstruing Booth as a Confederate agent who hated African-Americans. These quotations are so select, and the conclusions so contrary to the essence of the letter, as to seem a deliberate attempt to misportray Booth and keep the spotlight away from Lincoln's *real* political enemies.

Booth was a racist only by today's standards. His opinion of slavery wasn't derived from a cruel desire to condemn the African race to bondage. Rather, he believed, like so many other white people nationwide, that "this country was formed for the *white*, not the black man." He continued to explain:

> Heaven knows no one would be more willing to do more for the Negro race than I, could I but see a way to still better their condition. But Lincoln's policy is only preparing the way for their total annihilation. ... I thought then, as now, the abolitionists were the only traitors in the land ... not because they wish to abolish slavery, but on account of the means ... to effect that abolition.[3]

John Wilkes Booth did not know President Lincoln, nor did he understand that the President was working to amend all the tyranny and injustice that Booth had mistakenly blamed on him. However, Stanton did know and understand the President, but he and his coalition of Sumner, Stevens and Chase wanted the Union to carry on with the tyranny and injustice that had marked the Civil War, and had caused both governments to violate the United States Constitution.

The Radical coalition appointed Stanton to make arrangements to have Lincoln assassinated. Stanton needed not only to provide an assassin to carry out the plot, but he also needed to place the suspicion and blame on a defenseless victim. And what better defenseless victim was there to frame than the already hated Confederate government? The idea to use Booth as an assassin was the perfect choice in so many ways: his kidnapping accomplices were Southern sympathizers, could be connected to Confederate couriers, and had already been well infiltrated by several of Stanton's agents.

James Donaldson was just one of a number of Stanton's agents assigned to collect information on the Confederate Secret Service working in and around the Washington area, plus he was already in Booth's inner circle. Booth's kidnapping caper was known by many people in Washington, Baltimore, and

JAMES DONALDSON **in his trademark black suit, photographed in 1863 with ten of his State Department colleagues, including the Secretary, William Seward.**

the southern Maryland countryside. Donaldson posed as a willing accomplice to kidnapping Lincoln in order to gather inside information about Booth's Confederate agent friend, John Surratt, Jr.[4]

Another Stanton informant planted in Booth's gang was James Hall. He was hired by the National Chief of Police, Lafayette Baker, to watch the Post Office and intercept letters sent from Richmond, while he too posed as a Southern sympathizer.[5]

Louis Weichmann had also been hired by Baker to spy on John Surratt, Jr., who was Weichmann's old schoolmate from St. Charles College, Maryland. Baker had long known that Surratt was a Confederate Signal Corps spy. Baker had arrested Surratt on November 17, 1863, while John was the acting Postmaster for the Post Office in Charles County, Maryland. He charged Surratt with disloyalty, but John was only jailed for a few days, then released without further investigation or charges.[6] Baker replaced Surratt with his own postmaster before releasing him, allowing him to continue with his spying operations, but while the Police Chief monitored his every move. Baker's own postmaster-spy inspected the mail before it was delivered, and reported to Stanton any Confederate messages that he uncovered.

In 1862, at the age of 18, John Surratt began spying for the Confederate Signal Corps, and his job was to inform the blockade smugglers on the Potomac River about Union troop movements in and around the Maryland and Washington areas. John Surratt never realized Baker and Stanton knew about his spying missions, and John even gave talks years after the war had ended, bragging about how he fooled the United States government. In his talks he would say, "I confess that never in my life did I come across a more stupid set of detectives than those generally employed by the United States government. They seem to have no idea whatever how to search men."[7]

Those Union agents were in no way stupid, and keeping John Surratt in jail until the end of the war would have destroyed one of Baker's means of gathering Confederate secrets.[8]

In January, 1864, Louis Weichmann was persuaded by Baker to move to Washington to spy on Surratt and the other Confederate smugglers. Weichmann was given a job at the War Department, and by November, 1864, he had moved in with John at the boardinghouse owned by his mother, Mary Surratt.

A suspected civilian informant under Baker to monitor the mail was Thomas Harbin, who was also a Confederate agent, and whose coworker at the Allen's Fresh Post Office in Maryland was a French-speaking woman by the name of Sarah Antoinette Slater. Slater, too, was a Confederate bearer of dispatches.[9] Harbin is suspected of having struck a deal with Baker because he aided Booth in his escape after the assassination, and yet he was never charged by the War Department. Sarah Slater knew many merchants in the area who participated in smuggling contraband into Confederate territory, which was the black market enterprise Baker controlled.

But Stanton's most professional source of Confederate secrets came from William P. Wood, the warden of the Old Capitol Prison. William Wood was an agent appointed by Salmon Chase while Chase was still Lincoln's Treasury Secretary. Wood had some 30 agents and spies under his authority, and many agents, such as James Hall, intercepted mail deliveries between Richmond and Washington and brought the letters to Wood at the prison. Wood skillfully opened the letters, then read and copied the ones that had secret messages, sending the copies directly to Stanton.[10] After the war ended, Wood was appointed to head a new division for the Treasury Department (a secret service agency that would later become the FBI) as a reward for his service to Stanton during the war.[11]

There was still another very knowledgeable member in Booth's kidnapping gang who was also a double agent, and was also never arrested, nor even called to testify during the conspiracy trial. Her alias was Kate Thompson, and some knew her as Kate Brown. She stayed at the National Hotel with Booth, and was popular with all his gang members, even making trips to Richmond with Surratt and a Maryland blockade-runner named Augustus Howell.[12]

Howell was a well-known black market smuggler who made several trips between Richmond and Washington. He was capitalizing on the exchange rate between the cities' two separate economies and traded Federal greenbacks for the wholesale liquidation of Southern valuables.[13] Richmonders were selling or trading everything of worth to buy food and medicine, and even Jefferson and Varina Davis were trading clothing and jewelry to maintain their living conditions.[14] Washington's Chief of Detectives, Lafayette Baker, was at the head of this lucrative smuggling racket, and he was well familiar with Augustus Howell.

Because Howell had been arrested three weeks before the attacks on Lincoln and Seward, he could not be implicated. However, he was still called to testify as a defense witness for Mary Surratt during the conspiracy trial.[15] With John Surratt absent, the prosecution used Howell's close association with John to implicate Mary Surratt. During cross examination Augustus Howell admitted to the prosecution that he had been to the Surratt boardinghouse.[16] That was all Stanton's Judge Advocates needed to frame Mary Surratt as a Confederate agent. After the trial Mary Surratt was hanged.

Strangely, after Lincoln's death, Kate Thompson was never again mentioned, even though the prosecution investigators and all the military Judge Advocates knew she was a major conspirator in Booth's gang. She was much more involved in Booth's plans for Lincoln than any of Stanton's suspects who were hanged or given life in prison. Those suspects were also less involved than James Donaldson, who was also never arrested nor mentioned again.

Kate Thompson was in truth a double agent reporting to the War Department, and was originally hired as a detective for Allan Pinkerton in 1856. Her real name was Kate Warne and she was a young, attractive widow, who became the first woman detective in America. Kate Warne could easily infiltrate social situations without causing suspicion, because no one at the time suspected a female agent. Pinkerton himself described her as:

> eminently fitted for this task, … with clear cut, expressive features and an ease of manner that was quite captivating at times, she was calculated to make a favorable impression at once. She was of northern birth, but in order to vouch for her Southern opinions, she represented herself as from Montgomery, Alabama, a locality with which she was perfectly familiar.

She was useful in infiltrating sympathizer groups because she could make "remarkable progress in cultivating acquaintance with the wives and daughters of the conspirators." Prior to the formation of Booth's kidnapping gang—primar-

ily men from Baltimore—Mrs. Warne had been assigned to Baltimore to ferret
out sympathizers and Confederate provocateurs. Pinkerton wrote:

> Mrs. Warne displayed upon her breast, as did many of the ladies
> of Baltimore, the black and white cockade, which had been tem-
> porarily adopted as the emblem of secession, and many hints were
> dropped in her presence which found their way to my ears, and
> were of great benefit to me. [17]

Warne was so useful to Pinkerton, that within two years with his agency
she became a department head, the superintendent of all new female agents.
Her identity as an informant for Stanton had to be kept a secret. Kate [Warne]
Thompson was mentioned only one time in the conspirators' trial, and by only
one of the accused, even though every military prosecutor knew all about her.
She could never be called to court to reveal what she had learned as a secret
informant, because if it were ever known that she was an agent reporting on
Booth, Stanton would have to explain why Booth was never arrested for con-
spiracy to kidnap the President.

The entire myth that surrounds this unsolved mystery of who conspired
to help Booth kill Lincoln is exposed in the confession of George Atzerodt,
the fourth person hanged as a conspirator in the assassination plot. Atzerodt
attempted to save himself from certain execution by truthfully confessing to
everything he knew about Booth and his gang members. He made a prior
confession, but this confession to the Provost Marshall of Baltimore, James
McPhail, was recorded in a transcript in which he honestly admitted all that
he knew. He identified all the people who were involved in Booth's plot to
kidnap Lincoln. But what George Atzerodt did not realize (at the time) was
that he gave his confession to the very people who were behind the conspiracy
to murder Lincoln. Atzertodt's confession to McPhail was never allowed as
evidence in the conspiracy trial, and his story would be hidden away for 112
years.

George Atzerodt was a homeless German immigrant who spoke very poor
English, and was denied legal counsel while he awaited trial, chained and
shackled, hand and foot, in solitary confinement. He was entombed in the
chain locker of the ironclad U.S.S. Saugus while sweltering in the ship's stifling
heat, among snakes and spiders, with a canvas hood pulled down over his head
and tied at the neck.

On May 1, 1865, ten days following Atzerodt's arrest, Stanton was approached by Marshal James McPhail to ask the Secretary if he would grant him an interview with Atzerodt. George Atzerodt's brother-in-law, John L. Smith, was a detective working for MacPhail, and George's brother, John Atzerodt, had also worked as a detective for McPhail. Both detectives asked the Marshal if they could gain permission from Stanton for a pass to hear what George had to say. Stanton was very curious to find out what George knew and agreed to allow them an interview. However once Stanton read the contents of the interview he realized it, as well as Atzertodt, must be destroyed.

The Secretary of War Edwin Stanton, the Chief of Detectives Lafayette Baker, and the Judge Advocate General Joseph Holt, who was in charge of the trial proceedings and chief investigator for the War Department, were all parties to Lincoln's assassination and the cover-up that followed.

Secretary Stanton was a master at organization, and he tried to destroy every trace of evidence that could have possibly exposed his involvement in Lincoln's death. Until the present, every suspicion of Stanton's involvement has been dismissed as mere speculation because no one has provided any documented proof. However, Atzerodt's confession to McPhail is one piece of damning evidence Stanton believed to be destroyed forever, but a copy of it was found. Upon analysis the transcript makes Stanton's guilt for the conspiracy to kill Lincoln genuinely incontestable.

The named members of Booth's gang who were never arrested or even mentioned in the trial were Stanton's double agents: Kate [Warne] Thompson, James Donaldson, Charles Yates, Margaret Coleman and James Hall. Those uncovered gang members, mentioned in George Atzerodt's hidden confession, expose Stanton, Baker, and Joseph Holt as conspirators in Lincoln's murder. That's why his confession was never submitted as evidence, and that's the reason why the confession was intended by Stanton to be destroyed forever (*See* Appendix C).

Atzerodt's confession became his death sentence when he named the wrong people, and it was his mention of Kate Thompson (or Brown as she was known by both names) that would seal his doom. The diary found on Booth's body, but was never submitted in the conspiracy trial, most likely contained her name on the pages that were later cut out from the book. The diary and Atzerodt's confession were both withheld as evidence during the trial because of what they would reveal. Many of the pages in Booth's diary were removed, and just like those missing pages, those double agents were never considered at the trial or by anyone afterwards. This explains Stanton's purpose for inhumanely placing canvas bags over the heads of anyone who might expose the people he did not want to be known.

John Surratt, Augustus Howell, Louis Weichmann, Lewis Powell, David Herold, Edwin Stanton, Lafayette Baker, Joseph Holt and Thomas Eckert are just a few who knew Kate Thompson as a close member among Booth's followers. She was never called to testify, arrested, or even known to the public until 1977, when Atzerodt's confession was found by pure chance. Any member of Booth's gang who knew Kate Thompson never knew she was a double agent. They were either hanged, sentenced to a long prison term, or, as in the case of John Surratt and Augustus Howell, never had a reason or purpose to implicate her. Weichmann also knew Thompson, but he could never mention her name without implicating Baker and Stanton.

Weichmann's purpose as a witness during the trial was to cover for the Radical coalition's involvement in the assassination plot against the President. Any evidence that would expose the fact that Mary Surratt, David Herold and George Atzerodt were only conspirators in a kidnapping plot was withheld, while Weichmann was used to divert attention away from Stanton's many desperately guarded secrets and provide damning testimony against the accused. The serious charge of being an accomplice to assassination loomed over Weichmann's head, and his only salvation was to collaborate with the Judge Advocates' strategy to frame their ill-fated defendants as Confederate assassins. One of Weichmann's many assignments as the prosecution's star witness was to create the illusion that Kate Thompson and Sarah Slater were the same person.

Sarah Antoinette Slater was known to be a spy for the Confederacy, whose mission was to deliver secret messages. She lived in Baltimore and made only brief visits to Washington, staying at Mary Surratt's boardinghouse only on one occasion in late March. She was born Sarah Gilbert, married to Rowan Slater, and was well-known among the Confederate Signal Corps carriers. Members of her family were also known by many people. In contrast, Kate Thompson was posing as a childless, *widowed* Southern belle with no known family, and she also used the name Kate Brown. She did not live in Baltimore, but resided at the National Hotel with John Wilkes Booth. She was well acquainted with the entire kidnapping affair, and often seen at the Pennsylvania House where the kidnappers met. It is ridiculous to insist that Sarah Slater would pose as a childless widow named Kate with two different aliases

(Thompson and Brown) in the company of people who already knew her as the happily married Sarah Slater from Baltimore.

Kate Thompson was described by Atzerodt as young, good looking, and well dressed, with dark hair, dark eyes and a round face. The day after Atzerodt gave this account, his friend Louis Weichmann was in the Old Capital Prison, and would be interrogated about Confederate spies on the very next day. During Weichmann's questioning nothing was asked of him about Kate Thompson (or Brown), even though George Atzerodt had just revealed to McPhail the previous day that the widow Kate was clearly involved in the kidnapping plot, and that "young Weightman at Surratt's ought to know about this woman."[18] In fact, this double-named Kate would never be mentioned in official reports or by Weichmann at all.

Before Lincoln's assassination Kate Warne worked undercover for Pinkerton and the Secret Service using many different aliases. Her most often used disguise was that of a widowed "Southern belle," the same disguise that Kate Thompson used. In early 1861, Kate Warne played a key role in preventing an assassination attempt against Lincoln in Baltimore. She was described as a slender, brown-haired woman, but no other credible information has ever been disclosed to reveal her true identity. There are no pictures of her[19] or records of her service during the two years before Lincoln's assassination, but she worked for the agency up until at least 1867.

Many agents under cover chose to include some part of their real name as part of their aliases. This was to protect their alias if ever referred to by their true name. Allan Pinkerton chose the name E. J. Allen, changing one letter in the repeated name. Kate Warne almost always used the first name Kate, Kay, Kittie, or Katie, and often spelled Warne many different ways—Warn, Warren, etc. Even her headstone is inscribed differently than her known name. Kate Thompson or Brown was without question a Federal double agent, and reported to the War Department about the conspiracy to kidnap Lincoln for months before the President was shot. Her identity was deliberately hidden away, along with James Donaldson, Charles Yates, Margaret Coleman and James Hall, for no other reason than to hide how much information Stanton and Baker actually knew about Booth before Lincoln was assassinated. Only persons involved in Lincoln's murder would have a need to conceal this information; and only those in charge of the investigation and trial had the ability to withhold these crucial pieces of evidence.

7

A Band of Idiots

*T*he Confederate conspiracy theorists say that Booth was working closely with the Confederate government to kidnap Lincoln, and that his mission was to turn the President over to them. However, there is no evidence to substantiate this claim. Booth's only known connection to the Confederate government did not begin until January, 1865, after he won the confidence of John Surratt,[1, 2] a Confederate courier who traveled to and from Richmond. Other participants in the plot to kidnap Lincoln, such as Augustus Howell, Charles Yates and Kate Thompson, also traveled back and forth between Richmond and Washington,[3] but largely for reasons unknown.

By February the North had taken possession of eastern Virginia. Even if Booth had been able to succeed with his failed attempt to capture Lincoln on March 17th, he could only have turned his captured prize over to General Grant's *Union* army. The facts are that during late March, the Confederate capital was preparing for Union army occupation, and they could not have been making plans to capture Abraham Lincoln, but to save themselves from the advancing Union army. On April 2, Jefferson Davis boarded a train heading south to avoid being taken prisoner under the very serious threat of being executed as a traitor. The next day the Union army marched into Richmond and captured any Confederate administrators left in the city who had not fled.

The original purpose behind Booth's kidnapping plot was to exchange Lincoln for Confederate prisoners. General Grant had been complaining that the prisoner exchange program between the Union and Confederate armies gave an advantage to the South. The war strategy by Lincoln's administration was to force the Confederate states back into the Union by depleting Southern resources, which would in turn take away their ability to wage war. The naval blockade had cut off the import of manufactured goods; and ending the prisoner exchange program would deprive the Southern army from reenlisting their captured soldiers. Ending the exchange program would benefit the Union army because the South was running out of recruits, and the Union states had a population advantage of about 10 million more people. In February, 1864, Lincoln called for a new draft quota of 500,000 men to be filled by March 10,[4] (a number five times the size of Lee's Confederate Army).

In early September, 1864, Booth first devised his plot to capture Lincoln to barter for the release of Confederate prisoners, but he needed to enlist his own recruits to pull it off.

On a September evening, John Wilkes Booth sat in his room at the Barnum Hotel in Baltimore, and anxiously waited for his first accomplice to arrive. The hotel porter gave a quick knock on the door, then ushered into the room Samuel Arnold, Booth's old classmate from St. Timothy's Hall in Maryland, whom Booth had not seen in twelve years. Booth gave Arnold a warm reception, and the two men sat in elegant comfort, reminiscing about former school days. While Booth treated Arnold to fine wine and cigars, their conversation was interrupted by another knock at the door, and Booth's second recruit joined them in the plushy, smoke-filled hotel room. Michael O'Laughlen had come to the hotel prepared to discuss a business venture involving oil stocks, and both recruits were readily impressed by Booth's enterprising ideas about getting rich in the oil business. The three continued to become reacquainted, but Booth's guests still had not learned the true reason for their invitation to such an opulent gathering. However, as they talked their conversations gradually took on a more solemn and political tone.[5]

Both Arnold and O'Laughlen had previously been Confederate soldiers, but both men had deserted during the war and returned to civilian life. They both signed an oath of loyalty to the Union,[6] but just like Booth and many citizens of Maryland, their sentiments were still very much against the Lincoln administration. Booth felt assured he had recruited sympathizers to his cause, and he chose to reveal his plot to capture the President. His two guests were indeed very willing to help Booth trade Lincoln for the release of Confederate soldiers. However, though their aim was to add fighting men back to the hopeless Confederate army, none of the three men were willing to offer themselves as soldiers in open warfare. Both recruits agreed to take a new oath of secrecy with Booth, but it would not be until January, 1865, before they saw him again.[7]

Booth left the next day and traveled north to the oil region of Pennsylvania, New York, then onto Boston, and from there into Canada. He would not meet again with these collaborators until after New Year's Day. Before January, Booth had not yet made any definite plans or arrangements for an attempt to kidnap the President.

When Booth returned to Washington he brought with him a trunk filled with guns and knives for all his gang members, along with a pair of handcuffs for the President. His general idea was to intercept the unguarded presidential carriage during one of Lincoln's frequent trips back from the Old Soldiers' Home. Suspiciously, though maybe just coincidentally, Booth's knowledge of Lincoln's unguarded trips was the same information William Seward had revealed to his European agent F. H. Morse the previous summer.

In January, back in D.C., Booth obtained his third recruit, another Maryland native. This recruit had more than just a vendetta against the administration, he was a spy for the Confederate government. John Surratt, Jr., had been an agent for the Confederate Signal Corps since 1862. He had been arrested in November of 1863, suspected of being a spy, but was only jailed for a few days, then released. However, long before Surratt met Booth and joined his conspiracy to kidnap the President, he had been under close surveillance by Stanton's chief detective, Lafayette Baker. Having been once arrested as a spy, Surratt was suspicious of Northerners trying to collaborate with him. He had been introduced to Booth the previous Autumn, but was wary around the self-important and loud-mouthed actor, probably suspecting such an overt sympathizer might actually be a Union agent.[8]

JOHN HARRISON SURRATT, JR. had been under surveillance by the War Department since 1863.

While Booth had been out of town, Arnold and O'Laughlen took up residence together in Washington, and after Booth's return they all met frequently with him to help plan the kidnapping. But John Surratt soon became Booth's prime accomplice, leaving Arnold and O'Laughlen only vaguely aware of the specific details.[9]

At almost midnight on Wednesday, March 15, Samuel Arnold and Michael O'Laughlen were socializing with locals on the shared porch of Ruhlman's Hotel and the Lichau House restaurant when another recruit in Booth's gang, James Donaldson, called Michael aside and said Booth wished to see them both at Gautier's Saloon. O'Laughlen already knew James Donaldson, but this would be the first time Arnold had met him. After they arrived at the saloon, Arnold was also introduced to John Surratt for the first time, along with George Atzerodt, who was introduced by his nickname "Port Tobacco," and a strapping, young Confederate agent who went by the name "Mosby." This Mosby was actually a man named Lewis Powell, a name which he never revealed to anyone in Washington.[10]

Lewis Powell (aliases James Wood and Mosby) had been arrested earlier that week in Baltimore by Provost Marshal H. B. Smith, but not for being a spy. Mosby was charged with assault and battery of a black maid who worked at the Branson boardinghouse in Baltimore where Mosby stayed. He beat her just because she refused to clean his room.[11]

Lewis Powell had been wounded and captured on the Gettysburg battlefield. He was transferred from a makeshift hospital in Pennsylvania to a Baltimore prison, from which he escaped in late 1863 with helpers from the same Branson boardinghouse he had returned to in January, 1865. By March Mosby had gotten himself arrested in Baltimore, but he was not recognized as an escaped prisoner. Marshal Smith allowed his release after Powell agreed to sign an oath of allegiance, however this time Powell signed his name "Lewis Paine," using yet another alias. He was released on Tuesday, March 14, only a day before the conspirators met at Gautier's Saloon.

During the saloon meeting, Booth had provided an oyster feast with an open bar for his conspirators to enjoy while they listened to his revised kidnapping plot, in which Lincoln would be taken in Ford's Theatre. Each member was assigned a specific, coordinated duty to perform, with the exception of still another accomplice, David Herold. Herold was dimwitted and childish, and could only be trusted with simple tasks. His service to Booth was to run errands, do menial jobs, and look after the horses. David Herold was not at the saloon that night, neither was another member of the gang, Charles Yates.

In the new plan, Michael O'Laughlen and James Donaldson were given the assignment of extinguishing the theater's gaslights, while Powell (aliases Mosby and Wood) and Booth would handcuff the President and lower him down to Arnold, waiting on the stage. Atzerodt and Surratt were to wait on the other side of the East Branch Bridge. Atzerodt would then direct Lincoln's abductors to a hidden rowboat and turn the horses loose. Charles Yates (not at the meeting) would row the party across the Potomac River, and once in Virginia, Surratt (who knew the area) would act as their pilot to Richmond.[12, 13]

Samuel Arnold was opposed to the whole theater abduction idea, and he told Booth that just getting Lincoln from the theater box to the bridge was impossible to accomplish, surrounded by people, police and bridge guards. Arnold argued that they would be easily stopped, and O'Laughlen agreed with him. Arnold further stated that he wanted a "shadow of a chance" to succeed, and if they didn't come up with a feasible plan and execute it "this week, I will forever withdraw from it." Booth became very angry, and reminded Arnold of his oath of secrecy, and said he was liable to be shot for breaking the oath. Arnold told Booth that the plan had been changed to a futile suicide mission, and that Booth might as well shoot him there, though he would defend himself.[14]

The next day, Thursday, March 16, around 2:30 PM, Booth was still very angry with Arnold and he called only on O'Laughlen at the Lichau House. Arnold saw Booth outside with Michael and he interrupted their meeting to remind Booth of what he had said the night before. He again told Booth that if the kidnapping would not happen that week, he would drop out.

Under pressure, Booth agreed that they would use the original plot (to ambush the presidential carriage) on the following day, Friday, March 17. But the ambush failed because Lincoln did not show up. The President's agenda had been changed, and the carriage they thought would be the one carrying the President was actually some other carriage carrying someone else. Lincoln's change of plans had been announced in the metropolitan newspapers, and the President was instead rescheduled to attend a ceremony at the very same National Hotel[15] where Booth was a resident. But (according to several historians) the kidnappers had gathered on the 7th Street Road near Campbell Hospital to ambush Lincoln where Booth ignorantly assumed he would be.

Undaunted by his haphazard and foolish attempt to kidnap the President, the next evening Booth appeared as scheduled in the role of Duke Pescara in "The Apostate" at Ford's Theatre on March 18th. Days before, Booth had given out many complimentary tickets to the play. Surratt used one of his tickets to bring a guest, his friend (and Union informant) Louis Weichmann. O'Laughlen gave his extra ticket to the landlady of his boardinghouse, Mrs. Van Tine.[16, 17]

Booth's kidnapping attempt was so poorly planned and orchestrated that the gang began to break up, and a day or so later, Samuel Arnold and Michael O'Laughlen returned to their homes in Baltimore, while Booth left Washington for New York. On Thursday, March 23, Booth sent a coded telegram from Brooklyn, New York, to Louis Weichmann in Washington that was dispatched by telegraph officer A. R. Reeves. Weichmann had a cipher key used by the Confederate agents, and he relayed the message from Booth to John Surratt. During cross examination in the conspiracy trial, Weichmann admitted, "I made a confidante of Captain Gleason [at the War Department],"[18] and later "I spoke with him previously on various occasions,"[19] indicating he was reporting on Surratt while living with him at his mother's home. And the encrypted telegram proves Booth was in New York during late March.

There would never again be a reason or opportunity for Booth to kidnap the President. When Booth left New York he stopped in Baltimore on March 25th. During this same time President Lincoln was preparing to leave Washington for City Point, Virginia. Neither Booth nor the President had been in Washington after the failed ambush attempt. The President would not return to Washington until April 7. On April 9, General Lee surrendered, effectively ending prisoner exchanges, rendering any plot to kidnap Lincoln pointless.

Upon Booth's arrival in Baltimore he called on Samuel Arnold's father to send a message to his son in the country to come join him in the city for a meeting. But before Arnold could get to Baltimore from Hookstown, Booth had already left for Washington with Michael O'Laughlen.[20] Arnold was upset and angry that Booth did not wait for him. He complained to Booth in a letter that was later found in a trunk by detectives during their search of Booth's hotel room on April 15, the morning after the assassination.[21]

The letter would become known as the infamous "Sam letter" and it has often been purposely misinterpreted by Confederate conspiracy theorists in order to help cover up the truth about who persuaded Booth to change his kidnapping plot to assassination. They use only an edited section of the letter to portray Booth's conspirators as being Confederate agents, but the letter in its entirety actually tells a completely different story.

Arnold's letter to Booth was postmarked March 27, and it stated in part:

> When I left you, [March 17, after the failed ambush] you stated we would not meet for a month or so. [...] No one was more for the enterprise than myself and today [March, 25] would be there had you not done as you have.

Samuel Arnold was previously upset with Booth for revising the kidnapping plot from a road ambush to the absurdity of lowering Lincoln by rope from the state box of a crowded theater. Arnold was assigned to wait on the stage to catch the President. This plan was so stupid that it caused Arnold to drop out of the plot, and, along with Booth abandoning him in Baltimore, was the reason for his letter. On Friday morning, March 31, Samuel Arnold's brother Frank delivered to Samuel a letter from a Mr. Wharton, offering him employment at Old Point Comfort, Virginia. Sam departed for his new job the next day, Saturday, April 1, two weeks before the assassination, and Arnold never saw or heard from Booth again.

Arnold's "Sam" letter provides more evidence to prove that agents working for Stanton's Chief Detective, Lafayette Baker, were keeping close tabs on the gang well before the assassination. The letter stated: "you know full well the government suspects something is going on there. Why not, for the present desist, for various reasons, which, if you look into, you can readily see, without my making mention thereof."[22] The letter also proves that their surveillance on Booth was very obvious. Arnold's letter revealed just how many people as far north as Baltimore were aware of Booth and his "covert" plans when he wrote:

> I told my parents I had ceased with you. Suspicion rests upon me now from my whole family and even parties in the country.[23]

This statement corresponds with Atzerodt's confession when he also stated: "Plenty of parties in Charles County knew of the kidnapping affair."[24] This letter is further evidence that the Baltimore Provost Marshal James McPhail, Chief Detective Lafayette Baker, and Secretary Stanton all knew about every move Booth and his band of idiot followers were making long before Lincoln was assassinated, yet Stanton never ordered a single arrest for Booth and his gang.

George Atzerodt's brother, John Atzerodt, and his brother-in-law, John L. Smith, were *both* Maryland detectives for Marshal McPhail, and everyone in McPhail's small community was well acquainted. Provost Marshal McPhail knew Samuel Arnold, Michael O'Laughlen and their families. Everyone in the area knew each other very well, and was obviously aware of what was going on with Booth and his plans for Lincoln.

On the same day Samuel Arnold left Maryland to begin his job on the Eastern Shore of Virginia, and just three days before Richmond fell, John Surratt left on a mission to Montréal from the Confederate capital to deliver

CHRONOLOGY OF THE BOOTH GANG

This timeline of the Baltimore players in Booth's gang shows their assembly and their one feeble attempt at kidnapping the President before disbanding.

MARCH, 1865

Early March. James Donaldson stores Booth's weapons and supplies in his home.

12th, Sunday. Mosby (Lewis Powell) arrested in Baltimore for assault.

13th, Monday. Booth's coded telegram to O'Laughlen regarding Saloon meeting.

14th, Tuesday. Mosby signs an oath of loyalty as "Lewis Paine," then released from jail, takes the train to Washington, checks into Mary Surratt's house as "Reverend James Wood."

15th, Wednesday. Midnight meeting at Gaither's Saloon to introduce James Donaldson. Samuel Arnold strongly objects to the new theater-setting kidnapping plot.

16th, Thursday. Arnold stayed awake until 6 or 7 am, slept until noon. Booth calls on O'Laughlen only. Arnold threatens to quit the gang.

17th, Friday. Booth's and gang laid in wait to capture Lincoln by Campbell Hospital, but Lincoln was instead appearing at Booth's hotel.

18th, Saturday. Gang went to Ford's Theatre to watch Booth perform in a play.

continued

a dispatch from Judah P. Benjamin, the Confederate Secretary of State.[25] John's assignment was to convey orders to General Edwin G. Lee, who had recently been reassigned a new duty in Canada.[26] Lee was the second cousin of General Robert E. Lee, and he had replaced Jacob Thompson and Clement C. Clay as the new head of the Confederate secret service operations in Canada.

The blockade had dried up many resources in the South, and the lack of soldiers to fill the depleted Confederate ranks had left the Confederacy with no ability to continue the war. Less than a week later, on April 9, five days before Lincoln was shot at Ford's Theatre, the fighting war had ended and the Confederate administration in Richmond was trying to avoid execution by negotiating a deal for amnesty. Lincoln was their only salvation, because he had the power to pardon, and he was the only one that showed a willingness to save their lives. The last thing Confederate administrators would want after late March would be to lose their only chance for salvation by killing Lincoln.

Although Lee's surrender came less than a week after the fall of Richmond, the inevitable and obvious certainty of the war's end came as a bit of a sudden surprise to everyone. Even Lincoln had publicly expressed the previous summer that the war might continue three more years,[27] but things were quickly changing militarily and politically.

Politically, the sudden end to the war left the Radicals with no option but to replace Lincoln if they were to prevent the return of Southern congressmen to Congress, or to exclude former Confederates from returning to state and local government positions. The defeated former Confederate Congress had no say in these matters, and could only hope to not be hanged. The competition for political power was between two groups: Lincoln and his moderate supporters from both parties versus the Radical hard-liners.

Even after General Robert E. Lee surrendered his starving and depleted troops to Grant, General Edwin Lee in Canada wrote, "I cannot and will not believe that because Gen. Lee was compelled to surrender 22,000 men, we therefore have no more army, and can wage war no more."[28] However, Confederate armies rapidly disbanded, and by April 13 the reality of a totally defeated South had been painfully ac-

19–20th, Sunday.–Monday. Arnold and O'Laughlen check out of Van Tine's house and return to Baltimore.

21st, Tuesday. Arnold goes to his country village of Hookstown; Booth departs for New York.

22nd, Wednesday. Booth in New York.

23rd, Thursday. Booth (in New York) sends Weichmann a telegram for Surratt; Lincoln leaves D.C. for Virginia.

24–25th, Friday–Saturday. Booth arrived in Baltimore, sent for Arnold, but left for Washington with only O'Laughlen. Arnold writes his angry "Sam letter" to Booth.

26th, Sunday. Arnold returns to Hookstown.

27th, Monday. The "Sam letter" is postmarked.

28–30th, Tuesday–Thursday. Lincoln is in City Point, Virginia, and will be in Virginia until April 7th. O'Laughlen and Arnold in Baltimore and Hookstown, Maryland.

31st, Friday. Arnold receives an offer of employment from J. H. Wharton at Fort Monroe, Virginia.

APRIL, 1865

1st, Saturday. Arnold departs to Fort Monroe for his new job.

cepted by everyone in the Confederacy, its administration, and even fanatical Southern sympathizers, including John Wilkes Booth. Everyone realized that the war was truly all over, and on Thursday evening, April 13, Booth told his fellow kidnappers, "the thing had failed," and that he intended to open a theater in Richmond.[29] Only hours later, during the early morning of April

14, John Wilkes Booth scribbled out a short letter to his mother expressing his coming to terms with the war's end and he wrote to her:

> Dearest Mother:
>
> I know you expect a letter from me, and am sure you will hardly forgive me. But indeed I have nothing to write about. Everything is dull—that is, has been till last night [the Grand Illumination of D.C., a two-night candle-lit celebration of the Union victory].
>
> Everything was bright and splendid. More so in my eyes if it had been a display in a nobler cause. But so goes the world. Might makes right. I only drop you these few lines to let you know I am well, and to say I have not heard from you. Excuse brevity; am in haste. Had one from Rose. With best love to you all, I am your affectionate
>
> John[30]

The letter was written Friday, April 14th, 1865, at approximately 2:00 AM, the day Lincoln was murdered. It illustrates that Booth had no intentions to assassinate Lincoln even at that late hour. In sharp contrast to his grandiose and passionate kidnapping manifesto, this last letter pleads no cause, contains no finality, and shows his resignation over outcome of the war. In fact, he solicits a reply from his mother, obviously in the expectation to still be at the National Hotel in the future.

During the conspiracy trial, the prosecution never presented a single piece of physical evidence to substantiate their claim that John Wilkes Booth had a plot to assassinate Lincoln before the day of the assassination. Before any conspirator can be convicted of plotting to assassinate the President, it must first be proven they were involved after the plot began. Booth did not reveal to anyone that he had an *assassination* plot until 7:30 PM on Friday evening, less than three hours before he shot Lincoln.

Atzerodt's confession confirms John Wilkes Booth had given up on his kidnapping plot late Thursday evening, April 13, and Booth's letter to his mother also confirms that he had come to terms with the war's end. Lewis Powell also confessed to Reverend Gillette just before his execution that he and Booth had not planned to assassinate *until the last day*.[31] It was only sometime after the letter to Booth's mother was written that James Donaldson persuaded Booth to kill Lincoln. Only at that point in time would his kidnapping plot be revised to assassination.

Atzerodt's confession is also the physical evidence that proves Booth had an appointment to meet with James Donaldson on Friday evening. However, this crucial transcript was deliberately withheld from the evidence presented during the trial because it gave the names of Stanton's double agents, and it also would prove he was not involved with any assassination plot. The military commission completely ignored James Donaldson in order to keep his identity a secret, hiding the fact that the War Department had known for months about Booth and his plot abduct Lincoln.

Why were James Donaldson, Kate Thompson, and Charles Yates never arrested or questioned for their roles in Booth's circle, while every other suspect named in Atzerodt's confession was tracked down and arrested or called to testify? Other key individuals were also ignored in the trial, such as James Hall, Sarah A. Slater, and Margaret Coleman (a maid for Secretary of State Seward), whose roles were found to be significant in the alleged conspiracy.

John Surratt, Jr., escaped the country, but was arrested twice (once in Italy and again in Egypt) before being extradited back to the United States. John Surratt was tried for his involvement with Booth by a civilian court in 1867, but he was found to be not guilty of plotting to kill the President. The government went to great effort to pursue John Surratt. How or why did other conspirators named in Atzerodt's confession remain uninvestigated?

Everyone who read the confessions by Samuel Arnold and George Atzerodt knew James Donaldson was a long-time member of William Seward's staff,[32] and one of three State Department employees assigned to watch over the injured Secretary of State in his home.[33] Stanton and his investigators, the prosecutors, and the judges in the conspirators' trial all knew that Seward's aide was identified as a conspirator with Booth, yet Donaldson was hidden from the investigation and the trial testimonies.

Only Donaldson's bosses would want his role to never be known.

8

Weapon & Motive

*I*t was not the President who persuaded Stanton to remain with his second term administration. It was the Chief Justice, Salmon P. Chase, who changed his mind. Stanton agreed to stay on to help with the post-war reconstruction, but only under one condition: Lincoln had to go.

During his public address on April 11, Lincoln responded to the letter Chase had sent him earlier that morning. It would be the last speech he would ever make. A large crowd had gathered on the White House lawn to hear what the President had to say, and among the most intensely interested to hear his words were the Radicals.

The crowd anxiously looked on as Lincoln laid out his policy for the next four years, saying:[1]

> No one man has authority to give up the rebellion for any other man[.] Nor is it a small additional embarrassment that we, the loyal people, differ among ourselves as to the mode, manner, and means of reconstruction.[2] …
>
> I have been shown a letter on this subject … in which the writer expresses regret that my mind has not seemed to be definitely fixed … whether the seceded states … are in the Union or out of it.[3] …
>
> [N]o exclusive, and inflexible plan can safely be prescribed. … Such exclusive, and inflexible plan would surely become a new entanglement. Important principles may, and must, be inflexible.[4]

Chase responded to Lincoln's speech the very next morning, as he wrote to the President:

> Once I should have been … reasonably contented by suffrage for the more intelligent [blacks] & for those who have been soldiers;

now I am convinced that universal suffrage is demanded by sound policy and impartial justice alike.[5]

The monumental importance Salmon Chase had placed on a mandate for immediate black suffrage for former slaves was in truth only his desire to create a pro-North voting block in the South. At that time many social reforms were needed: in America's West immigrants were being exploited in dangerous occupations; in the North children were working hazardous factory jobs and denied educations, and across the country women were clamoring for greater rights and political participation. Women suffrage would not be enacted until 1920 and child labor laws a decade after that. Chase and the Radicals were pushing for black (male) suffrage *before* women—even their own wives and daughters—solely because freed blacks would vote pro-North, while white Southern women would vote pro-South.

Chase had failed to change the course Lincoln had set for post-war America. Saving the Radicals' objectives was now up to Edwin Stanton swaying the Cabinet, and his success or failure would decide Lincoln's fate.

Two days later (April 14), Lincoln was beginning his last Cabinet meeting. The President had invited General Grant to join with them to give him an opportunity to meet everyone in the new administration, although William Seward was still confined to bed and was unable to attend (his son, Frederick, was present and taking detailed notes in his place). The President was happy that Stanton chose to remain with the new administration, and the Secretary of War had come prepared to display the reconstruction plans by the Radicals.

The draft Stanton had put together was the issue that dominated the meeting, and the Secretary eagerly revealed the outline of the Radical vision for reconstruction to the new executive team. A quick review first featured the Treasury Department taking the responsibility for collecting all revenues (this was a main concern that Secretary Chase had written about in the letter to Lincoln two days before). The War and Navy Departments were to take full possession of all southern military and naval facilities. The Interior Department would deploy agents to survey land for the redistribution of confiscated property from southern citizens. The Postmaster General would be instructed to appoint his own postmasters to reestablish the mail delivery, while the Attorney General would appoint his own judges, marshals, and attorneys to reestablish Federal courts and law enforcement in the South. Any objections by private citizens to these specially selected government authorities were to be quickly repressed, enforced by military authority (martial law).[6, 7]

Stanton's reconstruction plan was a carbon copy of the correspondence Chase argued in his letter to Lincoln just two days earlier. The Southern states were to be disenfranchised, and anyone who protested would be "taught by new calamities." Lincoln sat quietly as Stanton explained to his Cabinet how the next administration should handle the defeated Southern states. After Stanton's long presentation, the President stood up and walked around the table, still in quiet thought, before looking up to address his staff. Lincoln was searching for way to persuade the next administration to bring the Civil War to a final end, and to bring Congress (once again) into accountability to the supreme authority of the Constitution. Stanton's proposal would only continue the unconstitutional Federal powers that had been necessary to win the war. However, it was now the wish of the President to reunite the Congress in equality, with the Bill of Rights equally applicable to all citizens, north and south.

Lincoln admitted he had not found the time to study Stanton's proposals, and he would probably make some modifications. He asked his Cabinet members to bring their suggestions and questions to be considered as to how they would bring the Southern states back into the Union.[8] Lincoln then added:

> If we were wise and discrete we would reanimate the states before Congress reconvened. These men in Congress [Sumner, Stevens, etc.] who, if their motives are good, are nevertheless impracticable and who possess feelings of hate and vindictiveness in which I have no sympathy and could not participate. I hope there will be no persecution, no bloody work. [...] No one need expect me to take part in hanging or killing those men, even the worst of them. We must extinguish our resentment. [... T]here has been too much of a desire on the part of some to be masters to these states [...] too little respect for their rights. I do not sympathize in these feelings.[9]

During Lincoln's second inaugural address, on March 4, 1865, he called for, "malice toward none, charity for all, to achieve and cherish a just and lasting peace."[10] But on the floor of the Senate the Radicals cried out, "to lay low in the dust under our feet, so that iron heels will rest upon it, this great rebel, this giant criminal, this guilty murderer, that is warring upon the existence of our country."[11]

Lincoln's cabinet meeting ended with no doubt or reservations in Stanton's mind about the need to carry out the plans Sumner, Stevens and Chase had made for the President. It was now up to Stanton to save their republic from a Confederate takeover of Congress.

The assassin sent from France, known only as "Johnston," had arrived in the United States sometime around the end of March or very early April. His mission was to eliminate Seward in order to keep the Secretary of State from interfering with Lincoln's lenient plans for the Southern states. By April 14th, however, Johnston would have had no way to collect his $5,000 bounty, and Seward's assassination would have been pointless for the Confederacy. Stanton needed an assassin that would take out *both* Lincoln and Seward, and for different reasons from that of the assassin Johnston.

William Seward had never tried to obstruct Lincoln's policy. The rebels in France were misinformed about what had been said at the Hampton Roads peace conference. Seward had supported the President's nomination over Chase, and now supported his reconstruction policy, making him a double traitor to his former Radical colleague, Charles Sumner.

Tracing the Weapon

John Wilkes Booth was the instrument that ended the life and Presidency of Abraham Lincoln. The question is, was he an instrument of the Confederacy or of a faction within the Union?

A clue to how Stanton recruited Booth is revealed in the hidden confession given by George Atzerodt. During the end of his interrogation on board the ironclad U.S.S. Saugus, Atzerodt said Booth had met a group in New York that had a plot "to get the President certain," and also stated they had access to an entrance to the White House that was near the War Department. Their plan was to plant a bomb and kill Lincoln by blowing up the President's house. Booth said if he "did not get him quick the New York crowd would."[12]

This access to the White House, Atzerodt said, would be through "friends of the President." The plan was "to get up an entertainment and they would mix it in, they would have a serenade and thus get at the President and party."[13] The New York assassins were collaborating with people who had White House access, describable as "friends of the President," not the Confederate Secret

Service. Atzerodt would not refer to anyone associated with the Confederate government as a "friends of the President." What Atzerodt was saying was that Booth had a close connection to some people who were allied with Lincoln, and those allies were the ones who wanted him assassinated. What political insiders would have connections to Booth, plus access to the White House, and wanted Lincoln dead? Atzerodt was unknowingly referring to Union agents when he said the New York assassins had "friends of the President." The reason it was so important to place a canvas bag over Atzerodt's head during his entire incarceration, and then have him hanged, was because he could tie so many conspirators directly to Stanton.

At this point removing Lincoln and Seward had become the only choice left for the Radicals to completely exterminate the Southern culture and end the threat of losing the majority of Congress.

Establishing Motive

By April, 1865, the institution of slavery was defunct, but the proposed amendment of emancipation before Congress threatened to reduce the legislative power of the Northeast. At the Philadelphia Convention of 1787, as the U.S. Constitution was being constructed, the states agreed that the number of representatives from each state elected to the House would be based on a state's total population. In what is called the Three-Fifths Compromise, slave states were to count their slave populations at three-fifths. Therefore, by 1865, the slave population in the South, numbering 4,000,000, was only counted as 2,400,000 people in determining House representatives for those states. Emancipation would make void the compromise in the Constitution, and the former slave states of the South would increase their representation in the House by two-fifths of the slave population—equivalent to 1,600,000 persons. Therefore, with emancipation the Southern Representatives would return to Congress in greater numbers. Without black suffrage, the white population alone would elect pro-South politicians to these posts. Black suffrage, however, would increase the pro-North voter base in the South by a substantial margin. This is the entire reason for Chase advocating for black suffrage. If Radicals failed to gain a support base in the South, the combined agricultural regions of the West and South would out-vote the industrial Northeast in Congress. At this point removing Lincoln was the only option left to the Radicals to prevent this catastrophic loss of power.

The Confederate states had unconditionally surrendered and their President Jefferson Davis was being hunted as a traitor. Lincoln had offered to pardon the Confederate leaders, to restore Southern representation in Congress, and even to return confiscated property to their original owners. In addition, Lincoln refused to mandate universal suffrage for former [male] slaves, allowing the former Confederate states to elect Congressmen with pro-agricultural agendas. If Lincoln were to die, the South had all that to lose.

The Radicals' ultimate wish was to render the South as territories, but as of April 14, 1865, doing so would only be possible if hostilities were to somehow resume. This would require a new act of war by the Confederacy. If the Radicals were to get their wish—new aggression by the South, and to lose Lincoln—they would have opportunity to gain the following:

- The Radical coalition could pressure Congress to hang every ex-Confederate general and administrator.

- The Confederate states would be placed under martial law.

- Southern confiscated property would not be returned to the people of the Confederate states as Lincoln had pledged.

- Protesters to these harsh policies would be "taught by new calamities" as Chase had insisted in his letter to the President.

- They could kill Lincoln's Reconstruction Plan and implement their own version of the Radical "Wade-Davis" Bill that Lincoln had vetoed.

- Union Congressmen would then have the power to change the requirements for readmitting former states back into the Union.

- Congress could bar any ex-Confederates from ever again holding a government office.

- Congress would have the power to redistribute all confiscated Southern property.

The former Confederate states had every reason to want Lincoln in office, and the Radicals had every reason to bring his second term to an abrupt end. If the Radicals were to assassinate Lincoln, it *must* appear to be the work of the Confederacy.

9

Reassurance

*P*resident Lincoln was not without his own informants, and in early 1864 his friends had notified him of a plan by Salmon Chase, with some help from Edwin Stanton, to deny him the nomination for a second term.[1, 2] In April of 1865 Lincoln felt that he again needed to consult with one of his trusted friends to find out the truth. Rumors going around Washington about assassination plots were more than just the usual speculation, and the President had become sincerely concerned. He knew just the friend he should call.

Noah Brooks, a reporter for the *Sacramento Daily Union*, had somehow learned about the European assassination plot that Secretary Seward had recently uncovered. On April 14th, just four hours before Lincoln was shot, Brooks informed the President about the assassin sent to Washington from France. This was the same threat that Stanton had known about for nine days, but had not told the President, and the same plot that Seward had been unable to relay to Lincoln because of his April 5th carriage accident.

On that last, fateful day of Lincoln's life, he was preoccupied with rumors of assassination and had uncharacteristically cut short his usual family time after his evening meal. Typically, at this part of his day he eagerly set aside other duties to laugh and joke with his son Tad and catch up on home matters. Lincoln's evening dinner had become his only chance to escape from the relentless burdens he carried, and he had nowhere else to find such blessed relief. He always viewed the evening meal as his personal emancipation.[3]

Lincoln had called Noah Brooks to the White House because he was such a trusted friend. They first became acquainted in the mid-1850s through business dealings in Illinois; and Brooks had traveled with Lincoln during his campaign for the state's Senate seat against Stephen Douglas. In 1862, Noah Brooks went on to become a Washington correspondent for the *Sacramento Daily Union*, and Brooks frequently made visits to see Lincoln at the White House throughout his first term as President. Lincoln so trusted in Brooks that he offered him John Hay's job as his personal secretary, as Hay was leaving for France to become Secretary of Legation in Paris.

Lincoln had always made his daily visits to the War Department to read the latest dispatches after his evening meal, but that evening he waited anxiously to meet Brooks before heading out. Lincoln suspected that Stanton might know much more about the assassination rumors than he was telling. This explains why Lincoln would be so desperate to meet with Noah Brooks *before* consulting with his Secretary of War, from whom credible threats ought to be reported. General and Mrs. Grant had suddenly, at Stanton's insistence, canceled their plans to attend the theater with the Lincolns.[4] The President was now asking everyone he could think of to please join him at Ford's Theatre to replace the Grants, who had already left Washington for New Jersey. However, the President did not realize that Mrs. Lincoln had already invited Clara Harris and her fiancé, Major Henry Reed Rathbone, to fill the void. Lincoln was also unaware that Stanton had warned General Grant not to go to the theater *specifically* because there were rumors of an assassination plot.

General Grant would never for a moment be intimidated by a threat of an attack, but his distaste for public appearances and his anxious anticipation to see his children in New Jersey was his true reason for retreating from Washington. But an even more persuasive reason for him to back out came from Mrs. Grant. She was never fond of Mrs. Lincoln and she too had every reason to cancel their invitation.

Mrs. Lincoln had called General Grant "a butcher," and the Radical faction in Washington considered Mary Lincoln just another hated Southerner.[5] Even her eldest son, Robert Lincoln, betrayed her after his father's assassination. With the aid of Leonard Swett and Judge David Davis they had Mary arrested and tried for insanity. Mary's attorney, Isaac Arnold, secretly plotted with Robert to have her committed to an asylum. However, only a few months later Mary hired her own female attorney and proved to the court that she was of sound mind, and obtained her release.

Less than four hours prior to the assassination Noah Brooks met with Lincoln and briefed him about what he knew before the President departed for the War Department. Williams H. Crook was just one of many police bodyguards for the President, and he recalled that Lincoln's mood had suddenly changed a great deal after his meeting with Brooks.[6] Crook noticed that the President was more depressed than he had ever seen him. The long strides and energetic pace with which Lincoln had moved ever since Lee's surrender had suddenly become slow and reluctant as the President and Crook followed the well-beaten path to the War Department.

Lincoln spoke quietly as the two slowly approached the steps of the War Department. Lincoln turned to his bewildered bodyguard and in a most somber tone said:

> Crook, do you know I believe there are men who want to take my life? And I have no doubt they will do it. Other men had been assassinated. I know no one could do it and escape alive. But if it is to be done it is impossible to prevent.[7]

WILLIAM H. CROOK recalled his final walk with Lincoln for the rest of his life.

Crook was taken so off guard by his comment he could only think to say, "I hope you are mistaken." William H. Crook would never forget that last walk he made with Lincoln only hours before the assassination. It remained etched in his mind, just as it happened, never to fade with time. Lincoln's eerie prophecy about the last few hours of his life was heard over again and again in Crook's conscience. Every word and vision in his memory of that evening could never be changed or forgotten.

The two men entered the War Department and the President met Stanton in front of his office. The short, squat Secretary of War and the towering frame of the President stood together in front of Crook for the last time. Lincoln's bodyguard watched as the President walked over to Stanton and draped his long, lanky arm around the Secretary's shoulder. Stanton without question was noticeably moved by the President's gesture, and Crook assumed these were expressions of mutual affection, but Stanton's reaction was not accurately interpreted. Crook did not realize that only Stanton could cause or prevent what lay in store for Lincoln later that night. The two most powerful men in the United States entered the office of the Secretary of War and closed the door behind them while Crook waited outside.

Crook noticed that the President's sudden melancholy, after having talked with Brooks, had just as suddenly vanished after his talk with Stanton. Obviously, Stanton had reassured the President during their private meeting that he had nothing to worry about.[8] As they walked together back to the White House, it was obvious John Parker, the President's personal guard for the four-until-midnight shift, was late once again. William Crook, still rattled by his previous conversation with Lincoln and concerned for his safety, offered to stay on the rest of the evening.

The President emphatically replied, "No, Crook. You have had a long, hard day's work already. Go home and rest."[9]

Earlier that morning, before the Cabinet meeting, Lincoln had insisted Stanton assign his Chief Telegraph Officer, Major Thomas Eckert, to be his presidential guest (and unofficial bodyguard) at Ford's Theatre that evening[10] in addition to the unreliable John Parker. Lincoln had always admired Major Eckert's brute strength, and his personal guard for that evening was really no protection at all. Stanton flatly refused Lincoln's request, arguing that Eckert had work that must be done that evening, and could not be spared. Lincoln immediately walked into the Chief Telegraph official's adjacent office and implored Eckert to accompany him, saying "Now, Major, you can do Stanton's work to-morrow."[11] David Homer Bates, one of the cofounders of the military telegraph department and eyewitness to this conversation, wrote that Eckert declined the President's invitation, reiterating Stanton's excuse about urgent work that must be done that evening, *knowing* General Grant was induced by Stanton to avoid Ford's Theatre due to an assassination threat.[12] Stanton and Eckert both knew there was no urgent work to be done and Major Eckert reportedly spent his entire evening at home.

10

"I Saw John Wilkes Booth!"

On Lincoln's last day he was busy following his daily, presidential routine. Meanwhile John Wilkes Booth was also having a very busy day, planning to end Lincoln's life. Prior to 10:15 PM that night Lincoln still had authority over the policy for the nation's future. However, only moments later, his murder would transfer power to a coalition of men in government who were at odds with the President's reconstruction plan. And that coalition stood to benefit greatly by Lincoln's removal from office.

Unlike the baseless claim that Lincoln's assassination was the end result of a Confederate plot, the facts exposing a Radical plot are not conjecture, nor biased opinions, but physical evidence and a logical motive. The written evidence left by Salmon P. Chase and his coalition supporters reveal a perfect motive for their intentions to have Lincoln and Seward prevented from serving a second term.

After April 2 there was no credible or logical motive for anyone who still remained in the former Confederate government to have Lincoln assassinated. If the Confederate government plotted to assassinate Lincoln, they would then be sacrificing Lincoln's promise of "malice toward none." Their murder of the President would result in them "laying low in the dust under the iron heel of a vengeful Congress." Jefferson Davis, as well as the entire Confederate administration, was accused of treason; they all faced the hangman's noose if the Radicals had their way.

Both motive and killer are traceable to the Radicals and Edwin Stanton. From this point the next aspect of the assassination to examine would be opportunity. The Confederates' only opportunity to assassinate Lincoln occurred on April 5, while the President walked openly through the streets of Richmond, not on April 14 in the heart of Washington, D.C.

Booth, who only had a kidnapping plot prior to April 14, had to be given a workable plan to assassinate Lincoln and be persuaded to do it. He did not need inside help to get close enough to take a shot at Lincoln, but he did need inside help to stand only two feet away from Lincoln, shoot him from behind, and then have any chance of getting away. Booth, who would not risk his life on the battlefield, who had hopes of becoming rich through oil investments, and whose greatest dream was to be a hero, would require an *insider's guarantee* that he would be allowed to escape. Confederates would not have given him such a task, nor could they assure him of an escape from a theater full of military and police. Only an authority with control over Lincoln's protection could have provided Booth access to the President and a means of escape out of Washington. The Confederate conspiracy theory originated with the prosecution's phony charges, supported by unchallenged testimonies, perjuries, and planted evidence.

Testimonies from the many eyewitnesses at Ford's Theatre concerning the assassination were as varied and contradictory as the imagination can conjure. Every witness who testified after the fact had a different description and interpretation of events, therefore only evidence and a credible motive can be trusted to arrive anywhere near the truth.

Many people testified they had seen Booth in the theater before the assassination, but the evidence demonstrates that *no one saw Booth* before he shot Lincoln. The actress playing the part of Mary Meredith that night was Jeannie Gourlay, and she said she saw Booth about 10 o'clock in the lobby,[1] no reference to his large knife, thigh-high riding boots with spurs, nor did she mentioned anything unusual about his attire. In fact, *every* person testifying, from army officers to theater employees (who knew Booth and his habits), spoke not a word of his odd choice of footwear just to watch a play.

On the night he shot Lincoln, Booth was dressed in long riding boots that came up well above his knees, equipped with spurs. He was wearing rough clothes, completely inappropriate for an evening in Presidential company. He also wore a large, foot-long dagger in a belt worn conspicuously around the *outside* of his coat. Jennie Gourlay testified that she saw John Wilkes Booth fifteen minutes before he shot Lincoln, and the only unusual thing she noticed about him was that he "looked pale." Booth was *always* pale, and he was also legendary for his "dandy" appearance. Earlier on that same day, Harry Ford (John T. Ford's brother) also described seeing Booth. He stated, "The well-known actor arrived with his usual elegant fashion, complete with kid gloves, tall silk hat and a walking cane."[2]

If Booth was seen that afternoon in rough riding clothes and spurred riding boots, it would have been very unusual, but even more so if he wore them that night to the theater. Booth lived just down the street at the National Ho-

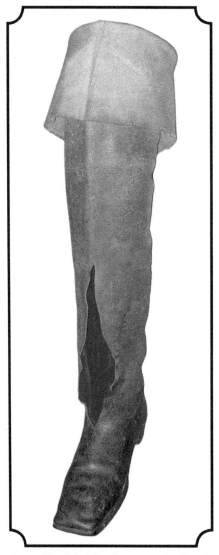

ABOVE: The left riding boot worn by Booth, which Dr. Mudd had to cut to remove from his badly swollen, broken ankle. BELOW: The boot's spur, recovered from Ford's Theatre, which had become detached in the flag draped from the presidential state box.

tel, only walking distance from Ford's Theatre. He had no obvious reason to be dressed so out-of-character, and yet somehow his odd appearance caught no one's attention nor raised suspicion. Not a single person who testified they saw Booth that night ever mentioned his riding boots or knife. One of the spurs he wore on his boots was detached when it caught in the flag as he jumped off the state box, and it was recovered the next day. The spur was then turned over to the Metro Chief of Police Almarin C. Richards for investigation, and Richards called on John Pumphrey to identify the spur.[3]

Pumphrey owned the livery stable that Booth used from time to time, and he identified the spur as one belonging to the assassin.[4] The boot that covered Booth's broken and badly swollen ankle had to be cut off with a knife by Dr. Mudd to set and splint his leg. The boot was recovered and used as evidence to convict Dr. Mudd as an accomplice aiding in Booth's escape. There can be no doubt from physical evidence that Booth was wearing heavy riding boots as he fled Ford's Theatre, but not a single witness corroborated that fact.

All those witnesses claimed they noticed so many intimate details about Booth, and yet they all overlooked every unusual and out-of-place aspect of his appearance. No two testimonies matched. The only possible answer to

According to many historians, the photo of John Wilkes Booth on the left was the one shown to alleged witnesses, and which influenced their description of the assassin. That night Booth was actually dressed for an escape through rugged terrain, as depicted on the right by an artist.

why they all gave accounts different from the facts would be that *none of them* actually saw Booth that evening; they only assumed after-the-fact that they must have seen him. How Booth actually entered Lincoln's state box has never been proven with evidence, but has only been assumed, if not fabricated, and built from dubious testimonies.

Lieutenant Alexander M. S. Crawford was seated close to the President's state box. He was the first to report to Stanton about the shooting.[5] Crawford testified that the man he saw entering the state box was wearing a slouch hat. The second person Stanton interviewed was Harry Hawk (the only actor on the stage when Booth jumped out of the box). Hawk said Booth was not wearing a hat when he saw him jump to the stage, only moments after Lieutenant Crawford reportedly saw a man wearing a hat. There is no explanation for

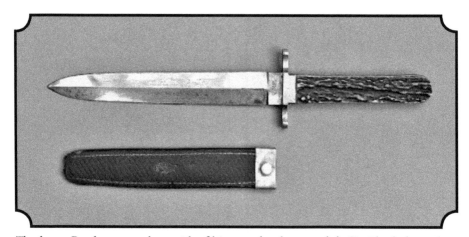

The dagger Booth wore on the outside of his coat when he entered the President's theater box, with which he injured Major Rathbone.

where the assassin's hat went, and the only hat recovered from the crime scene was Lincoln's beaver top hat.[6]

Captain Theodore McGowan was seated only a few feet from the corridor leading to the President, and he identified Booth from a photograph shown to him during the trial. He said the man he saw about to enter the presidential box was the man in the photograph. McGowan described the man he saw as a dark-haired man of medium height, dressed in a black coat, and dark pants, and wearing a black, stiff-rimmed, flat-top, round-crowned hat.[7] This was the same type of hat that Booth was wearing in the photograph, and not the slouch hat that Lieutenant Crawford testified he saw on the man who entered the state box. But no one made any reference to the large knife tucked in his belt, or his unusual, heavy riding boots and spurs.

It is also conspicuous when the testimonies agree. Captain McGowan, George B. Todd (a Navy surgeon), and Dr. Charles A. Leale (the doctor who came to Lincoln's aid after the shooting) all stated they clearly noticed seeing Booth hand the President's attendant, Charles Forbes, a card before he entered the presidential box.[8] The vindication given to Forbes for allowing Booth to enter was that he took the card into the presidential box to Lincoln and received permission for Booth to enter. The witness George B. Todd testified; "Forbes took the card into the box and in a minute the door was opened and Booth walked in." But another witness, James P. Ferguson, a restaurant owner next door to Ford's Theatre, testified he remembered seeing Booth push the door open with his knee, then enter.[9] Ferguson later changed his testimony to resemble the others.[10]

No card was ever recovered as evidence, and no explanation was given to explain why a mere card could allow a *visibly armed man* to enter Lincoln's state box. Not one testimony can be trusted as an accurate account of what truly happened. How Booth was able to get so close to Lincoln is still unknown, along with why his guard, John Parker, was not held accountable for deserting his post, resulting in the death of the President. For certain to understand why these occurred would require a cross-examination of John Parker's excuse and the physical evidence of the card allegedly given to Charles Forbes, but this scrutiny was never allowed to take place.

An undeniable truth is that Lincoln's assigned bodyguard, John Parker, was absent from his post. The reason Parker was not on duty can never be proven because he never had to account in the conspiracy trial for his absence. Furthermore, Charles Forbes never produced as evidence the card he claimed Booth had given him, and no card was recovered at the scene. The physical evidence disputes the accounts given by the eyewitnesses, and only demonstrates that no one actually saw Booth before he shot Lincoln.

After his re-election, Lincoln consented to having an around-the-clock bodyguard, and several men were chosen by the War Department for this duty. Thomas Pendel was one of the original guards selected, but later that year he became a bookkeeper for the White House; then William H. Crook was appointed as his replacement. Crook was the bodyguard to be relieved by John F. Parker for the four-to-midnight shift the evening of April 14, but, true to form, Parker was once again late for duty. He did, however, finally show up, but for what purpose will never be known. How he became a bodyguard to the President is the only thing more mysterious than why he was even hired to be a Metropolitan policeman.

Before John Parker worked for the police, he was a carpenter by trade. He was selected to be a presidential guard on the very day Lincoln was reelected, from a choice of 150 other patrolmen. Parker's entire police service record was marred by conduct unbecoming of an officer. On many occasions he was late for duty. He had also been reported for drinking, sleeping and even visiting brothels while on duty, and for public profanity. As a presidential guard, failure to be at his post, for whatever reason, allowed Booth to enter the state box unchallenged. It was not until August 13, 1868, that Parker was finally dismissed from the police department over repeated charges of gross negligence of duty. But in the conspiracy trial of 1865, he was not even called to explain his absence from the time prior to the assassination until his reappearance around 6:00 AM the following day.

An effort has been made by Confederate conspiracy theorists to excuse John Parker. Some surmise that Lincoln gave Parker permission to find a better seat to watch the play. But there is absolutely no proof that Lincoln ever said such a thing (besides, he was concerned that day about threats against his life), and the evidence proves that Parker was nowhere to be found in the theater. In fact, when he showed up at dawn the next morning, he was with a woman whom he asserted was a prostitute.[11] Others have asserted Parker was only assigned to escort Lincoln to the theatre, ignoring the fact that Forbes, Crook and the citation issued against Parker by the police department for neglect of duty, stated he was "detailed to attend and protect the President."[12] No one will ever know where he was during this time because all of the records relating to his trial before the Board of the Metropolitan Police to account for his absence have completely disappeared from the National Archives.[13] Parker was excused from appearing at the conspiracy trial on June 2, without explanation, and no newspapers ever followed up the investigation into Parker's neglect of duty, nor did they even mention his name when writing about the conspiracy trial.

11

The Chamber Maid[1]

*D*uring the same time John Wilkes Booth was entering Ford's Theater to assassinate Lincoln, William Seward's doorbell was ringing. The young, colored house servant, William Bell, opened the door to find a large man holding up a small package for Bell to clearly see. Lewis Powell stepped into the hallway, and Bell closed the door behind him. The large stranger paced toward the stairs, telling William Bell he had come to deliver medicine sent from Dr. Verdi. "I must go up and administer this medicine to Mr. Seward," Powell told Bell, more as an order than as a request. William Bell protested that he had orders not to disturb Mr. Seward, and he said that Dr. Verdi had just left the house only about an hour before. But Lewis Powell ignored him and continued walking down the hall towards the steps that led to Secretary Seward's bedroom (he somehow knew the way).

The much smaller doorman kept arguing with Powell that he must not go upstairs. But William Bell realized he could not stop the larger Powell from going up the steps, and he began to think that maybe he would be in trouble if Powell was, in fact, just following orders from Dr. Verdi. Bell asked Powell to excuse him for talking so rough, to which Powell replied, "Oh, I know. That's all right." Bell had followed slightly behind Powell on their walk to the stairs, but he quickly took the lead before they started together for the third floor. Powell wore a large, brown hat that he had pulled down low over his face. He had on black pants, a light coat, and weighty, hard-soled boots that rang throughout the house with every step he took on the hardwood stairs. Bell turned to Powell halfway up the steps and told him, "don't walk so heavy."

As they reached the third floor they found Seward's oldest son Frederick standing on the top step. Powell's clamorous footfalls had brought Frederick from his bedroom to see who was calling so late at night. Powell repeated the same story that he had given Bell at the front door, but Frederick blocked the way. After a full five minutes of debate, Seward's son insisted Powell leave the medicine with him, or he could leave with the medicine, but he could not wake his father. Bell had been standing behind Powell the whole time during the argument with Frederick, and as he and Powell started back down the stairs, Bell leading the way, he turned to Powell to tell him once again to not walk so heavily. Just as Bell looked back he heard Powell say, "you," and saw something in Powell's hand that appeared to be "round, mounted all over with silver, and about 10 inches long." Powell attacked Frederick with what Bell had taken to be a knife. Powell hit Frederick twice in his head, knocking him backwards into his sister's room that was two doors down from Mr. Seward's bedroom. Bell was horrified, and he turned and ran down the stairs and out the front door hollering, "Murder!"

The noise from Powell's attack on Frederick brought Mr. Seward's male nurse, Sgt. George F. Robinson, from Seward's bedside to the bedroom door to see what the trouble was. As Robinson opened the door Powell was there before him, and, as the Sergeant later testified, Powell struck him "with a knife in the forehead." Pushing past Robinson, Powell attacked the barely conscious Secretary of State, wildly stabbing at him. William Seward laid there, completely defenseless, as he received two slashes to the face and neck in the dark bedroom. The steel brace supporting Seward's broken jaw had deflected the blade from its fatal course.

Sgt. Robinson quickly recovered and jumped to his feet, grabbing Powell and pulling him away. Powell again turned his attack on Robinson. Mr. Seward's other son, Major Augustus Seward, had been awakened by his sister's screams and ran into the dark room to see a struggle between two men at the foot of his father's bed. Augustus grabbed one of the men in the dimly lit bedroom, thinking it was his father and that he had become delirious. Immediately Augustus realized it was not his father, and then supposed it must be Robinson who had become delirious. Not yet realizing this was an assassination attempt against his father, Augustus clung to the intruder, shoving him toward the door.

While wrestling with Augustus, Powell lashed out at him with his knife, striking him five or six times, and in the melee lost his hat. Now engaged with two men Powell's attack seemed hopeless. At close range in the well-lit hallway Augustus stared into the face of the assassin. Powell hollered to a secret accomplice (who was within the house), "I'm made! I'm made!" Then, breaking away from Augustus and Robinson, Powell charged down the stairs and disappeared out the door.

Augustus Seward had misunderstood Powell's Alabama drawl when he heard him call out, as saying, "I'm mad! I'm mad!" while Powell struggled to break free from the army Major. Powell was actually hollering to Seward's chamber maid, that he had been *made*—clearly seen. He had lost his hat and his face had been revealed, and he knew Augustus could now identify him.

The chamber maid at Mr. Seward's home was identified in Atzerodt's confession as being in a relationship with Booth.[2] She and James Donaldson were secret agents in the War Department's assassination plots against Seward and Lincoln.

Donaldson first infiltrated Booth's kidnapping conspiracy, winning Booth's trust by posing as a double agent for the Democratic Copperheads, but he was actually on a mission for Edwin Stanton. Two months later, and just hours before Lincoln departed for Ford's Theatre, Donaldson gave Booth the plan for the President's assassination. He also provided Booth with the name of Seward's doctor, a bottle of medicine, and the location of Seward's bedroom on the third floor.[3] Donaldson was originally scheduled to be Seward's guard for the evening, but he traded his shift with Robinson.[4]

Donaldson's instructions for Powell were to make his way into Seward's bedroom, quietly kill the Secretary with a knife, and then discreetly depart. Powell was assured that the chamber maid would help him with his mission. However, her actual purpose was to plant a very rare, broken, Confederate-made pistol at the crime scene. The pistol would be used as evidence to prove that a Confederate assassin murdered Mr. Seward.

Baker and Stanton already knew that Booth had given each of his gang members a pistol and a knife, and Stanton preplanned to use those weapons as evidence to frame Booth's kidnapping accomplices as Confederate agents, therefore implicating the Confederacy as committing "a new act of war." Stanton knew about the weapons because John Surratt's close friend, Louis Weichmann, was a civilian informant, living in Mary Surratt's boardinghouse, and for two months he had been reporting his surveillances about Booth and his associates to Captain D. H. Gleason at the War Department.[5]

Weichmann reported to Gleason that John Surratt's friend from Baltimore, James Wood, was a Confederate agent who always wore a long, gray coat.[6] The pistol and coat were preplanned by Stanton to be used as evidence to identify James Wood (Powell) as Seward's Confederate murderer.

Powell stabbed one more victim before he fled the Seward house. His last attack was on Emerick W. Hansell, the third State Department messenger assigned to watch over the Secretary of State since his carriage accident.[7] As Powell was running from the house he collided with Hansell, then stabbed him in the back. After Powell descended the staircase, Major Augustus Seward scrambled back to his room and dug down into his carpetbag where he kept his pistol. He then hurried downstairs to the front door to shoot the intruder if he attempted to return.

William Bell had run down the street to General Augur's headquarters to get help. After not finding anyone on duty, he raced back to the house, and on his way three soldiers ran out of the building and fell in behind him, maintaining a short distance. As Bell turned the corner he saw the assassin jump on a horse. Bell had not noticed a horse when he answered the door, nor was a horse there when Bell ran down to General Augur's headquarters. Only after Bell returned to the house did he see the horse for the first time. Bell hollered to the three soldiers, "There he is, going on a horse!" The soldiers slacked their pace, and stopped running. Bell fell in behind the rider, and kept up with the assassin all the way up to I Street at 15-1/2 Street. The assassin just rode away at an easy pace with Bell running only about 20 feet behind him. After turning right on Vermont Avenue the assassin spurred his horse and galloped out of sight. The three soldiers who had followed Bell back to Mr. Seward's home for some unknown reason never joined Bell in his pursuit of the assassin.

Augustus was still standing at the doorway when Bell returned to the house. The breathless servant told Augustus that the "man with the knife" had ridden off on a horse. Bell was sure that Powell had attacked Frederick with a knife, and testified that it was a knife, but that he was told by the investigators that Powell used a pistol.

Major Augustus left Bell at the front door, and returned to Mr. Seward's bedroom. Only then did he realize how severe his own injuries were. After all five stabbing victims had been bandaged and cared for, Augustus again checked on his father. The family wouldn't know until the next morning that the other son, Frederick, was seriously injured, with his brain exposed through a hole in his shattered skull.

During the trial Augustus said that the wound on Frederick's head looked just like it had been made with a knife, but "surgeons said" Frederick's wound appeared to be created by the hammer of a pistol. Some people said that the pistol was found in Seward's bedroom, but Augustus heard it was recovered in the front yard of the home. In either case Augustus never saw the pistol in his father's room, and after he returned to the room he only found Powell's hat on the floor.

If Powell attacked Frederick at the top of the stairs with the butt of a pistol and then immediately turned to attack nurse Robinson with a knife, the pistol and its broken pieces would have been found in the room where

Frederick was knocked down: two doors away, and not in Mr. Seward's bedroom. Powell obviously would not have bothered to pick up the useless, broken pistol and carry it with him into Mr. Seward's bedroom, or carry it outside with him, and then drop it in the front yard during his escape. The pistol was without question planted, which exposes

The pistol that appeared at the Seward home was a rare, 36-caliber Confederate Navy revolver made by Spiller & Burr of Atlanta. The pistols Booth obtained in New York for his followers were 44-caliber Colt revolvers. This blue steel gun could not have been mistaken for a silvery knife.

a premeditated set-up to Seward's murder. Donaldson and the chamber maid were working with Stanton to use the pistol and the long, gray coat as evidence, even before Powell was given a plan commit the crime.

Surgeon Joseph K. Barnes treated Frederick Seward's head wound and said it seemed to have been inflicted by some blunt instrument. William Bell said he saw Powell attack Frederick with something silver "about ten inches long." That could only be a knife held with the blade pointing out in front of Powell's hand. The blunt handle was used to come down on Frederick's head because he was holding the knife with the blade pointing forward. The attacker could only use the knife to cut with an *upward* swinging motion while held in that position. Powell never had a pistol when he entered the house, only a ten-inch silver knife mounted on a blunt handle.

The pistol used as evidence against Powell did not belong to him, but was planted by Mr. Seward's chamber maid after he had attacked five people with a knife. Though it was known a maid was in the house, she was never called to testify. She was the same person Powell was calling to when he lost his hat and abandoned his attack, yelling, "I'm made! I'm made!" This chamber maid was identified in George Atzerodt's confession as being in a close relationship with John Wilkes Booth:

> I overheard Booth when in conversation with Wood say, That he visited a chambermaid at Seward's House & that she was pretty. He said he had a great mind to give her his diamond pin.[8]

This precious, monogrammed pin was found on Booth's body when he was captured.[9] Atzerodt's confession was withheld from the trial.

Minutes after Powell fled Seward's house, James Donaldson showed up.[10]

12

Obstruction of Justice

After assassinating Lincoln, Booth spent the next two weeks trying to avoid capture by Stanton's military or Baker's detectives. Few hard facts are known about what really happened during that two-week period, but that stretch of time has inspired some of the most speculative and biased conjecture ever written. The mainstream historical accounts explaining Lincoln's murder and Booth's escape have been based almost exclusively on the War Department's fabricated rendition. The investigation and conspiracy trial to determine the assassins and conspirators were both conducted under the authority of the military and run by the very man who planned the assassination. Only reliable evidence (disregarding the trial's perjured testimonies) can solve many of the mysteries about the assassination conspiracy and restore the truth from the War Department's fictional accounts. Reconstructing Lincoln's murder and Booth's escape by using the previously unconsidered evidence will reveal what was probable, and what would have been impossible.

Despite having a theater full of witnesses that heard the shot and saw Booth drop to the stage, not even Mrs. Lincoln's guest, Major Rathbone, could say with certainty what Booth yelled out after he shot the President (or if he actually yelled anything at all). Booth broke his leg when he crashed awkwardly onto the stage, but some historians have even disputed that fact because evidence was not considered. David Herold admitted to news reporters on the same day of Booth's capture that Booth broke his leg on the stage,[1] but that statement has gone unnoticed in those escape and capture recreations.

What is known as fact—not just an assumption—is that Edwin Stanton deliberately hid away the diary found on Booth when he was captured. Not only was the diary withheld, but also evidence that would prove how John Wilkes Booth was fatally shot. Two surgeons were called on to perform an autopsy on Booth's body before a crowd of military officials and the press. The corpse and its injuries were photographed, and the plates and two medical reports were sent directly to Stanton, but those photographic plates were never seen by anyone ever again.

The two separate autopsy reports, submitted by Surgeon General Joseph K. Barnes and Dr. Joseph J. Woodward, gave opposing descriptions of Booth's fatal neck wound. Barnes described the bullet as traversing the neck, severing the spinal cord, in a slight upward direction, exiting the right side; Woodward described the bullet descending and exiting out the left of Booth's neck.[2] Without an opportunity by the defense to examine those two reports, and without the autopsy photographs, an important

Dr. Barnes

Dr. Woodward

The two autopsy reports on Booth's corpse disagreed on which side of his neck the bullet exited. The autopsies agreed, however, that Booth was shot from the side by a pistol, and from a distance of about four yards, refuting any claim of suicide.

clue to how Booth was shot has been overlooked. Because there was no autopsy photographs to view, or conflicting medical reports to examine, Booth's execution was swept aside, and the actual shooter was never truthfully identified.

Stanton did not wish to have any conflicting testimonies clarified, as they would explain how and why Booth was shot while he was trapped in a barn

Booth's autopsy aboard the U.S.S. Montauk, April 27, 1865, by Drs. Woodward and Barnes. They each separately submitted autopsy reports addressed to Edwin Stanton.

Even the newspapers parodied the conflicting testimonies of how Booth was shot. Combining the two separate accounts, Booth supports himself on a crutch while juggling a pistol, a long rifle, and a second crutch, as he faces the man who shot him through the side of the neck. On the right, David Herold is surrendering.

without any chance of escape. During the trial, Boston Corbett (the alleged shooter) testified that Booth was making a move towards the door but aiming a carbine in the general direction of Corbett. It was at that point when Corbett stated he shot Booth to see he did no harm. Another soldier's testimony agreed Booth was aiming a carbine in the direction of Corbett.

Booth had to use a crutch to stand, and he could only *aim* a heavy rifle while facing in that same direction. Even without the conflicting exit wound reports, the obvious fact is Booth was shot while facing approximately 90° to the shooter. Booth was shot through the side of the neck. There was no explanation given for how Booth could have been shot in the side of the neck while facing the shooter. The accounts given by both men about Booth's execution, was a deliberate deception to hide the truth about who actually shot Booth, or why he needed to be shot. Stanton's handpicked judges knew for a fact that Corbett was not Booth's shooter, but they went along with the false testimonies and gave Corbett credit for the shooting to end any further investigation.[3]

A written transcript of George Atzerodt's voluntary confession to Marshal McPhail was also deliberately excluded as evidence, and Stanton saw that it was destroyed,[4] but a copy Stanton didn't know existed providentially resurfaced 112 years later. In 1977, a descendent of Captain W. E. Doster (Atzerodt's attorney) happened to find his confession among several other old documents from Captain Doster's files.[5] Atzerodt's confession explained his role and named the people involved in the entire kidnapping affair. His confession proved his innocence by accounting for all the alleged evidence the military commission used to convict him for conspiracy to assassinate Vice President Andrew Johnson. It can only be concluded that Atzerodt's confession contained information Stanton did not want exposed during the trial. That information would undeniably interfere with the preconcerted guilty verdict.

One more piece of evidence excluded from the trial was John Wilkes Booth himself. Had he been able to speak openly in his defense he could have divulged his accomplices in the assassination plot. Booth and his diary had to be destroyed to keep that information unknown. Booth also left a letter naming his accomplices—*his Federal government assassination accomplices*—and it explained their motives for killing Lincoln (as he understood them), but it too was destroyed.

Even the Derringer that Booth used in the assassination was overlooked as another important piece of evidence. Booth went to Ford's Theatre with a weapon good for only one shot, and only at point blank range. In the conspirator's trial, the prosecution alleged that Booth supplied Lewis Powell with a *six-shooter* to kill a defenseless William Seward in his sleep; and yet to kill the President Booth chose a weapon that could not even get him past the minimum of two guards. In order to shoot Lincoln with a Derringer, Booth would have expected to get within feet of the President. Booth only armed himself equal to the situation he was told to expect: unopposed access to Lincoln's unguarded back. Booth arrived at Ford's Theatre dressed for his escape and armed with the confidence that he would need to fire only a single shot.

The question arises: why did Booth not anticipate the need for a second shot, even to aid in his escape? Samuel Arnold dropped out of the kidnapping plot after he argued with Booth that it would be impossible to get Lincoln out of Washington before being stopped by the sentinels. Booth answered Arnold, "Shoot the sentinels."[6] *That* was Booth's plan for dealing with any guards who attempted to disrupt the kidnapping and their escape from D.C. Considering Booth had access to better firearms, one must ponder why he would place himself in a situation, to escape from the midst of a crowd of military personnel in the heart of the Union capital, with only a *knife* to fend off the sentinels. Booth had to have been guaranteed access to Lincoln, plus the liberty to escape, and such guarantees could have only come from someone who could manage Lincoln's security.

Had there been a civilian murder trial, complete with probing questions, cross examination, statements of the accused, plus the inclusion of the Derringer as evidence, Stanton's involvement in the assassination would have been revealed. A fair and impartial trial would have found that none of the accused accomplices could have helped Booth get within arm's reach of Lincoln, or provided any means to help him escape Washington's military and police security.

Booth entered Lincoln's state box by passing, conspicuously dressed, through a theater full of military officers and police. However, no one became concerned, because apparently no one saw him until he leapt to the stage. Charles Forbes and John Parker were the last obstacles to the state box and the only protection provided for Lincoln's security. Once inside the box, Booth faced only a single army major who was unarmed and unable to stop Booth from escaping.

Stanton was the man who had compiled all the evidence against Booth and the accused conspirators. He began collecting his information sometime around the middle of the previous year, using his spies that had infiltrated Booth's gang.

Booth shot Lincoln in a crowded public theater in the heart of Washington, D.C., and in plain view for all to witness. His escape route was into Virginia, where the burned out, occupied capital city of Richmond, along with the entire state, had unconditionally surrendered to General Grant's Army five days before. It could hardly provide refuge for a fugitive running from Federal agents, and Booth began his flight without provisions and little more than $100 cash in his pocket.[7]

The killer was John Wilkes Booth and his "motive" was an unrealistic and pointless fantasy by a deranged and unstable mind. His decision to kill Lincoln made no logical sense because there would be no possible benefit for Booth to jeopardize everything in his future just to kill the President. There was also no benefit for the Confederate government to have Lincoln assassinated, as he was their only protection against the vengeful Radical coalition who wanted to hang them all. On the other hand, killing Lincoln would benefit that coalition which had tried for so long to take away Lincoln's nomination to a second term. But a deranged mind uses faulty logic, so it remains credible that Booth would agree to kill Lincoln.

It was Booth's *opportunity* to kill Lincoln that provides clues that have been grossly overlooked. Stanton knew all about Booth's malice towards Lincoln, and with such short notice only someone within the administration could change the President's venue to Ford's Theatre (a perfectly suited location for Booth to get to Lincoln). John T. Ford's two sons testified that the theater wasn't notified that Lincoln was coming until late morning that same day. Factor in the absent security along with Booth's choice of weapon and a flood of logical questions arise.

The state box itself had been well-prepared ahead of time for Booth's fateful deed. A peephole had been cut into the state box door. Booth also planned a means to secure the door from being opened after he entered the box. A music stand was fashioned into a brace that fit perfectly into a notch cut into the floor.[8] He then timed his shot at a precise moment during the play, synchronized with the attack on Secretary of State William Seward. This is all proof of a professionally-planned, premeditated attack.

So what arrangements did Booth make to gain access past Lincoln's guards? How could Booth be certain that Forbes would not challenge his access, or that Parker would be absent from his post at the exact moment both Lincoln and Seward were to be attacked? All his prior arrangements would be useless without the certainty that he would be provided access past those two guards.

After reviewing the capabilities of every possible conspirator, it is only Stanton who could have guaranteed Booth that he could get close enough to assassinate Lincoln with one shot at very close range, and then escape from the city using only a knife.

13

Lie or Die!

At three o'clock in the morning, as Lincoln lingered near death, investigators raided Mary Surratt's boardinghouse, looking for clues about the assassin. After the officers left, her anxious resident, Louis Weichmann, along with another boarder, checked out of Mary's home before sunrise and made a full report to the Metropolitan police. They were then deputized for the manhunt to find the Booth gang, and left with police the very next day for Canada to help locate and capture John Surratt, Jr.

Throughout that same morning, after Lincoln had died, Stanton was becoming frantic over his loss of control. He had developed an exclusive system of first-hand intelligence gathering, and had always orchestrated every situation, but now he was losing his concealment. As days passed, the reward money offered for capturing the fugitives divided investigators into competing agencies, while clues and evidence were independently gathered and selfishly guarded. No longer was everyone involved reporting directly to him; no longer could he determine what was concealed and what was revealed.

Stanton immediately recalled his chief investigator, Lafayette Baker, back to Washington from New York. Baker quickly discovered that General Christopher Augur had assumed authority over the Washington detectives and soldiers, while the police department was conducting their own separate investigation.[1] The city of Washington was steadily becoming engulfed with detectives and reporters from every northeastern state, all joining the search for Booth and his gang, hoping to collect the ever-increasing reward money, and be cast as a hero in this now world-famous spectacle.

Major James O'Beirne took charge of a large company of military detectives, while Baker was left covering the least likely escape route north of Washington. James McPhail claimed his home range of lower Maryland, and he worked on finding Michael O'Laughlin and Samuel Arnold. Colonels H. H. Wells and David R. Clendenin (who would later serve as one of the Judge advocates in the conspiracy trial) led another division of military detectives independently from O'Beirne.

Weichmann had reported to detective James McDevitt at the police head-quarters, accompanied by his fellow boarder from Mary Surratt's home, John Holohan. They were both made deputies and stayed the night at McDevitt's home before they too joined in the manhunt.[2]

Get Weichmann!

Weichmann was a treasure trove of inside information, and Stanton was horri-fied when he found out that he was cooperating with the Police Department. The police had Weichmann, and Stanton desperately needed to have him back and under his control. Stanton was throwing a fit over Weichmann, but completely unconcerned about Holohan. What did Stanton *know* about Sur-ratt's boarders, Weichmann and Holohan, that he panicked over one and was indifferent to the other?

The assassination had been committed by a known civilian in civilian territory, thus falling in the jurisdiction of the District of Columbia. Stanton's top priority in successfully framing the Confederacy would be to have his hand-picked suspects tried by his own, hand-picked judges and prosecutors. Stanton held evidence that could connect Booth with Andrew Johnson, and he threatened him with the note Booth left the Vice President on the morning of the assassination. Against the wishes of officials across Washington, Stanton succeeded in pressuring the new President Andrew Johnson to issue an execu-tive order giving the military full authority over the conspirators' trial.

Stanton first regrouped by taking authority away from Almarin C. Rich-ards, who had replaced Baker as the head of Washington security. And then Stanton had to take possession of the evidence gathered by nonmilitary in-vestigators, while at the same time calling in his own investigators. Detective Baker had been called back to Washington from his previous assignment in New York, and Colonel H. L. Burnett was called to Washington from Cin-cinnati to be a Stanton investigator and organizer of the military tribunal. Burnett was provided a room at the War Department so he could work under Stanton's watchful eye.[3]

After learning Weichmann was in Richard's custody and somewhere in Canada, Stanton went berserk and demanded to the Police Chief in no uncer-tain terms that he was to immediately return Weichmann to Washington and place him under military arrest.[4] Richards was so intimidated by such a stern command from the Secretary of War that he dropped everything and personally traveled to New York to pick up Weichmann, handcuff Weichmann to himself, and deliver him to Burnett's office at the War Department.

Weichmann reported to Burnett the details of his trip to Canada. Burnett was thoroughly impressed that Weichmann was not part of the assassination conspiracy, nor a threat to the public in any way, and chose to release him. When Stanton learned Weichmann had been freed, he exploded, threatening to discharge Burnett from the Army. Of course, Burnett tried to justify his decision, but Stanton ignored Burnett's arguments and ranted inconsolably that Weichmann *must* be in his office as fast as he could be delivered.

Burnett quickly called for Weichmann's arrest and returned him to Stanton along with his resignation as Judge Advocate. Burnett could not understand Stanton's panic and unreasonable attitude, and he wanted no more of Stanton's abuse. After Stanton realized he had lost an important ally, he begged Burnett to forgive him.[5] He needed Burnett to help him frame the kidnappers as assassins, and he blamed his rage on the pressure and responsibility of the investigation while grieving over his friend, Lincoln. Everyone from Burnett to historians have explained Stanton's bizarre behavior, accepting this ludicrous excuse that the Secretary of War, who had handled every issue during the entire Civil War, could not handle the pressure of this investigation. As soon as Weichmann was returned to Stanton's office the Secretary of War immediately resumed his composure, handling every situation in the investigation as well as the elaborate memorial services, including the train trip conveying Lincoln's body back to Springfield. The 20-year-old corporal James Tanner, who took shorthand statements for Stanton, described the Secretary as a man of steel. "The stern Stanton barked out a steady stream of orders and took command of the chaotic situation, which he did not relinquish for several months."[6]

The truth behind Stanton's temporary nervous breakdown was that he knew that if Weichmann were to be put under pressure by investigators outside Stanton's circle of collaborators, young Louis might try to defend himself by revealing he had been a paid informant to Baker while in Booth's gang. Stanton realized that his entire charade would fail if Weichmann were to talk. Baker, Stanton, Eckert, and Holt would fall like dominoes, one by one, if Weichmann were forced to admit his connection to the War Department.

Confederate conspiracy theorists try to cover up the extensive knowledge Stanton possessed about Booth before the assassination, and they deny Weichmann's service to him as an informant. They profess that Stanton went berserk only because he actually believed that Louis Weichmann was a dangerous conspirator. The Metro police and Stanton's own investigator, Colonel Burnett, had no doubt whatsoever that Weichmann was not a danger. Stanton alone was upset to learn Weichmann was free to help find John Surratt, Jr., who was known by everyone as a true suspect and a known conspirator with Booth.

Stanton was building a case with which to frame the kidnappers as Confederate assassins and he needed a military tribunal under his complete control to be able to manipulate the outcome. The timid Weichmann could be a tremendous liability or asset to his elaborate deception. The Secretary of War's entire case would depend on the testimony of Weichmann, who would become the prosecution's prime witness. Stanton had a two-hour talk with Weichmann after he was returned from Canada, not only to ascertain what he'd already shared with investigators, but to instruct him that he had better come up with a very convincing reason why he should not be included with the other accused conspirators. Stanton, of course, had no intentions to release Weichmann, and had him transferred directly to the Old Capital Prison to join the ever-increasing inmate population of suspects and witnesses collected by the detective and military investigators.

Arresting Mary

Two days after Lincoln's death, a team of investigators under Col. H. H. Wells returned to Mary Surratt's boardinghouse for a second search and to place everyone under arrest. While Mary was being interrogated, her doorbell rang and Officer Richard Morgan (under the orders of Colonel Olcott) answered the door to see a strange-looking man standing there, wearing a long, dark coat with the sleeve of a shirt on his head as a skullcap. The man carried a pickaxe on his shoulder and his boots were covered with mud. The stranger was set back at seeing an officer answering the door and he quickly replied, "I must be mistaken." Morgan asked who he came to see and the man answered, "Mary Surratt." Officer Morgan firmly replied with his gun drawn, "You are right; walk in." Powell entered and took a seat.

Officer Morgan began to question the stranger about why he was calling so late at night, and the odd man told Morgan that Mary had hired him to dig a gutter. Morgan continued probing to find out exactly who this man really was. Another question as to where he came from led the stranger to offer a document—an oath of allegiance—he had signed in Baltimore a month before. It was signed *Lewis Paine* and dated March 14, 1865.

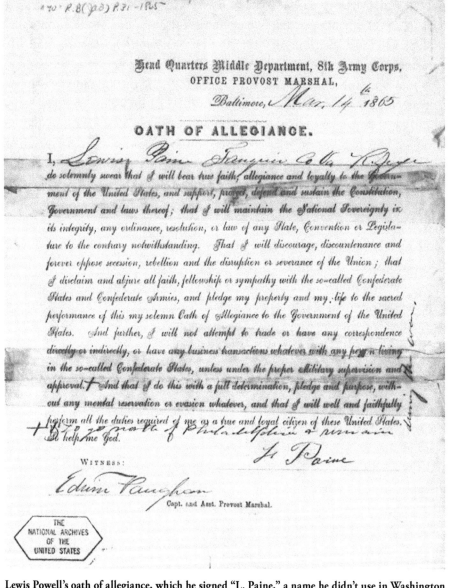

Lewis Powell's oath of allegiance, which he signed "L. Paine," a name he didn't use in Washington (Powell used the alias "James Wood"). Louis Weichmann was *told* of the alias "Paine," and went on to inform the court that "James Wood" had changed his name to "Payne" prior to the assassination.

Mary was called into the room to confirm the stranger's story, that she had hired him to dig a gutter, but she frantically denied knowing him or ever seeing him. At that the investigating team for Colonel Wells and General Clendenin had captured James Wood, Stanton's prearranged assassin for Seward. But Wood (Powell) was now wearing a different colored coat and identifying himself as "Paine." Only *after* his arrest did James Wood first become known as Lewis Paine. However, Stanton and Baker had been informed by Weichmann, since February, that the stranger was a Confederate spy who went by the alias of James Wood, and he also reported that Wood always wore a long, gray coat.[7]

That night Mary was taken into custody along with Powell, now alias Lewis Paine, who would later be charged as the man who attacked the household of Secretary of State William Seward. In the press Lewis Powell would become Stanton's "Mystery Man" of many aliases. He only used one alias (Wood) while he had been free in Washington, but the reason he was called "The Mystery Man" was because each independent investigating agency knew him by a different name. Lewis Thornton Powell was his real name. James Wood, with the nickname "Mosby," was his Washington alias; Lewis Paine was the false name he used in Baltimore and signed on his oath of allegiance; and which he presented to the investigators when he was arrested at the boardinghouse.

Louis Weichmann testified that March 14 was the day that James Wood returned to Mary Surratt's boardinghouse for a second visit, and that Wood had changed his name to Lewis *Payne* (spelled as such), a name he could have learned only from investigators *by word of mouth*, and only *after* Powell's arrest. Weichmann said on that March day "Payne" was dressed in a complete suit of gray. Louis Weichmann was the only witness who ever testified that he knew Seward's assassin as "Lewis Payne" before the day he was arrested at the boardinghouse. Weichmann even thought Paine's *actual* name was Wood. The truth is Powell never used the name Paine in Washington until he presented his oath of allegiance to the detectives three days after the assassination. Stanton needed Weichmann to prove for him that the man in the long gray coat who attacked William Seward was this same "Paine" they arrested at the Surratt house. Even at the start of the trial they had yet to learn his real name was Powell.

Arresting Arnold & O'Laughlen

It is obvious that after the assassination, when Louis Weichmann went to the authorities, he identified the members of Booth's gang. But before arrests could be made, some type of physical evidence needed to be collected to justify why the suspects were being held. More evidence provided more suspects, and Samuel Arnold was arrested on April 17, while at his new job as a clerk near Fortress Monroe in Virginia. Arnold worked and slept at John W. Whaton's storehouse in Old Point Comfort, where Officers Eaton G. Horner and Voltaire Randall tracked him down. Arnold cooperated fully with the police and confessed to the kidnapping plot and gave them the names of Michael O'Laughlen, George Atzerodt, and John Surratt, Jr., as co-conspirators. But neither Surratt nor Arnold had been in Washington the night of the assassination, and O'Laughlen had an ironclad alibi for his whereabouts from many credible witnesses.[8] When Michael O'Laughlen learned he was wanted for questioning he turned himself over to that same, well-known neighbor of all the accused conspirators from Baltimore, Marshal McPhail.

It was proven in the trial that Arnold had dropped out of the group, shortly after the meeting at Gautier's Saloon, and left Washington two weeks before Booth shot Lincoln. During that meeting Arnold called the kidnapping plot suicide, and he began to suspect that Booth was delusional and mentally unstable. The letter he wrote to Booth explaining why he dropped out of the kidnapping conspiracy was called the "Sam" letter, and used as evidence against him as a assassination conspirator. The letter was found in the trunk in Booth's room at the National Hotel after the assassination. This letter reveals an obvious secret informant, because the letter was signed only "Sam." For investigators to know Sam was Samuel Arnold, someone had to have given his full name and identity to the authorities prior to them finding the letter. That someone was Louis Weichmann, an inside informant reporting on Confederate couriers, and it can be sure whatever information he knew prior to the assassination, so did Stanton.

Arresting Atzerodt

Investigators had George Atzerodt's name, but needed an excuse to arrest him. On May 18, 1865, Louis Weichmann was lying when he explained to the defense attorneys why he reported to the police so very early the morning after the assassination. He stated, "I read the newspapers on the morning after the assassination and I learned that the assassin of Seward wore a long, gray coat, so I thought it was George Atzerodt." Judge Holt, who had worked for months with the informants under Stanton, knew full well that Weichmann had always used the long, gray coat to identify James Wood (Lewis Powell) in his reports to the War Department.

Major O'Beirne used the long, gray coat as his excuse to investigate George Atzerodt's room at the Kirkwood Hotel, and Weichmann's lie in court was to cover for him. The Defense Attorney, Mr. Atkins, questioned Weichmann about how he came to connect what he read in the newspaper with any of the people in Booth's gang. Judge Bingham protected Weichmann from that intimidating question by ruling that, "It is no matter how a man's mental processes work."[9] The defense was restricted from proving Weichmann's testimony was perjury.

George Atzerodt was not apprehended until April 20, even though his rented room at the Kirkwood Hotel had been searched on April 15, where incriminating evidence was found. He was arrested five days later in Germantown, Maryland, while asleep in the home of his uncle, Hartman Richer, who was also taken into custody and later released.

April 13th, the day before the assassination, George Atzerodt rented room 126 at the Kirkwood Hotel, one floor above the suite where Vice President Andrew Johnson lived.[10, 11, 12] The next evening, just three hours before Lincoln was shot, he received a visit from David Herold summoning him to meet with Booth. As they departed the hotel (never to return), Herold left his coat, gun and knife in Atzerodt's room.[13, 14] During the trial proceedings, John Lee, a military policeman testifying for the prosecution, stated that on the night of April 15, he was ordered by Major O'Beirne to investigate the Kirkwood Hotel, but he never explained why he was ordered there, or what he was to investigate. Only after he arrived at the hotel did an employee familiar to Lee inform him that the day before a rather *suspicious looking man in a gray coat* was seen around the hotel.[15] Why would investigators be looking for a man in a long gray coat, when the witnesses to Seward's attack could not even agree if the assassin wore a coat?

According to his testimony, this newly discovered information prompted John Lee to check the hotel register, and in doing so he found G. A. Atzerodt, written very badly, assigned to room 126. Lee did not explain why the poor handwriting was a clue. People who knew Atzerodt and those who laundered his clothes testified they never saw him in a long gray coat,[16, 17] and the suspect, Lewis Payne (Powell), whom Weichmann reported *always* wore a long gray coat, had no features that even vaguely resembled those of Atzerodt. At the trial, John Lee neither identified his employee friend at the hotel who gave him the useful tip about the gray coat, nor gave the reason why O'Bernie ordered an investigation of the Kirkwood.

John Lee found the door of room 126 was locked and no key was available. For that reason, said a clerk, the chambermaid had not been able to enter the room to clean it.[18] The fact that the door was locked was an important point for the prosecution to establish. A locked door, one might argue, would prove that the investigators could not have planted the evidence found in room 126.

Lee got authorization to break the door down with a clerk from the hotel, Lyman S. Sprague, present.[19] Upon entering the room Lee noticed the bed had never been used and was still made and untouched. Atzerodt confessed he stayed at least one night at the Kirkwood, so how did the bed get made if the chambermaid had not been able to enter the room?

Officer Lee testified that although nothing on the bed appeared disturbed, he checked it over thoroughly and under the pillow he discovered a loaded pistol. He explained that when he removed the sheets from the mattress he found a large Bowie knife. In the room was hanging a black coat, and in the pocket the detective allegedly found a bankbook belonging to J. Wilkes Booth. It was from the Ontario Bank of Canada, showing a deposit of $455 made on October 27, 1864. Also in the coat pocket, he said, were three handkerchiefs, and on the floor a brass spur, a pair of socks, two collars, and a map of Virginia.[20]

The hotel clerk, Lyman S. Sprague, testified that he went into the room with Detective Lee, however the only thing he witnessed Detective Lee find was the revolver under the pillow. It is more likely that the bankbook was originally found in the trunk in Booth's room at the National Hotel (where with the "Sam" letter was found) and then planted by Officer John Lee into Herold's black coat pocket to provide enough evidence to link Atzerodt to Booth and the assassination. If Herold had truly gone to the trouble to hide his knife and gun, why would he leave his coat to be found with a bankbook belonging to Booth in the pocket?

It would be very doubtful Booth would have trusted David Herold with his bankbook. Furthermore, the Kirkwood Hotel clerk testified he only witnessed Detective Lee finding a pistol. Also, at least two of the three handkerchiefs found in Herold's coat pocket clearly belonged to Booth, and may have also been found in Booth's hotel room before being planted in Herold's coat pocket. The map of Virginia was obviously planted to allege Booth's premeditated plan get away to the south.

Fabrications

Louis Weichmann realized that his life de-
pended on whether he would be a cooperative prosecution witness, otherwise he
would be hanged for being a Confederate
accomplice to assassination. He had no
way to prove that he worked for Baker as
a civilian informant, reporting about espionage against the administration, and
Weichmann's close personal relationship
to John and Mary Surratt, along with his
association with Booth (which included
telegrams and secret meetings), would be
enough to charge him as a primary conspirator in Booth's gang. Weichmann was
easily persuaded by the prosecution to lie

LOUIS J. WEICHMANN, the prosecution's
star witness, provided testimony to ensure swift guilty verdicts for all four of
the hanged defendants.

to conceal the fact that Booth and Powell were the only conspirators in the
assassination plot, and that in actuality the other prisoners had been only civilian, *would-be* kidnappers.

By May 1, Booth was dead and his entire cohort had been rounded up.
The process of depicting Lincoln's demise as the result of a Confederate plot
now rested in the hands of the War Department's Judge Advocates and the
testimonies from the hundreds of suspects and witnesses, much of whom were
held under armed guard in the Old Capitol Prison.

On May 2, the day after George Atzerodt gave his confession to McPhail,
Louis Weichmann was interrogated by the War Department's investigating
officer, Colonel Foster. Oddly, there were no questions asked about Kate
Thompson (or Brown), even though Atzerodt had just revealed to McPhail
"young Weightman ought to know about this woman." Weichmann did, however, give conflicting and confusing accounts about what he had witnessed
while living at Mary Surratt's boardinghouse, and backtracked on his story
several times. Louis remained incarcerated.[21]

Being jailed was a nightmare for Louis. He was not a rugged or worldly
man, but an aspiring minister, mainly to please his mother. As an informant,
young Louis appealed to John Surratt to be included in his operations, but
John refused him, saying he could neither ride nor shoot. Three days after his

interrogation, Weichmann wrote a long letter to Colonel Burnett, who was also the third member of Judge Advocate Holt's prosecution team. Louis wrote that he was so scared and upset that he could not think straight, but wanted to clarify the confusing statements he had given to Colonel Foster. However, his new information about Howell and Slater was still of no consequence, and much of it demonstrably false.[22]

On the third floor of the Old Capitol Prison, which had previously served as the Washington Arsenal, a new courtroom was constructed for the trial. On May 12, only eight days after Lincoln was buried, the conspiracy trial proceedings began. Despite the fact that Judge Advocate John Bingham protected the prosecution witnesses from cross-examination with his numerous dubious objections to rational questions (which the tribunal often upheld), Weichmann's testimony was plagued with many conspicuous inconsistencies.

Weichmann's letter to Burnett failed to get him out of prison, and he remained another 23 days in the same clothes he was wearing when arrested, all the while sharing the prison with Augustus Howell (whom he had testified against) and facing the possibility of sharing the same fates as his friend George Atzerotdt.

The completely desperate young man wrote a second letter to Burnett. This time he claimed that Howell had threatened him, and that he was, at last, determined to tell the truth "at all hazards," and would do so "though the heavens fall." He then spun a most far-fetched web of stories, trying to prove his value as a witness, claiming Howell was well known as "the most notorious blockade-runner ever to cross the Potomac." He said that he had forgotten, but now remembered, sensational facts about Howell and Slater and their doings in Vermont and Canada, and things he'd overheard about Robert E. Lee, Jefferson Davis and the head of the Confederate Secret Service, Jacob Thompson.[23] This second desperate letter by Weichmann proved to the War Department that they now had an insider from Booth's circle willing to . agree to make any statement that would save his neck. Louis would sell out Mary Surratt, who had been like a mother to him, and his boyhood friend, her son John.

Weichmann's testimony was used by the prosecution to directly tie Powell, Atzerodt and John Surratt to the pistols, spurs and Bowie knives that the prosecution presented as physical evidence. The planted spur in room 126 was purposely placed there in order to connect Atzerodt to Booth. On May 13, 1865, Weichmann testified, he saw "Surratt and Payne (Powell) seated on a bed, playing with bowie-knives. There were also two revolvers and four sets of new spurs."[24] Weichmann then identified the recovered brass spur found in room 126 as the missing spur to a set of three pairs of spurs found in the closet of his room at Mary's boardinghouse, leaving the impression that Booth wore one set, and the other three sets were left in the closet in his room. The prosecution never had to explain how or why only one spur made its way onto the *floor* of room 126, a room whose bed had been made, and the clerk testified he witnessed only a gun was recovered.

Planting evidence was a common practice during the entire investigation. False charges and perjured testimony were introduced and encouraged throughout the trial. The judge tribunal protected the prosecution witnesses from cross-examination, and the judge advocates (military prosecuting attorneys), some of whom had participated in the investigations, presented planted evidence and provided perjured testimony from their captured witnesses.

Another example of phony evidence, planted strictly to blame Lincoln's death on a Confederate plot, occurred when military police detective R. C. Morgan testified on May 19 that he recovered photographs from Mary Surratt's boardinghouse of General Beauregard, Jefferson Davis, and the Confederate Vice President Alexander Stephens. A card was claimed to be recovered reading, "Thus Will It Ever Be with Tyrants—Virginia the Mighty" written on it, along with two Confederate flags embroidered with the Virginia state slogan, *Sic Semper Tyrannis*.[25] Consequently the Virginia slogan is what the War Department claimed Booth yelled out after he shot Lincoln, but this was never substantiated, and was asserted specifically to link Booth to Mary, and paint the whole gang as Confederate agents.

Found in the boardinghouse were carte-de-visite photographs of John Wilkes Booth and the Democrat candidate for president, General George McClellan; and allegedly, in Mary's bedroom, was a bullet mold along with percussion caps. The Derringer Booth used to shoot Lincoln was a muzzle-loader which used percussion caps. The mold and caps were planted evidence to tie Mary to the murder weapon, and also to allege that she was a member of the phony Confederate assassination plot.[26]

The defense attorneys tried to discover where the photographs might have originated, but they were prevented from asking any questions relating to that evidence. One defense witness, George B. Wood from Boston, was called to testify that he had seen photographs of the rebellion leaders readily available for sale in public places in the North. The Defense asked him if he had seen them in possession of any "loyal" persons (inferring War Department investigators). The Judge Advocates objected, saying the question was irrelevant and immaterial, and the questions were withdrawn.[27]

Anna Surratt was trying to save her mother from being convicted as a Confederate spy by accounting for the incriminating photographs. She claimed that the pictures belonged to her, because her father had given them to her before he died. But Mr. Surratt died suddenly of a stroke in August of 1862. At that time General George McClellan was not considered friendly to the Southern cause, and only became a threat to the Radicals a year after Mr. John Surratt had died. It would be ridiculous to assume that Anna's father would have admired a photograph of the *Union* General George McClellan.[28]

Louis Weichmann also claimed in an affidavit regarding the first raid on the boardinghouse the night of the assassination, "When the detectives came at three o'clock the next morning, I rapped at Mary's door for permission to let them in. 'For God sakes, let them in! I expected the house to be searched,' said she."[29] It was not on the first raid, but on the second raid of Mary's house two days later when she was arrested, and during subsequent searches, when evidence was recovered. Mary's home had now been raided once, and she knew she was a person of interest while Booth was still at large. Why would she have allowed there to be *so much* incriminating evidence so easily found in her boardinghouse? This was obviously perjured testimony by Weichmann, or else the evidence found was planted, or both.

The contrived evidence was planted to support the fabricated story created by the War Department of a Confederate plot. The prosecution and the judges were under the direction of Stanton (one judge, John A. Bingham, later became a Radical Congressman), while the defense attorneys were under the strict limitations set by the rules of the War Department.

Conflicts of interest were given little or no consideration in gathering and presenting evidence. Among the investigators who had recovered items from the boardinghouse was an Army Lieutenant named Dempsey, who had been a Confederate prisoner for two years. One clear attempt at planting deceiving evidence is exposed in the charges against John Surratt, Jr. The prosecution demonstrated their deliberate, but sloppy practice of falsifying evidence when investigators Captains Potts and Newcomb conducted just one of many repeated searches of Mary Surratt's boardinghouse, during which they uncovered a scrap of paper with the name "Gen. Suratt CSA" written on it. This was used to allege John Surratt, Jr., was a high-ranking Confederate officer.

However, when they fabricated this evidence they spelled Surratt with only one "r" attesting this evidence was a forgery.[30]

Every effort was made by the War Department to either plant fake evidence, relocate personal effects to contrive connections, or to destroy or withhold legitimate evidence that might vindicate the accused. The singular purpose of Stanton was to disguise the true conspiracy against Lincoln by the Radical coalition. The judge advocates who ran the prosecution used empty, pretentious charges that Lincoln's assassination was a Confederate plot. The evidence and transcripts from the military commission easily prove the proceedings were a sham, clumsily sidestepping the obvious truth that the Confederate government had no motive, ability, or opportunity to help Booth in any way with Lincoln's assassination.

14

Following the Script

Stanton easily recognized that Booth's plot to capture Lincoln was an impossible and absurd idea. The kidnapping buffoons never posed a serious threat to the President, nor had a remote chance to carry out a successful capture. Since late 1863 it had always been John Surratt, and not Booth, whom Baker and Stanton believed was the ringleader of the Washington gang. Stanton's initial reason for his surveillance on the kidnappers was to gather information about the Confederate spy, John Surratt, Jr. Once Lincoln was killed, Stanton began to publicly portray Booth as the chief operative of a diabolical Confederate plot of assassination. But in truth, Booth and his conspiracy to capture Lincoln were such a trivial threat to the President's security that Booth and his cohort would never have entered into the pages of history had he not been persuaded to murder Lincoln.

On April 15, the day after the assassination, John Surratt was in New York City buying shirts when he heard the news about Lincoln's murder. He immediately dropped everything and made directly for the St. Lawrence Hall Hotel in Montréal, Canada, the city's well-known headquarters for Confederate agents. From there he was provided assistance to leave the country by the Confederate Secret Serivce.[1] Had Booth actually been a Confederate agent as John Surratt, he too would have made for the Canadian safe house, not the swamps of northern Virginia. The facts are that John Surratt had no knowledge of a plot to kill Lincoln, and John Wilkes Booth had no plans to run further than the outskirts of D.C.

Before the assassination the kidnapping gang was considered by Stanton and Baker as just a band of halfwit sympathizers with a pipe dream about apprehending the President right from under the nose of the War Department and the Metropolitan police force. The gang's only ridiculous attempt to capture the President ended without ever beginning because they allegedly waited for him in the wrong location; meanwhile, Lincoln was appearing at Booth's very hotel (they even missed that announcement in the newspapers). After that debacle the gang split up, and well before Booth and Powell turned into assassins. By the time Booth was considering assassination John Surratt had been out of Washington for two weeks and was in New York; Samuel Arnold had moved to Fortress Monroe, Virginia; and his neighbor Michael O'Laughlen was living with his brother-in-law back in Baltimore. The War Department's choice of candidates to frame and execute as Confederate assassins consisted of a homeless immigrant, a young man with the mind of a child, plus the *mother* of John Surratt. The War Department had been hoping to use the Confederate agent John Surratt to make their case (they weren't even sure who Lewis Powell was), but instead they tried and convicted John's mother, the first woman executed in America.

The only truly guilty prisoner of the four hanged was the Confederate message carrier, Lewis Powell (alias James Wood), whom they called "Payne" throughout the trial and in the press. But even he had been an incapable failure in his own attempt to assassinate Secretary of State William Seward. The Confederate conspiracy theory claims that it was these four prisoners who fooled the War Department's intelligence gathering division and were the masterminds who launched attacks on the Secretary of State and the President.

After those four prisoners were arrested, and before the conspiracy trial began, Stanton's War Department fed the media their prefabricated story about the assassination conspiracy. The investigators provided newspaper reporters descriptions and explanations of the individual roles for each of the four accused. The prisoners were said to be Confederate spies carrying out orders given to them by Jefferson Davis. All four of these specially selected suspects were accused by the War Department of being Confederate assassins and were hanged.

The prosecution strictly controlled the testimonies of the defense witnesses and they presented contrived evidence to the court to convict the suspects. Any evidence that could prove that any of the defendants were not involved in the murder conspiracy was withheld or destroyed.

Lewis Powell was marketed to the media as a mysterious Confederate spy using several aliases to disguise his covert activities. The Federal investigators reported to the newspapers that the "Mystery Man" boarded at Mary Surratt's home, and while there he called himself the Reverend Lewis Payne (spelled as such), and he always wore a long, gray coat. But in truth the name *Payne* was not known by anyone in Washington until three days after the assassination.

The newspapers depicted Mary Surratt as a spy providing a meeting place to plan the assassination, while masquerading as an innocent businesswoman running a boardinghouse. Articles such as those had no basis in truth whatsoever. Mary Surratt was found guilty of assassination conspiracy after the testimony of Stanton's prime prosecuting witness, Louis Weichmann, who, unlike Mary, was part of Booth's gang, and present at every event that was used to convict her. The military prosecution claimed Weichmann was completely unaware and uninvolved as Mary aided Booth with Lincoln's murder. Weichmann, a civilian informant for Lafayette Baker, was how Baker and Stanton knew so much about Booth and his followers.

The young David Herold, captured along with Booth in the Virginia tobacco barn, was described to the public as "second only to Booth." *The Washington Evening Star* claimed the 22-year-old Herold was "Booth's most important accomplice," and *The New York Times* reported that he was "Booth's nearest accomplice."[2] But during the trial, David Herold's lifelong neighbor (who was also his doctor) testified about the David Herold he had always known. In Dr. Samuel A. H. McKim's description of Herold, *Booth's most important accomplice*, the doctor said, "In mind I consider David Herold about eleven years old."[3] In all, five people intimately familiar with Herold testified in agreement with the doctor, saying he was immature, unreliable, trivial, and according to a Dr. Charles W. Davis, also a neighbor, "far more like a boy than a man."[4]

George Atzerodt was reported to be a notorious Confederate blockaderunner. But he was actually a homeless immigrant who spoke broken English. Atzerodt was convicted in the media with descriptions such as: "the general contour of his features stamp him as a man of low character, who would stoop to any action, no matter how vile, for money,"[5] and "a villainous-looking man … there is little doubt of his criminality."[6] His defense attorney, under the command of Secretary of War Stanton, was Captain W. E. Doster, who asked the military tribunal to dismiss the transcript of Atzerodt's confession, which they did.[7] That evidence would have revealed the true conspiracy and proven him not guilty. Captain Doster chose instead to defend Atzerodt as being too cowardly to carry out the crime he was charged with: an assassination attempt against Vice President, Andrew Johnson.

On the afternoon of Lincoln's assassination, Booth headed to the Kirkwood Hotel to make a quick call on the Vice President. Johnson was not there, so Booth left a personal note that said, "I do not wish to disturb you. Are you at home?" The note was not found until five o'clock that evening, but not by Johnson. It was mistakenly placed in the mailbox of his personal secretary,

William Browning.[8] Booth needed to travel south to meet with John T. Ford who was already in Virginia preparing to reopen his Richmond theater.

Johnson had previously told Booth that he would provide him passes to go to Richmond, but he had backed out of his promise and was now avoiding Booth.[9] Getting those passes was the purpose for the personal note Booth left Johnson at the Kirkwood Hotel, and getting the passes from Johnson was why Booth paid George Atzerodt to rent a room at that same hotel. Atzerodt was accused in court of being at the hotel, asking where he could find Johnson, allegedly on a mission to kill him. This event was reported to have taken place on April 12th, two days before Booth had any assassination plans.[10] Furthermore, Booth would have certainly *not* sent Atzerodt to assassinate the Vice President *before* his surprise attack on Lincoln. The reason Lincoln and Seward were attacked simultaneously was to take advantage of the element of surprise: each needed to be killed before the other could be protected.

While at the Kirkwood, Atzerodt did inquire about Johnson, but the real reason Atzerodt was asking where he could find the Vice President was because he was trying to get the papers Johnson had promised.[11] Booth assumed passes were necessary to get through the military checkpoints south of Washington, because he had not yet learned that Lincoln had declared passes were no longer needed.[12]

Booth first met Johnson in February, 1864, while Johnson was the military governor of Tennessee and Booth was performing at the Wood's Theatre in Nashville. Johnson and Booth socialized together in Tennessee with a couple of prostitute sisters.[13] The note Booth left Johnson at the Kirkwood Hotel would later be used by Stanton as blackmail against the new president. Stanton threatened he could charge Johnson as a conspirator in Lincoln's assassination, and he used Booth's note to force Johnson to do his bidding, beginning with ordering a military trail for the Southern sympathizers Stanton intended to frame for Lincoln's murder.

Stanton had to change Booth's kidnapping plot into an assassination plot, and blame the assassination on the Confederate government. To accomplish this he heavily relied on the prosecution's judge advocates to hide evidence along with the perjured testimony of his civilian informant, Louis Weichmann. Between hiding evidence and presenting false testimony, Stanton could cover up his own involvement in the plot and disguise what truly happened.

Before the gang had given up on the kidnapping plot, Booth had a buggy, which he purchased for the purpose of transporting his presidential hostage.

On Tuesday, April 11, the day Lincoln gave his last public address, Mary Surratt sent Louis Weichmann to ask Booth if she could borrow his buggy to go on an errand to Surrattsville, which was to collect on a debt from a Mr. Nothe. Booth had sold his buggy, but he gave Weichmann $10 to rent a buggy for Mary to use for that day. Then Friday afternoon, April 14, Mary needed to call again on her debtor in Surrattsville. Weichmann was again asked to find her a buggy, and this time he would rent it from Howard's stable using money Mary had given him.

At about the same time that day Booth was spotted in the alley behind Ford's Theatre by Mary Jane Anderson, who testified:

> I saw him … between 2 and 3 o'clock in the afternoon, standing in the theater back-door, in the alley, talking to a lady. … He and this lady were pointing up and down the alley as if they were talking about it. They stood there a considerable time, and then Booth went into the theater.[14]

Could this lady have been Margaret Coleman, William Seward's chambermaid? John Miles, a stagehand at Ford's Theater, also testified he saw Booth "about 3 o'clock in the afternoon … in the stable… not more than five yards from the theater."[15]

Weichmann claimed that he saw George Atzerodt round 2:30 PM at Howard's stable while he was there renting the buggy.[16] His account contained two lies. First, Weichmann testified that Atzerodt told him that he was going to see "Lewis Payne." George Atzerodt only knew Powell as Wood.[17] Second, Weichmann did not see Atzerodt at Howard's stable. Atzerodt admitted that he saw Weichmann on that same day, but it was earlier in the day at the Post Office.[18] Weichmann had claimed they were at Howard's stable because he was trying to hide the fact that he was a spy working for Baker and Stanton at the Post Office. Weichmann needed to keep secret that one of his jobs for Baker was to check out the mail deliveries sent from Richmond.

The unarguable truth is that Powell was only known in Washington as James Wood or his nickname Mosby. Miss Honara Fitzpatrick and Miss Dean were boarders at Mary's home and they both testified that before the assassination they knew Payne only as James Wood.[19] Anna Surratt, John Holohan, and Eliza Holohan all testified they never knew Lewis Powell by any other name than the Reverend James Wood.[20, 21, 22] Even Mrs. Martha Murray, the landlady at the Herndon House where James Wood stayed for two weeks while he was in Washington, never once referred to him as Payne. George Atzerodt and Samuel Arnold also confessed they never knew Lewis Powell by any other name than James Wood or by his nickname Mosby. *Only* Louis Weichmann pretended to have known James Wood as "Lewis Payne" prior to the arrest at which he presented his oath of allegiance.

Weichmann testified in court, "A man calling himself Wood first visited Mary's wearing a black coat. Three weeks later on March 14, he came back calling himself the Baptist preacher *Payne*, and he was dressed in a complete suit of gray." Louis Weichmann was a civilian informant for Baker, and he had been reporting to Captain Gleason at the War Department about Lewis Powell since February, but during this entire time he too did not know Lewis Powell by any other name than the Reverend James Wood. Chief of Detectives Baker recorded Weichmann's reports on page 486 in the book he published after the assassination. Baker wrote that "Payne" had been identified by a lodger at Mary Surratt's boardinghouse, that the man had visited Mary's twice under the name of Wood.[23]

In order for Stanton to identify James Wood as also being the same man who was arrested at Mary Surratt's boardinghouse three days after the assassination, he had to account for the dark coat, and prove that James Wood was the same man who had presented an oath of allegiance signed "Lewis Paine." Weichmann had to falsify his testimony to prove that Lewis Paine was the same man as James Wood.

Weichmann's testimony could only be substantiated with some help from Stanton's judge advocates. Captain W. M. Wermerskirch was the officer who arrested *Paine* at Mary's boardinghouse. He testified that on the night he arrested Paine, "He was dressed in a dark coat and pants that seemed to be black." That testimony was not what the judge wanted to hear, so the judge ordered Paine to put on a white and brown, mixed-colored coat that the prosecution was presenting as evidence, and for Wermerskirch to then identify that coat. Captain Wermerskirch then said, "That is the coat" but he paused and added, "I would not positively swear to the coat, but it is near the color and shape of that coat as can be."[24]

The prosecution was determined to use a coat to identify Powell as Seward's assassin. The white and brown coat was claimed to have been recovered from woods three miles west of Washington by detective Thomas Price on April 16.[25] Wermerskirch testified that was the same coat Powell wore when

The War Department dressed up their captive, Lewis Powell, for the newspapers. LEFT: the "mixed brown and white" coat Powell was allegedly wearing when arrested, though the arresting officer first described it as "dark," and police claimed the coat was in their possession the day *before* his arrest. RIGHT: a long, gray coat, similar to the one Powell was known to wear, which Weichmann also associated with Atzerodt. Neither coat was covered in blood.

he was arrested on April 17th! Of course Colonel H. H. Wells also testified Powell was arrested in a "dark gray" coat.[26] The white and brown coat was allegedly the coat Powell wore when he attacked the Sewards, and was said to have "traces of blood" on the inside of a sleeve. The nurse, Sgt. George F. Robinson, testified that in the Secretary of State's bedroom, he had pulled Powell "off the bed,"[27] and Dr. T. S. Verdi described "his bed [as] covered with blood, with blood all around him, blood under the bed, and blood on the handles of the doors."[28] The coat Powell wore would have been soaked in blood. Bell had described the assassin's overcoat as "light," while Augustus Seward said the attacker had "no coat."[29, 30]

Weichmann was Stanton's only witness who could identify Seward's at-tacker, Lewis Payne, as being the same Confederate agent in Booth's gang who had always worn a long, gray coat. Of course Powell's famous gray coat never materialized, but in order to be able to associate Powell with Booth's gray-coat associate, and with Seward's attacker, Powell was photographed for the newspapers dressed up in two separate coats—a long, gray coat, and then the white and brown coat the prosecution claimed he once wore (to which no witness would positively swear).

Though members of Seward's household didn't agree on whether the at-tacker even wore a coat, Stanton's investigators were busy looking for a coat, with *traces* of blood, that would fit James Wood. They were looking for some-thing witnesses hadn't described, but that suited Stanton's prosecutors. This further demonstrates a connection between Stanton and the attack on William Seward. Stanton's problem was when James Wood was arrested he was wearing a black coat, and he had a document to prove he was not James Wood but Lewis Paine. The coat investigators "found" was said to have been recovered west of Washington, as Seward's attacker was expected to flee with Lincoln's assassin. Powell, of course, remained right there in Washington. Stanton was sure he needed to present a coat as evidence to prove that the man he chose to be Seward's assassin was the same man the War Department had always known as James Wood in Booth's gang.

Stanton had preplanned the assassinations of Lincoln and Seward, and called on his double agent, James Donaldson, to convince Booth and Powell to be the assassins.[31] He knew that Seward's assassin could be identified by his coat, but when Lewis Powell (alias James Wood) was arrested he was wear-ing a dark coat, and he presented an oath of allegiance that he had signed "Lewis Paine" a month before in Baltimore. This unexpected development left Stanton with a difficult situation that he could only solve with the perjured testimony from his prime witness, Louis Weichmann. The testimonies of Louis Weichmann and Captain W. M. Wermerskirch about Paine's identity and coat were accepted by the military court, yet the court disregarded that every other testimony was contrary.

Stanton assigned his secret division's most trusted agent, Major Thomas Eckert, the duty of photographing all the accused Confederate spies in candid poses. The photographs were then given to the media for a visual image of this alleged Confederate spy ring said to have been working for Jefferson Davis. The War Department provided the newspapers with several photographs of the "Mystery Man" wearing the brown hat recovered from the crime scene, and the two coats provided by the prosecution. Though the trial's presentation of the coats made little sense, if any, the judges and the public seemed satisfied they had a Confederate assassin, and Booth was considered the same.

15

One Man

$\mathcal{E}$dwin M. Stanton was the J. Edgar Hoover of his day, with secret agents answering only to him, along with Lafayette Baker who kept dossiers, photo files, and an unrecorded slush fund to hire unlisted, civilian informers.[1] Stanton's agents had infiltrated the Confederate message carriers, and William P. Wood (the warden at the Old Capitol Prison) provided him with exclusive access to the mail being passed between Richmond and Canada.[2]

The ridiculous assumption that Louis Weichmann was just an innocent and unaware bystander boarding in Mary Surratt's home cannot be disproved with direct physical evidence because Baker kept no discernible records of his informants' identities. In addition, Stanton destroyed anything that could expose his many agents who fed him decoded Confederate messages.

How else could Stanton have known from the very start of the investigation that Charles Forbes, John Parker and Boston Corbett (credited with silencing Booth) were uninvolved in the plot to kill Lincoln? He somehow knew those men needed no further investigation while he doggedly pursued other suspects, and some only remotely acquainted with Booth.

John T. Ford, the owner of Ford's Theatre, was made a prime Stanton suspect because of his long friendship with the popular actor, and because he was in Richmond during the assassination.[3] Before Booth killed Lincoln he had many long-time friends in Washington, and in addition to Ford's Theatre, John Ford managed theaters in Richmond and Baltimore. Ford had a legitimate business reason to be in Richmond. Ford sent appeals to Stanton for his release, and he offered his help in the investigation to solve the crimes. But John T. Ford did not understand that his ability to help in the investigation was the reason he was being held in prison. The personal information he knew about Booth's accomplices could provide exactly what Stanton did not want known. Ford suggested a bond be set for his release at whatever amount Stanton wanted. Despite Ford reaching out to numerous government officials, from Senators to the Governor of Maryland, Stanton ignored his appeals and kept him in prison until the investigation was complete and the trail was in progress.[4]

All the while Ford was incarcerated, many of Booth's known associates—Charles Yates, James Donaldson, James Hall, Margaret Coleman and Kate Thompson—were never investigated, or to this very day ever identified. Immediately after the assassination Sarah A. Slater was never again seen by anyone, even by her family.[5] She disappeared from the face of the earth. What is even stranger about these major suspects is the fact that history writers, like the prosecutors, have ignored the roles they all played in Booth's gang, while the Confederate conspiracy theorists work so hard to justify Stanton's charges against Dr. Samuel Mudd.

It is without question Dr. Mudd was aware of the kidnapping plot, but so was Stanton, Baker and the Provost Marshal of Baltimore James McPhail, just to name a few. If Dr. Mudd were a part of Booth's planned escape, then Booth also would have had to plan his broken leg, because that was the only reason he went to Dr. Mudd's home on his run from Washington. Why is it so important to historians that Dr. Mudd be accepted as a key conspirator, while other major conspirators have remained unnamed? Stanton wanted Mudd convicted, and the theorists must vindicate Stanton to protect the premise of a Confederate plot.

So many conspiracy theories still linger because Stanton destroyed everything he did not want known. The man shot in the tobacco barn in Virginia could not have been anyone other than John Wilkes Booth, but even his identity became a conspiracy theory because there is no physical evidence to prove it was Booth. Tales and even books circulated for a century that Booth escaped and lived out his life under an assumed identity. The physical evidence establishing who was killed in Garrett's barn was in the photographic plates sent to Stanton, only to vanish before the trial began. Because of Stanton's obstruction of justice, the Confederate conspiracy theorists (even many who know better) will not admit that Colonel Everton Conger shot Booth. They still stick to the claim that Boston Corbett shot Booth, or they try to claim it was a suicide.

Another suspicion due to Stanton's interference was the mysterious card Booth allegedly gave to Charles Forbes, which Forbes never had to account for. No card was ever produced as physical evidence to prove how Booth was able to enter Lincoln's state box. It cannot be proven that such a card ever existed. That crucial evidence was said to have been lost while every other article in the theater that night was recovered—all the papers in Lincoln's pocket, the Derringer and even the spur lost when Booth jumped out of the box.

Why did Stanton not want Booth's diary submitted as evidence? Why was Booth's manifesto confiscated and hidden from the public? Why did Stanton insist on a military trial under his direct supervision? Why didn't Stanton reveal he had infiltrated Booth's gang months before? Why didn't Stanton provide reliable security for the President on a day when Lincoln himself expressed a fear of being assassinated? Why were the accused locked away on a gunboat in cramped cells with bags over their heads instead of being granted access to fair legal counsel? Why, if Edwin Stanton loved Lincoln so much, did he support Chase in the 1864 elections? Why did Stanton pick trial judges from among Lincoln and Johnson's political enemies?

Edwin Stanton orchestrated nearly every facet of the alleged conspirators' investigation and trial proceedings so he could cover his own tracks. How well could Edwin Stanton have fared if the investigation and trial had *not* been run by his subordinates? Motive, opportunity and a mountain of credible suspicion were not only suppressed, along with physical evidence, they are still passionately suppressed and protected by Confederate conspiracy theorists even to this day. History scholars and renowned authors whine and complain that the suspicion about Stanton won't go away, and his involvement in the assassination is all just some baseless theory.

The only baseless theory is the accusation that Lincoln's assassination was the result of some Confederate plot. Suspicions about the Radical plot won't go away because the conspiracy behind Lincoln's assassination has never been solved. But what can be known for sure is that Stanton quickly knew he needed to investigate Mary Surratt's boardinghouse even before Lincoln had died, although nothing was found that night that could be used to implicate her in the assassination plot. Only after *subsequent* searches did investigators begin to gather their mountain of incriminating, planted and phony evidence.

Well before the assassination, Stanton would order anyone followed who might be suspected of covert activity. Post Master General Montgomery Blair became witness to the extent that Stanton would investigate suspects. His niece, Louisa Buckner, was on a shopping trip through Washington and she carried with her a military pass from her uncle, along with a personal note from President Lincoln. Even with these credentials a detective was assigned to follow Mrs. Buckner, and she was caught with 600 ounces of quinine, a desperately needed drug for sufferers from yellow fever. This drug was considered contraband, which could have been smuggled through the Union blockade. Mrs. Buckner, her mother, and a minister friend who accompanied her while shopping were all arrested and imprisoned.[6] Very little ever escaped Stanton's watchful eye, but biased historians insist that before the assassination Stanton was completely unaware of Booth, and he had no motive to remove Lincoln from serving his second term. Throughout the trial Stanton succeeded in withholding any evidence that would arouse suspicion about his conspiracy charges against Booth and his selectively-targeted gang members.

The Diary

When Booth entered Ford's Theatre just before the assassination did he not know he would never return to Washington? He carried with him hardly any essential items. His riding boots and spurs were for his getaway, and his muzzle-loaded Derringer would only provide him a single shot. Oddly, he carried only a knife for a backup weapon. The only other item he felt necessary to have with him was his diary. He would use it to record his account of his infamous deed, not realizing at the time that his despicable act would soon be condemned by the entire nation.

Any prosecutor who had access to the recorded personal accounts written by the assassin himself, confessing to the murder and admitting treason against his country, would eagerly have submitted the diary as evidence. So why did Judge Advocate General Joseph Holt withhold the diary as evidence? Why was the diary withheld from public display? More than just a confession, the contents of the diary proved a conspiracy.

In an effort to account for the missing pages removed from Booth's diary, authors writing about this story refer to it as being only an appointment book, even though it is clearly a diary. It was obvious that Booth had chosen to use the book for addresses and appointments before his April 14 entry because the diary was outdated (it was for the year 1864). But if the first pages of the diary had not been destroyed, it might have revealed names and addresses of his contacts, thus adding to its value as evidence. But even without those undeniably missing pages, the diary would have been a most valuable and incriminating piece of evidence. The pages that remained revealed that Booth expected he could be *cleared of the crime*—an indication that his act was sanctioned by someone at the highest levels of government.[7]

The confession in the diary spans only a few, short pages, in which Booth confessed to the crime and at the same time exposed the fact that his delusional mind had little grasp of reality. For five days Booth and David Herold were provided a hiding place in Zekiah Swamp by Samuel Cox, and Cox brought Booth the newspaper stories of the assassination. It was during this time that Booth learned that he had shouted "sic semper tyrranis" before fleeing Ford's Theatre, and while he surely liked that account, he was astonished at other reports. His diary entries were largely reactions answering the newspaper accounts of his deed.

After recounting his short, rambling, glorified rendition of the murder, a few interesting facts stick out that have previously gone unnoticed. Each sheet of the book is divided into six separate days, with three days named on the front of a page, and three days on the

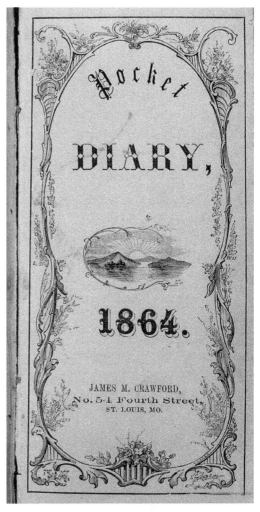

The title page of John Wilkes Booth's diary, clearly marked "DIARY." Though there is a calendar and schedule of tides, dawns and sunsets within the book, it was most certainly not an "appointment book" as some have argued.

reverse. Booth's first entry begins on the page for Monday, June 11 (again, the days printed in the diary do not correspond with the days, or year, in which Booth was writing). That would mean there were 27 *calendar* pages, printed with January 1 through June 10, cut out from the book before he began his first entry.

He began on the middle of sheet one by scratching over Sunday, [June] 12, and writing; "April 14, Friday the Ides." Each page was labeled three days, thus each sheet six days, and the confession spanned three sheets. However, the middle sheet in the confession is empty of any text. What makes this fact so interesting is that the empty sheet was after Booth began to reveal the contents of the letter he entrusted to fellow actor John Matthews. Matthews agreed to post the letter in *The National Intelligencer* on the fifteenth, but that letter was suspiciously destroyed. The contents of the letter Booth was desperately hoping would appear in the paper was never printed.

Just before the empty second sheet, Booth mentions this letter and begins to reveal the identity of someone crucial:

> I wrote a long article and left it for one of the editors of the National Intelligencer, in which I fully set forth our reasons for our proceedings. He or the gov'mt [thus ends the text before the blank page][8]

Booth was sharing credit for his deed with others. Booth was about to reveal his conspirators in the assassination plot. The empty second sheet was printed with the dates *Friday 17, Saturday 18, Sunday 19* on the front page and *Monday 20, Tuesday 21, Wednesday 22* on the reverse, but nothing is written on the page. Booth then began a completely new entry on the front of sheet three (Thursday the 23rd), writing:

> After being hunted like a dog through swamps, woods, and last night being chased by gunboats till I was forced to return wet, cold, and starving, with every man's hand against me. ...[9]

It is also obvious that Booth had read the newspapers, finding that every account condemned his murder. "I am abandoned with the curse of Cain upon me." This was not merely the Union he was referring to but the entire nation, north and south. Booth began to question his deed and to fear his fate would be to die like a criminal. He realized he was not portrayed as the story's hero, "Brutus," who struck down the evil tyrant, Caesar, but nothing more than a common cutthroat. The assassin had, overnight, transformed Lincoln from the victorious savior of a restored Union into a martyred symbol of the Radical cause to impose harsh retribution against the Confederate states.

If it could be proven that Booth and his accomplices were Confederates, then Stanton would achieve his goal to break the peace by condemning Lincoln's murder as an *act of war*. Reconciliation would be replaced by subjugation and vindictive punishment.

Reality replaced delusion, and Booth wrote, "Behold the cold hands they extend to me." He considered returning to Washington and he once again referred to the letter he left with John Matthews. This letter contained some mysterious justification for his actions. He wrote on the back of sheet three:

> The little, the very little, I left behind to clear my name the government will not allow to be printed. ... Tonight I will once more try the [Potomac] river with the intent to cross, though I have a greater desire and almost a mind to return to Washington and in a measure clear my name—which I feel I can do.[10]

Booth did not know that the letter he entrusted to John Matthews (that he felt could clear his name) had been destroyed, and he thought that "the government" was withholding the letter from being printed, perhaps the same party he intended when he described "our proceedings."

Why would Booth believe "the government" was preventing his letter to *The National Intelligencer* from being printed? And, why would the government withhold the letter (or his diary) if he was naming *Confederate* accomplices? Booth's letter included the accomplices who plotted Lincoln's assassination with him. Why would he be so passionately upset to not see those names in print? And after confessing to the murder, *why*, with the Confederacy wiped out, would he expect to return to the *Union capital* to clear his name?

Booth appears to have stopped writing in mid-sentence on the back of the first sheet. The rest of this page, instead of the conclusion of this most desperate and revealing passage, is a pointless calendar drawn sideways. The second sheet, front and back, contains no text to manifest the reason he and his accomplices "set forth their proceedings" to remove Lincoln from serving his second term.

The mystery of the empty second sheet is all that remains of the last piece of a 150-year-old puzzle to find out, once and for all, who helped John Wilkes Booth kill Lincoln. Oddly, there has been a united effort and commitment to hide clues that would solve this mystery and prove the real conspiracy. At the same time there has been an equal commitment to continue condemning those who have already been proven not guilty.

Further study of the surviving text of the diary does, however, give tantalizing clues that, when added with all the other overlooked evidence, substantiate the suspicion of a cover-up, and one orchestrated by a large and powerful authority with a guiding hand in politics, education and the media.

Booth justified his act by claiming, "God simply made me the instrument of his punishment." What stands out about this phrase is that a month later Louis Weichmann accused Mary Surratt of having said, "I think J. Wilkes Booth was only an instrument in the hands of the Almighty to punish …"[11] How did Booth end up recording in his diary a phrase nearly identical to what Mary was accused of saying only a few hours after the assassination without any contact between them? Had Louis Weichmann been coached on what to say by someone who had already read Booth's diary? Weichmann gave that statement to Judge Advocate Col. Burnett in an affidavit on August 11, 1865, over a month after Mary Surratt had been hanged. At the time Weichmann gave his testimony only Stanton, Baker, Conger and the Judge advocates had read Booth's diary. Did she actually say that, or was that just another one of Weichmann's many false testimonies he was forced to give to protect Secretary Stanton?

Nothing in his diary would explain why Stanton, Holt and Bingham would not submit to the court Booth's written confession to the assassination and his admitted betrayal of his country. The diary would have proven a conspiracy and provided the unquestioned evidence to every charge against him and any suspected accomplices.

Besides the withheld diary, the two conflicting autopsy reports, and the photographic plates of the deceased Booth, there was another key piece of evidence that was withheld for no reason other than to hide the truth. This was evidence given to the prosecution by one of Booth's kidnapping gang, George Atzerodt. He had been arrested and held in custody, while being tortured without legal counsel, facing almost certain execution. The prisoner thought that by confessing everything he knew he might be granted an opportunity to be transferred out of the nightmarish bowels of the ironclad. However, the interview was granted only because Stanton needed to learn how much the prisoner really knew. Stanton had no intentions of allowing any evidence that might contradict his charges or that would expose his secret informants.

Stanton not only had authority over all the evidence and prisoners, he had authority over the careers of the judge advocates, the chief of police Lafayette Baker and every officer involved with the military tribunal. Soon after

Lincoln's death the entire investigation, military commission, and every player in the proceedings were answerable to one man: the Secretary of War, Edwin M. Stanton.

16

Means of Escape

*T*here was never any doubt that Booth was Lincoln's assassin, because a theater full of witnesses instantly recognized the famous actor.[1] Booth's escape plan included a drop onto a stage for one last curtain call ("breaking a leg"), announcing to everyone in the theater that it was *J. Wilkes Booth* who fired the killing shot.

Stanton had no question from the very instant of the assassination the correct person he needed to pursue to apprehend Lincoln's murderer. The War Department had compiled a great deal of knowledge about Booth prior to his attack on the Lincoln administration, but Stanton needed Booth *dead*, not captured. If Booth were captured alive he would expose Stanton and his agents, who had previously uncovered the kidnapping plot. Stanton had no fear that Booth might actually escape into some protected, Southern sanctuary. By April of 1865, the Federal government had won complete supremacy over the South, and even the Confederate president was on the run, trying to escape from the same authorities that were also in pursuit of Booth.

Lincoln had been progressively lifting the state of martial law over the surrendered territories, but with the South accused of his murder, harsh resentment induced a renewed frenzy of revenge and punishment. Without Lincoln's initiatives of moderation and reunification the entire country fell under the jurisdiction of Stanton's Army, which required little accountability for violating anyone's Constitutional rights. After the demonstrations by Sherman and Grant, showing what the Union Army was capable of doing, there would be no illusions in anyone's mind what repercussions could follow if one dared to challenge the runaway authority of the War Department.

The ridiculous vindication given for Stanton's cruelty to his accused prisoners, or for his complete abortion to any rule of law, was his claim that the South could still pose some type of threat that needed to be guarded against. But the fact was that people were so intimidated and scared of military retribution, that throughout the South their fugitive president, Jefferson Davis, often had to sleep under the stars. Southerners were too afraid to even provide him a bed for the night. It is safe to assume that Stanton had no concerns about a possible threat from the demoralized South, and that his actions were an obvious attempt to hide his many secrets. One of those secrets was the nature of an alliance between him and his closest agent Thomas Eckert, the War Department's chief telegraph officer.

Eckert was born in Ohio in 1825, and spent most of his adult life as a telegraph operator. At the age of 36, the robust Eckert had worked his way down to North Carolina, and by 1861, was employed as the manager of a gold mine. This position involved directing rigid surveillance and brutal security over a large work force. After secession led to war, he left the South and returned to his home state of Ohio to join the Union Army. Being a telegraph worker by trade for most of his adult life, and having experience governing the flow of a precious commodity, won him a military commission in 1862 from the newly appointed Secretary of War, Edwin Stanton. Eckert was made the War Department's Chief Telegraph Officer, where he would govern the flow of a different precious commodity—military secrets. His senior position gave him a broad range of authority, answerable almost exclusively to Stanton.

Stanton resented having any interference with "his department," and rather than reporting to the White House, the White House would come to him. Lincoln made trips to the War Department daily, often spending much of his day in Eckert's office to receive the most recent reports of the war's progress or setbacks. Lincoln found the telegraph office a place where he could write and think with fewer interruptions, plus being there allowed him to get latest first-hand information coming directly from his generals on the front.[2] In Stanton's view those generals belonged to him, and the less Lincoln knew, the less he could interfere in the War Department's affairs.

Stanton's opinion of the Commander-in-Chief can be best summed up in a remark that he once made after the first Battle of Bull Run, referring to Lincoln as "the original gorilla."[3] Six months before Stanton began his Cabinet post, he wrote to his former boss, James Buchanan, and referred to Lincoln's administration as an "imbecility," producing only "irretrievable misfortune" and "national disgrace."[4] Lincoln was well aware of Stanton's contrary nature and his lust for authority, but he based his appointment on ability (and politics), believing that Stanton's contributions would far outweigh his habitual insubordination. That decision might have aided in the war effort, but without doubt it would later cost Lincoln his life.

GENERAL ALBERT JAMES MYER (1828–1880) is not only remembered today as the father of the Signal Corps, but also the U.S. Weather Bureau. Myer first developed the practice of applying the telegraphy service to directing artillery fire. Stanton removed Myer in 1863, but Congress forced Stanton to reinstate Myer to his previous post as Chief Signal Officer in 1866.

The telegraph service was the nerve center of Stanton's first-hand information gathering network, managed by his chief officer. It received incoming information from every agent stationed throughout the entire country, as well as Canada and Europe. It could even dictate executive policy. In its day the telegraph office was the hub of power.

The Signal Corps under General Albert J. Myer directed artillery fire using the same telegraph lines Stanton used to receive covert communiqués from his agents. General Myer and the Signal Corps were not part of Stanton's personal spy division, but Myer had access to all telegraphs, including Stanton's secret communiqués. On November 10, 1863, Stanton ordered General Myer to turn over all his telegraph equipment to the newly-appointed *civilian* chief telegraph official, Anson Stager, a former Western Union superintendent.[5] Stager was a close friend of Stanton, overseeing almost 1,500 telegraph operators.[6] Stanton sent General Myer far away to Memphis, Tennessee, and Major Thomas Eckert, the War Department's Chief Telegraph Officer, became Stanton's personal telegraph liaison.

After all the time Lincoln spent in the telegraph office, appreciating Thomas Eckert's professional attributes (along with his brute strength), Lincoln chose Eckert to be his bodyguard for the presidential outing to Ford's Theatre. But Stanton flatly refused Lincoln's order to assign Eckert the duty, arguing to Lincoln that Eckert could not be spared that night.

Stanton's purpose for keeping Eckert from accompanying the President was not to deny Lincoln a competent bodyguard. Booth could have shot Lincoln just the same had Eckert been present, but there would have been no way

Booth could have escaped the state box with Eckert there. Booth had been persuaded to use only a single-shot firearm, leaving him with just a knife, useful against only a single, unarmed person. Eckert and Rathbone together would have surely wrestled Booth to the floor. It can be certain that Eckert did not wish to be the one stabbed in such a struggle. It made no sense to leave the President unguarded in a public place with credible assassination rumors circulating. However, for the architect of Lincoln's assassination, it made perfect sense to ensure Thomas Eckert would be "too busy" to attend the play that evening.

About a month before the assassination, Booth attempted to carry out the kidnapping ambush that he had been working on for almost six months. But his ambush failed because of his inability to plan anything on his own, and his lack of reliable or first-hand information. His March 17th attempt to capture Lincoln was nothing less than an embarrassing disaster that left Booth humiliated and his gang discouraged and disillusioned. The next day the kidnappers began to drift apart, while Booth made his only theatrical appearance of the year the very next night. Soon afterward, Booth sold the buggy he had planned to use to transport the President to the Potomac River.

Immediately following the failed ambush, Booth told Samuel Arnold they would not meet again for a month or so,[7] but before that period passed the President was shot to death in the very theater Booth had included in his various plans since September of 1864. Lincoln's life may have been spared if Booth had captured him on that mid-March day, because had he done so, none of the kidnappers would have made it out of the city. Had Booth tried to smuggle the President out of Washington, the telegraph lines would have been buzzing with the news of Lincoln's abduction, and all avenues out of the capital city would have been alerted. The kidnappers, rather than the President, would have been the ones captured. Booth's kidnapping preparations included no arrangements to disrupt telegraph lines, nor did he even conceive the need. He did not realize that all the military checkpoints would have been alerted at the instant the President was discovered missing.

However, a month later, precisely at the time of the assassination, someone with specific knowledge of the telegraph terminals *did* know to plot the sabotage of the capital city's outgoing wires. According to Chief Detective Lafayette Baker's book, page 485:

Within fifteen minutes after the murder the wires were severed entirely round the city, excepting only a secret wire for Government uses, which leads to Old Point. ... This information comes to me from so many credible channels that I must concede it.[8]

While questioned in a Congressional hearing two years later, Thomas Eckert himself testified that the telegraph lines were sabotaged:

Q: Did you have knowledge of the telegraph lines at or about the time of the assassination of President Lincoln?

A: I did.

Q: Was there any interruption of the lines that night?

A: Yes, sir.

Q: What was it?

A: It was my impression they were cut, but we got circuit again very early the next morning.[9]

It was neither a Confederate agent nor even a member of Booth's gang who blocked all transmissions going out from Washington. Only a *Union* telegraph agent could engineer the disruption of the city's communication grid at such a critical moment. Booth's escape went unreported the entire night, until the next morning, after the telegraph lines were repaired.

After Lincoln's death, Thomas Eckert was promoted (by Stanton) to Assistant Secretary of War, and two years later Stanton helped him start his career with Western Union, where he became president, and later chairman of the board.

17

The Stacked Deck

*D*irectly after the shooting, Lincoln was carried to the home of William Peterson, a German immigrant who lived across the street from Ford's Theatre. As Lincoln lay mortally wounded, information began pouring in about the assassination, some real and some only speculation. Lincoln lingered over the next nine hours, never regaining consciousness, attended by at least seven surgeons, all knowing that the wound was fatal. Abraham Lincoln died at 7:22 AM on the morning of April 15. Edwin Stanton, also present throughout the evening, was said to have declared, "Now he belongs to the ages." Some present thought he said "the angels." He immediately took charge of the "investigation."

After Lincoln's body was removed souvenir hunters ransacked Peterson's house, and nothing in the room where Lincoln died was left untouched. Even the plaster and carpet in the room had been stripped from the house, while angry mobs took to the streets in both northern and southern cities. Little more than a few basic facts from that evening can be proven or known for sure, and the rest will be argued and debated forever.

The Confederate conspiracy theory has attributed Lincoln's assassination to a Confederate plot, without evidence, a plausible motive, or establishing an opportunity by Confederate agents to help Booth in his access to or escape from the scene. Their accounts of the assassination suppress or ignore many facts—facts that tell a different story than the popular tale they would prefer the public believe. The prevailing theory insists that Lincoln could not have possibly been killed by members of his own administration.

Opposing theories and accusations have gone unresolved mainly because Stanton destroyed so much evidence that could have exposed the full truth about a conspiracy and cover-up by the coalition of which he was a most active partner. Their motive for helping to conceal Stanton's involvement was that they also approved of preventing Lincoln from serving a second term, and covered every trace of their own prior knowledge of an assassination plot.

The surprising amount of evidence that yet survives points strongly to Stanton's involvement in the assassination. The possibility of his guilt has always been dismissed as only a theory, or that the evidence is merely circumstantial. But what cannot just be argued away as an unsubstantiated theory is what Stanton did next.

Stanton's Man Baker

The President of the United States had been attacked in a presidential state box in the heart of Washington, D.C., while in the presence of the military and metropolitan police force. Answering *how* and *why* this could have happened fell upon the head official of the War Department. Stanton needed help quickly, and realized he must call to his aid a government official who was just as corrupt and brutal as he, easily bribed, yet credible enough to be accepted as a chief investigator. Stanton had just the perfect candidate for the position, and he called on Lafayette Baker.

After Stanton became Secretary of War, Baker replaced Allan Pinkerton as the new head of the National Detective Service (the precursor to the U.S. Secret Service). Baker began his illustrious police career around 1856, after the California gold rush days, where he had been an enforcer in the Vigilance Command, an organization created to bring law and order to San Francisco, and lynching was their style of justice.[1] The Civil War furthered his career by making him a hero in the eyes of General Winfield Scott, who admired his skill as a double agent. Baker had convinced both the Union and the Confederacy that he was working for them, but in truth Baker never worked for anyone other than himself.

In 1862, after learning of Baker's expertise in deception, Stanton appointed him to uncover any subversive organizations plotting against the government, and to spy on whomever the Secretary needed to know about, regardless of position or reputation.[2] Baker went on to claim successes as head of the Union intelligence service, but his methods of brutal interrogation and inhumane treatment of suspects caused some objections and concerns from many in Washington.[3] These concerns included more than just a suspicion that he was taking advantage of his unrestricted authority. Baker used arrest and imprisonment to threaten the smugglers and thieves who would not agree to his payoff demands.[4] His shakedown operations were of no concern to Stanton until Baker was caught tapping the telegraph lines between Nashville and Stanton's own office.

Lafayette Baker had always been devoted only to himself, and loyal only to the cause that would be the most profitable to him. After being caught spying on his own boss, Baker was transferred to New York, and was there when Lincoln was shot. Stanton sent Baker a telegram on April 15 ordering him to "come here immediately and see if you can find the murderer of the president."[5]

It is pointless to argue over the many versions detailing what Booth and Herold did during the two weeks they eluded capture. Many accounts have been written

LAFAYETTE CURRY BAKER, the cunning and ferocious Chief Investigator for Stanton's War Department and instrumental in coordinating the hunt for Lincoln's assassins.

about their adventure, but few would disagree that the truth can never be known. The only detail that can be trusted as factual is that Booth was shot to death at the spot he was cornered without any chance of escape.

On April 23, Baker put in a request to Major Thomas Eckert for a telegraph transmitter, along with someone who could receive and send communiqués. Major Eckert appointed Theodore Woodall to be Baker's telegraph operator; however Woodall also had to be available to all the other independent investigators.[6] Before Woodall left Washington for his assignment, Eckert gave him special instructions warning him not to transmit all his information over the open lines. After a witness reported some breaking information on Booth's whereabouts, Woodall carried out Eckert's orders and choose not to use his open line to relay this valuable clue. The witness reported to Woodall that he saw two men crossing the Rappahannock River near Port Royal, and one of them was using a crutch. With that exclusive information Woodall traveled immediately to Baker's headquarters in Washington and had the witness report his story in person directly to Baker.[7]

The day before Baker received this exclusive tip from Woodall, Major O'Beirne's team of investigators found some tracks made by a person also using a crutch, and those tracks headed towards the Rappahannock River.[8] O'Beirne telegraphed his findings to Stanton, and with that tip and Baker's secret information, a detachment of 26 cavalrymen were gathered to follow up on Stanton's exclusive lead. Lieutenant Edward P. Doherty was assigned to lead the detachment, which also included the chief detective's cousin, Luther Baker, and a special agent from Baker's investigating team named Colonel Everton J. Conger, whom Baker personally called in from disability leave to aid the detachment.

When the cavalry reached Booth and Herold at Garrett's farm near Port Royal, the suspects were already locked in the tobacco barn from the *outside* with a padlock.[9] The reason the barn was locked from the outside can only be speculation, and will never be truly known. But what is not speculation is that Booth and Herold were already being held in captivity before the soldiers arrived, and with little chance of escape.

Sergeant Boston Corbett was just one of the specially selected 26 soldiers assigned the duty of apprehending Lincoln's assassin. He allegedly shot Booth while the suspected assassin was trapped in the barn. Corbett was still under arrest for the shooting of Booth when he returned to Washington, but his reason for taking the shot was never investigated, because Edwin Stanton ordered his release. Stanton proclaimed Boston Corbett a "patriot hero," and he declared, "The Rebel is dead, the Patriot lives," and with that he ended any further investigation into the reason for Booth's execution.[10]

Sergeant Corbett was a man of very questionable mental faculties, who likely suffered from mercury poisoning, or "mad Hatter's disease," and had previously castrated himself. Yet this man was assigned by Baker to be on this elite, military detachment. Surely Stanton and Baker felt they could easily take advantage of his mental disorder, promising him fame and fortune. Boston Corbett would become their perfect patsy.

If Booth had not been shot to death, he would have been brought back to Washington to stand trial. If Stanton truly believed he was part of a Confederate plot, then Stanton should have been furious to know Booth had been shot for no apparent reason. If Booth had been tried for murder the investigation and evidence would have exposed all the conspirators who provided him help to assassinate Lincoln, and then escape from Washington.

The photographs of John Wilkes Booth's dead body that were captured on board the U.S.S. Montauk on April 27 by Alexander Gardner and Timothy H. O'Sullivan should have been used as evidence in the conspirators' trial. Those plates were intended to be a record of Booth's true identity, and the physical proof of how he died. But for some unexplained reason, they were confiscated by the military under Stanton's orders and taken directly to him, never to be seen again.[11] The reason Stanton destroyed so much evidence was to cover up the truth. A photograph of Booth's dead body would have helped prove who killed him and why.

BOSTON CORBETT, prior to being assigned to the detachment that cornered Booth and Herold, was court-martialed for insubordination and suffered from mercury poisoning. Corbett was known to be unstable, and had even castrated himself with scissors.

It was proven that Boston Corbett did not kill Booth;[12] he was shot by Colonel Everton J. Conger, Lafayette Baker's specially-assigned detective.[13, 14] At the conspiracy trial Corbett was called to testify, and he was expected by the prosecution to make only a short statement. Corbett, however, gave a long, theatrical account that was clearly contrary to all the evidence presented about the shooting. The Military Commission fully realized his testimony, along with the evidence, proved there was no possible way that it could have been Corbett who shot Booth, but despite the obvious, the judges still gave him credit for killing Lincoln's assassin.

The autopsy report found that Booth had been shot with a pistol from about 12 feet away, but Corbett carried only a rifle. Colonel Conger testified that he heard a pistol shot and assumed that Booth had committed suicide. He also added Booth was found with a pistol in his hand which directly disputed Corbett's account.[15]

Every witness who was at the barn when Booth was shot gave a perjured testimony. The only purpose for lying about what truly happened would be to hide the truth. During a civilian trial, conflicting testimonies would be cross-examined and scrutinized to find out what really happened. This was a primary reason why Stanton demanded a military tribunal.

The autopsy reports prove that Booth could not have shot himself. The surgeons, well versed in gunshot wounds, stated with certainty Booth was shot at a distance of not less than four yards, and by a pistol. If, in fact, Booth did shoot himself—*through the neck*—he would have had to have held the pistol twelve feet away from his body to keep the powder burns from singeing the hair off the back of his head. And the pistol could not have been found in his hand because he was instantly paralyzed from the neck down after the shot. It was reported that about 7:00 AM Booth, with the aid of a soldier, was shown his hands, at which he moaned his last words, "Useless, useless!" With useless hands, how could he have still held on to the pistol after shooting himself from twelve feet away?

Stanton's omission of the autopsy report withheld the evidence that could prove Colonel Everton Conger shot Booth. Conger was following orders from Baker and Stanton to make sure the detachment did not bring Booth back to Washington to stand trial. Had Booth not been killed, and were he instead brought back alive to face a murder trial, Stanton would have had to submit all physical evidence. Instead, the diary, Booth's two conflicting autopsy reports, and the photographs of the killer's corpse were never submitted.

Stanton the Puppet Master

Because Stanton was allowed to play puppet master, he succeeded in not having to account for skewing the investigation, as well as for his glaring failures in the chain of events that resulted in Lincoln's death. Charles Forbes and John Parker were the only bodyguards provided for the President in a public theater at a time when Stanton was well aware that Lincoln had a pile of death threats lying on his desk back at the White House. Stanton warned several people, including General Grant, not to accompany Lincoln to the theater because of a credible assassination rumor, and he also refused an invitation himself. Stanton lied to Lincoln about Eckert, his chief telegraph officer, being *too busy* to be assigned as the president's guest; and as Lincoln was killed that night the city's telegraph lines were cut, allowing the killer to escape the capital.

A week prior to Lincoln's murder, Secretary Seward warned Stanton of credible assassination plots, but Stanton never informed Lincoln, even after Seward was almost killed only hours later. Charles Forbes was Lincoln's personal aide, and he had every reason to question why Booth (who was visibly armed with a knife) should be permitted to enter Lincoln's state box. John Parker had been one of the least dependable patrolmen, yet was chosen out of 150 police officers to be trusted with the important assignment of guarding the President. He was chosen mainly *because of* his poor service record. Stanton did not require either man to fully account for his actions, removing them both from scrutiny.

If Booth had been captured alive, then in his murder trial Stanton himself would have been called to testify, and would have been cross-examined, because he was the one in charge of Lincoln's security. Stanton would have had to account for all that he knew about Booth and his gang before the assassination, and then could not have claimed to be so unaware. Without Booth and a civilian trial, the focus of the entire investigation into Lincoln's assassination came only from the conspiracy trial. A *military tribunal,* with judges under Stanton's complete authority, insured that he would be able to orchestrate the desired outcome.

Within a few hours of Lincoln's death Stanton ordered, "if the military authorities arrest the murderer of the President [we will] put him in a monitor and anchor the ironclad out in the stream with strong guard on the vessel, wharf and Navy Yard."[16] That evening Stanton ordered an ironclad to be made immediately ready, and maintained day and night. Stanton commanded that all prisoners must be heavily secured in irons. He also ordered no one should be permitted to communicate with the prisoners without a pass signed by both himself and the Secretary of the Navy. He also ordered canvas bags to be placed over the prisoners' heads.[17]

Some argue these measures prove that Stanton wanted to keep Booth alive and dispel the accusations he was attempting a cover-up. On the contrary, this is further proof he was safeguarding information the prisoners knew—the names of his double agents—which could reveal his own involvement in the assassination. If an agency other than his coalition of spies captured any of Booth's gang members alive they would have to be transferred to Stanton's floating dungeon. Stanton could still prevent any information they knew from leaking out with his tightly controlled security. The last thing Stanton wanted was a witness who could shed light on the truth.

John T. Ford was one such witness, therefore he was imprisoned only on suspicion. Meanwhile there were so many others who were directly involved with the assassination, but they were assumed innocent without any further investigation.

Ed Spangler was Booth's close friend who might have known some of Stanton's informants who had infiltrated the kidnapping gang. Spangler was only a circumstantial suspect, arrested on hearsay, but he was included with the select group of Stanton's chosen conspirators. Ed Spangler was moved from the Old Capitol Prison to the ironclad under Stanton's strict security, and he too was ordered to wear a canvas bag over his head. All the while Stanton somehow insisted, without any investigation, that neither John Parker, Charles Forbes, nor Boston Corbett were to be implicated in the assassination plot.

Stanton's Man Holt

The Judge Advocate General, Joseph Holt, was Stanton's chief prosecutor under the military conspiracy tribunal. Holt had been a close associate of Stanton since their cabinet appointments in the Buchanan administration, and had worked under Stanton during the Lincoln administration. In the summer of 1864, Stanton ordered Holt to carry out an extensive examination of what became referred to as the Confederate "fifth column." This was an organization of Peace Democrats working out of Canada, who took advantage of the northern public becoming sick of the war, and were allegedly engaged in espionage.[18] They had followers from Ohio, Indiana, Illinois, Kentucky, New York and Missouri. The mayor of New York City, Fernando Wood, and Clement Vallandigham, a peace Democrat congressman from Ohio, were just two suspects under Holt's investigation. They both were opposed to the Republican administration, and they were calling for an end to the war. Included in the investigation were anti-war Copperhead groups such as the The Sons on Liberty and the Order of American Knights, but despite their large following of saboteurs seeking to depose the current administration, little, if any sabotage ever took place. Stanton's double agents had secretly infiltrated every facet of subversion against the administration and prevented their plots.[19, 20, 21]

On October 8, 1864, Joseph Holt submitted his extensive report and findings to Stanton about espionage threats a full six months before Booth attacked Lincoln. If Booth had any association with these groups Stanton would have surely known. In any event Stanton was, in fact, well aware that Booth was a card-carrying Southern sympathizer in the heart of Washington, D.C., with a police record for being an outspoken agitator against Lincoln and his administration.[22]

Lafayette Baker, Thomas Eckert, and Joseph Holt managed Edwin Stanton's secret division, and they reported only to the Secretary of War. Joseph Holt's assignment as chief prosecutor for the military tribunal would ensure the privileged knowledge Stanton and his spies held of the events surrounding Lincoln's murder remained exclusively their own. Joseph Holt knew almost as much as Stanton knew, and along with Baker and Conger, he was one of the chosen few who had read Booth's dairy before the trial began. Holt had also read the full

JUDGE ADVOCATE GENERAL JOSEPH HOLT, likely aware of Booth's conspiracies months before the assassination, was privy to Booth's diary and Atzerodt's confession, and therefore knew Mary Surratt to be innocent as he labored on Stanton's behalf to have her put to death.

text of George Atzertdot's confession to Marshal McPhail, which identified Stanton's double agents—Kate Thompson, Charles Yates, Margaret Coleman and James Donaldson. With Stanton directly controlling the prosecution and all access to the defendants, and with Joseph Holt also functioning as *advisor to the panel of judges*,[23] it's no mystery why the defense never called on these witnesses to account for their significant involvement in Booth's plot.

18

Testimony vs. Evidence

*T*here was never a murder trial to prosecute Lincoln's assassin because John Wilkes Booth was shot to death allegedly while resisting arrest. The reason Booth chose to resist arrest (with no other option but to die on the spot) remains just another mystery surrounding the assassination that has never been solved.

Each eyewitness who claimed to see how Booth was shot told a different story. This does not necessarily imply that every eyewitness was lying, but it does demonstrate how eyewitness accounts cannot be trusted to be the undisputed truth. An eyewitness testimony is only reliable if it is congruent to the available evidence, a logical sequence of events, and other credible witnesses. The best means of establishing facts is through untainted physical evidence. No one understood that fact better than Edwin Stanton and he was a master of destroying physical evidence.

Stanton exhibited to those around him an exterior façade opposite from his true, but hidden intentions. The loyal defender of the Union and Lincoln's dear and most trusted friend was the exterior personality he portrayed for others to believe. "Lincoln's dear friend" is the way many history writers have chosen to depict Stanton. But evidence and collaborating testimony reveal the real Stanton and expose the obvious truth about the conspiracy to kill Lincoln.

Just two days before Booth was shot he wrote in his diary, "Tonight I will once more try the river with the intent to cross. Though I have a greater desire and almost a mind to return to Washington and in a measure clear my name, which I feel I can do." But most historians writing about his death have assumed he chose instead to die rather than to be captured.

During their escape from Washington, Booth and Herold stopped at the Surrattsville Tavern, run by John Lloyd, to pick up the weapons that had been placed there five to six weeks earlier as part of his kidnapping plot. Lloyd testified that Herold took one of the two carbines, but Booth elected to leave his carbine behind at the Tavern, because he could not use anything other than a pistol while nursing his broken leg. Booth had to support himself with a crutch in order to be able to walk. Two eyewitnesses of Booth's corpse (a surgeon and a reporter) described his fractured leg as considerably swollen and discolored.

Boston Corbett was the soldier who was given credit for shooting Booth in the tobacco barn, and he claimed that he did so because Booth was *taking aim* with his carbine. While locked in a burning barn, surrounded by 26 soldiers waiting to arrest him, it is said Booth had the choice of using either two pistols or one carbine to fight them off. During Lloyd's testimony he said Booth's carbine was left behind at the tavern. This testimony was substantiated when Booth's carbine was recovered at the tavern by investigators. The carbine left behind is evidence that Booth would *not* carry a rifle while trying to hobble on a crutch. Neither could Booth *aim* a carbine while using his crutch, and he was shot while heading for the door of the barn. Colonel Conger, the first to reach him, testified the fallen Booth had a pistol in his hand. This illustrates how much the testimonies regarding Booth's escape and murder varied depending upon who was telling the story. The illegitimate trial of the accused conspirators failed to substantiate testimonies with physical evidence or proper cross-examination, therefore the mystery of Booth's death, among many other things, was never resolved.

The long list of mysteries surrounding the assassination comes from the restrictions placed on the defense counsel, the lack of submitted evidence, along with unchallenged and unsubstantiated testimonies. The omitted evidence and the conflicting testimonies have caused later investigations into Lincoln's murder to be answered by speculation. The reason for so much conjecture is the interference of Edwin Stanton, the man who had exercised authority over everyone, even the new President, Andrew Johnson.

To hide the reasons Lincoln and Booth were assassinated Stanton needed to retain full control over every facet of the proceedings. The War Department's purpose for using a military tribunal was to portray Lincoln's assassination as an act of war issued by Jefferson Davis, and carried out by the Confederate Secret Service. The situation that led to using a Military Commission to try Lincoln's conspirators first began with Stanton's challenge to the authority of the Supreme Court. Only a few months before the murder, James Speed had been appointed as the new Attorney General, and he as well as President Johnson became little more than puppets to Stanton's demands.

Speed's insecurity, due to his limited experience compared to Stanton, who was a former Attorney General,[1] left him unsure of his position and

A fitting illustration from the March 7, 1868 edition of *Harper's Weekly*, depicting Edwin Stanton and his War Department holding President Johnson captive with a canon marked "Congress." Johnson is holding a document inscribed with "coup de etat" and hiding behind Lorenzo Thomas, while Stanton is flanked by Grant and clutching a ramrod styled "Tenure of Office Act."

susceptible to Stanton's overbearing nature. Stanton was also blackmailing the new President with a threat of bringing charges against him as an accomplice to the assassination conspiracy. Stanton was threatening Johnson with the personal note Booth left him at the Kirkwood Hotel. The Secretary of War promised Johnson that if he interfered with the investigation and trial, then charges would ensue. Stanton's Radical coalition did, in fact, do just that during their subsequent attempt to impeach Andrew Johnson half-way through his term.[2]

After Stanton had the President and Attorney General under his control he could then quash other arguments against using a Military Commission to try civilians. The power of the military in trying civilians in military courts was largely decided in 1864 in the case of *Ex parte Vallandigham,* where it was ruled that even the Supreme Court had no power to issue a writ of *habeas corpus* to a military tribunal. The former Attorney General, Edward Bates, was Stanton's only credible opposition against this unconstitutional act, but the retired Bates was a poor match to the runaway power of the War Department, which, at the time was dominating the Federal government. The generals and colonels under Secretary Stanton's command won the jurisdiction over the proceedings, and the depth of their bias would leave (to this day) the conspirators behind Lincoln's assassination an unsolved mystery.

This so-called "loyal" panel of judges under Stanton's authority ignored the most basic rules of law adopted by a free nation: that a prisoner is innocent until proven guilty, the right to a fair and impartial trial, and the right to a proper legal defense. The trial was a disgrace to every principle of American justice and was concocted to frame others for Stanton's own conspiracy.

Two of the original judges appointed to serve the Commission were outspoken about the methods and limits put on the defense counsel, and they complained about the closed-door sessions by the judges. These detractors, General Horace Porter and General Cyrus B. Comstock, were both dismissed under Special Order Number 216 issued by President Johnson in accordance with Stanton's demands.[3, 4] Stanton justified their removal by arguing that since those officers were members of Grant's staff, and Grant had been an object of the assassination plot, it was necessary to remove them from the Commission. However Stanton was the only one accusing the prisoners of including General Grant as a target for assassination, without any kind of proof or evidence.

By the time of the trial Stanton had succeeded in providing the Judge Advocate General, Joseph Holt, a united panel of cooperative justices who would be willing to hide or withhold evidence, control testimony, and place confining restrictions on the defense counsel. The goal of the military commission was to blame the assassination on Confederate agents. To do this the prosecution would need falsified evidence, perjured testimony and, most importantly, the tribunal itself would have to be willing to withhold credible evidence and testimony that would expose the truth, namely the involvement of Stanton's secret agents and informants.

It had become obvious that Booth needed to have more help than he could have gotten from his small band of incapable accomplices. If the War Department could not prove that the Confederate government was involved in the conspiracy, then they would have to accuse some other accomplice, one with a believable motive, who would also have the ability to provide Booth with the means and opportunity to assassinate the President and escape Washington.

Part of the prosecution's strategy was to make the attacks on Lincoln and Seward appear to be just two among numerous atrocities perpetrated by the Confederate Secret Service. The allegations designed to implicate Jefferson

Davis were based on circumstantial evidence, plus unfounded rumors that had gained traction prior to Lincoln's assassination. The testimonies against the Confederacy about sabotage and conspiracy were given by released convicts and captured ex-Confederates under intimidation to validate preconceived allegations, but none of the terrorist acts described were ever committed. Later it was proven all the testimonies were perjury.[5, 6]

Jacob Thompson was the former Secretary of the Interior before secession, and Clement Clay was a former U.S. Senator from Alabama. They both ran the Confederate Secret Service out of Canada, and they were both accused of conducting Confederate terrorist attacks.

One alleged atrocity in the trial was that the Confederacy had carried out a biological attack of yellow fever against the Union Army. Prosecuting Judge Advocate, John A. Bingham, alleged that 2,000 deaths were the results a chest of infested clothing planted on an army base in New Bern, North Carolina, by Confederate saboteurs. The prosecution's witness, Godfrey Hyams (a captured Confederate and suspected secret agent) identified Dr. Luke P. Blackburn as the plot's mastermind, asserting that the doctor stated, "an infested trunk of clothing could kill at 60 yards distance." Bingham named Clement Clay as the headman in charge of "this diabolical attack of the yellow fever epidemic."[7] Yellow fever, also known as "American plague," was a long-standing epidemic in the United States, often killing thousands of victims per outbreak, until a vaccine was developed in the 20th Century. It was learned in 1900 that the virus was spread by mosquitos, and could not infest clothing. However, in the conspiracy trial the War Department was determined to bamboozle the court and the public with atrocity allegations. The outbreak in North Carolina, spread by mosquitos, resulted in the deaths of Union soldiers and Southern citizens alike, but like the Salem Witch Trials, Bingham presented accusations of "an infamous and fiendish project of importing pestilence," without evidence, and with a coerced witness. Had the South actually planted a trunk of clothing at a location where no plague was present, nothing would have happened, and no such allegations would have been invented. The charge is itself evidence of the prosecution fabricating its case.

Jacob Thompson was accused of being the man heading the plot to leave the government without leadership. The prosecution's witness to prove this charge was a captured Confederate Secret Service agent, Charles Durham, testifying under the false name of Stanford Conover. The War Department asserted that, other than Lincoln and Seward, there were *three* other targets for assassination: Vice President Johnson, General Grant and the Secretary of War Edwin Stanton. This latter charge would help divert suspicion away from Stanton and the Radical coalition behind him.

Before the 1864 elections, the Radicals were trying to have Lincoln and Seward prevented from serving a second term by advancing their own candidates over the incumbent. After Lincoln was killed, Johnson became a Tennessee Democrat President. The Radicals felt Johnson could easily be held in check as a weak president, and as it turned out they were right. Stanton ran Johnson's administration, and he even called and presided over the President's own cabinet meetings.[8, 9, 10] During the Radical-led impeachment trial of Andrew Johnson, the President finally fired Stanton. Instead of departing from his position, Stanton locked himself in his office in defiance for several months, counting on the Senate to impeach Johnson. When the impeachment charges against Johnson were defeated (by a one-vote margin), Stanton finally relinquished his post. During this standoff the Radicals tried to overturn Johnson's authority to fire Stanton using the Tenure of Office Act, but with only temporary success. Despite this victory, Johnson remained such a weak president he did not even receive his party's nomination to a second term.

When the Radicals failed to prevent Lincoln's second term, he and Seward both became targets for assassinations. Even if Johnson had been considered as a target, no attempt was made against him, plus his ties to Booth were leverage that would render him easy to control. Neither Grant, Johnson, nor Stanton had been actual targets for assassination, but such was claimed by the War Department during the conspiracy trial. The only legitimate assassination targets after Lee's surrender were Lincoln and Seward, but not by the South. In late 1863, Lincoln issued his Proclamation for Amnesty and Reconstruction, measures fiercely opposed by half of his party. The Radical coalition wanted to hang the Confederate leaders and strip the South of Congressional power. Secretary Seward had been a supporter of Lincoln's Reconstruction Plan, and he opposed Chase, Sumner, Stevens and Stanton.

Hans Von Winkiestein was a Union soldier imprisoned for desertion, but he testified under the name of Henry Van Steinacker. He claimed that Thompson and Clay were frequently seen with Booth in Canada to plot the abduction and assassination of Union leaders. Winkiestein had a powerful incentive to commit perjury: after testifying for the prosecution he was released from prison, while his fellow deserters were shot or hanged.[11]

Richard Montgomery claimed to have been a double agent in Canada, and testified that Thompson was overheard saying: "it would be a blessing to rid the world of Lincoln, Johnson and Grant." Montgomery's testimony was also found to be fabricated.[12]

The key witness for the military's prosecutors, responsible for the convictions of Booth's eight gang members, was Louis Weichmann. He was as much involved with the events leading up to the assassination as any of the convicted conspirators, but he was never charged with any crime. Weichmann's testimony provided ammunition against all the key conspirators and he was obviously very knowledgeable about every player and scene. But his questionable testimony was never challenged, nor was he ever implicated.

John Lloyd, the Surrattsville tavern keeper, who had a close association to the conspirators, was another witness with detailed knowledge of Booth's gang, but he too was never implicated for having known of the kidnapping plot. The prosecution's witness Daniel Thomas (a civilian informant for Baker) alleged that Dr. Mudd had prior knowledge of the kidnapping, and his testimony was accepted on hearsay four months old. Daniel Thomas had also favored the Confederate cause early in the war, and obviously knew as much about the kidnapping plot as Dr. Mudd, but he was never implicated. Thomas Harbin, a known Confederate spy, *aided in Booth's escape* by providing him with fresh horses that were obtained previously for the kidnapping plot. Prior to the trial, investigators knew and had physical evidence that he made arrangements for Booth and Herold, during their escape, to be harbored by a Dr. Richard Stuart. Harbin was named by Atzerodt as an accomplice and known to the prosecution, but was never charged.

Among the credible, physical, undisputable evidence that could have been presented (but wasn't), were the diary found on Booth, his 1864 manifesto, the autopsy reports, the Derringer, Atzerodt's confessions, and the photographic plates of Booth's dead body. But none of these crucial pieces of evidence were ever submitted to the military tribunal. Also the persons of interest identified by the accused—Kate Thompson, Margaret Coleman, Charles Yates, James Hall, Sarah Slater, and most importantly, James Donaldson—were known by the entire prosecution, but never arrested, called to testify, or even pursued.

In contrast, John Surratt, Jr., the best arguable connection between the condemned and the Confederacy, was tracked down as far away as Egypt and extradited back to the United States. The civilian court that tried him in 1867 failed to find him guilty of conspiracy to assassinate Lincoln and declared a mistrial. Surratt did acknowledge being personally complicit in the *kidnapping* plot, but the court ruled that the statute of limitations had expired for that crime, and he was released. Surratt's legitimate trial proved just how selective, illegal and ineffective the military tribunal had been in finding the *real* conspirators.

In 1866, the Supreme Court ruled in *Ex Parte Milligan* that a military trial of civilians was unconstitutional.

19

"How Impotent Is Justice!"

On June 29th, 1865, the military judges secretly met, and they reached their verdict by the next day. Eight prisoners were convicted of conspiracy charges, four of which were sentenced to hang by the neck until dead. The executions of Mary Surratt, George Atzerodt, David Herold, and Lewis Powell were carried out on July 7, 1865. The sentence of hard labor for life was given to Samuel Arnold, Dr. Mudd, and Michael O'Laughlen. These men had only played minor roles in Booth's kidnapping plot, and two of these were not even in or around Washington the night of the assassination. Theater employee Ed Spangler was given six years for aiding and abetting the escape of Booth on hearsay, while Lincoln's guard, John Parker, was acquitted of deserting his post (resulting in the President's death). Charles Forbes, who allegedly allowed a visibly-armed John Wilkes Booth to enter Lincoln's state box, was never charged with any crime.

Jefferson Davis was captured on May 10, 1865, in Irwinsville, Georgia, and was charged with inciting, encouraging and conspiring to "kill and murder" Abraham Lincoln, Andrew Johnson, William Seward, and Ulysses S. Grant."[1] Though Davis was in Union custody, Stanton's military tribunal proceeded to try him *in absentia*, accusing him and the Confederate Secret Service of numerous acts of terrorism. The testimonies from a select list of alleged witnesses were used to arrive at a guilty verdict. The military tribunal issued these verdicts without providing proper legal defenses, conclusive evidence, or consideration of the fact that the alleged acts of terror (other than the attacks on Seward and Lincoln) never took place. Davis was imprisoned for two years at Fort Monroe, not because there was evidence to convict him, but because he could not prove that he was not guilty.

Whoever was *truly* behind the assassination conspiracy, and their reasons for it, has never been proven. Very little of the prosecution's presentation had any corroboration with evidence, and much of the testimony was undoubtedly falsified. The entire trial by the military court under Stanton's complete control was a fraud and a violation of every principle of American justice, with corrupt and biased judges, intimidation and abuse of witnesses and the defendants. There was little scrutiny allowed of the prosecution's charges, testimonies or evidence. The conflicting recollections of the prosecution witnesses were accepted over the far more harmonious accounts from the defense.

Four civilian prisoners were executed by the United States military, convicted of collaborating with the Confederate President to assassinate Lincoln. Jefferson Davis, meanwhile, was held in a tiny cell with no human comforts, no exercise, no books to read, and was intentionally deprived of sleep.[2] All of his letters were censored, and two years passed without a court hearing. His eyesight was ruined and his body diminished to a frail and malnourished shell.[3] Another year of such torture would surely have caused his death.

On January 8, 1866, Stanton's chief investigator, Lafayette Baker, was caught red-handed in Johnson's office while spying on the President. Baker put the blame on Stanton, saying the Secretary of War ordered him to gather information that might be used against the President. Over the next thirteen months Stanton and the Radical coalition were building a case to impeach Johnson,[4] but in the impeachment trial they failed to convince enough members of Congress to remove him from office. They used intimidation and even death threats against fellow congressmen[5] who would not vote with them, and Johnson escaped impeachment by only one vote in the Senate.

In early 1867, Lafayette Baker published *History of the United States Secret Service*, a book ghost-written for him, containing a glamorized account of his own career. Included in this volume was mention of the "forgotten" diary that had been found on John Wilkes Booth's body. The diary became public knowledge during Johnson's impeachment trial and while John Surratt, Jr., was using it in his own defense. The House Judiciary Committee examined the diary, whereupon they realized, for the first time, that the kidnapping and assassination plots were two separate conspiracies.[6]

Edwin Stanton, Joseph Holt and the prosecuting judge advocates had read the diary before the trial, and they all knew that Booth's confessions within it would have cleared Mary Surratt of the charge of assassination conspiracy. The committee also realized that the diary proved Jefferson Davis had no role in the assassination. This new information, once viewed by Congress, resulted in the dismissal of the charges against Davis, and he was released from his cell at Fortress Monroe to live as a free man for the rest of his life. Davis traveled back to his two former homes on the Mississippi river, but found them both destroyed. Mrs. Sarah Ann Dorsey from Biloxi, Mississippi, provided Jefferson and Varina Davis a tenant house in which to live. From there he wrote his memoirs. The former Confederate President lived in poverty until his death on December 13, 1889.[7]

In February 1867, the United States House of Representatives, led by the Radicals, began impeachment proceedings against President Andrew Johnson in an effort to remove him (too) from office. During the investigation Baker was called to testify before the Judiciary Committee and in his testimony he brought up Booth's forgotten diary. Baker said, "I think there was a great deal more of the original diary than appears here now."[8] His statement was a spiteful attempt to implicate Stanton in Lincoln's assassination. After Johnson caught Baker in his office, the President banned Washington's chief detective from access to the White House. Baker blamed his actions on Stanton and Stanton in turn forced Baker's resignation from the Army. By 1867, Stanton and Baker had broken their common cause alliance, and Baker threw at Stanton a fictional accusation in retaliation for their mutual betrayals. This partnership ended as one would expect an alliance between liars and murderers would.

In May 1867, after Baker's testimony, the text of Booth's diary was, for the first time, released to the press. Two years earlier the diary had been turned over to Stanton when Booth's body was brought back to Washington. After a close examination by the Secretary of War the diary was given to Judge Advocate General Joseph Holt just before the conspiracy trial began.[9] Holt held the book in his hands, in public view, during the conspiracy trial, but it was not presented in any way or even mentioned. Some newspaper reporters witnessed the diary, but no questions were raised about its contents or why it was not included with Booth's other belongings exhibited in the conspiracy trial.[10]

During the continued investigation of President Johnson, Baker's wild accusations about the diary's missing pages began to crumble under cross-examination. Not one person (not even his cousin Luther) who had been involved in the investigation into Lincoln's assassination would back his story. His testimony about the pages of the diary disappearing after Booth's death fell on deaf ears, until his next claim accused President Johnson of being a Confederate spy. That testimony caught the interest of many Congressional Radicals. Baker professed that he could obtain wartime correspondence between President Andrew Johnson and Jefferson Davis.[11, 12] The diary quickly took on a whole new purpose after Baker told the congressional inquiry that he could provide documentation to prove the President of the United States was actually a Confederate spy.

Lafayette Baker, the man who had been stripped of all his previous police authority, suddenly became a star witness for the Radicals. Because of Baker's illegal and almost treasonous behavior, he had been banned from the White House and forced out of the Army by Stanton. But the former chief detective in Lincoln's murder investigation could now possibly prove, once and for all for the Radicals, that the Confederates killed Lincoln.

The War Department's military commission had argued with unwavering persistence two years earlier that Johnson was a target for assassination by Confederates, but all that had been suddenly forgotten, based on the proclamation of such a despicable and disreputable character as Baker. Forgotten was the fact that David Herold and George Atzerodt were convicted by the War Department for conspiring to assassinate Andrew Johnson, and for their crime they hanged by their necks until dead. Another great hypocrisy was that Michael O'Laughlen had been convicted by the War Department for being a Confederate assassin assigned to kill General Grant and Secretary Stanton. O'Laughlen died in prison of yellow fever, serving his life sentence at Fort Jefferson, Florda, which was known to be infested with the epidemic. Judge advocate Bingham had accused the Confederates of importing the pestilence of yellow fever, condemning that act as a *diabolical* method of killing. However, Bingham knew full well that his charges of Confederate terrorism were deliberate perjury to hide the truth. Bingham used that same yellow fever pestilence as his diabolical method to kill any chosen conspirators he could not kill by hanging. Had Michael O'Laughlen survived long enough to be pardoned (like Spangler, Arnold and Mudd were), he too would have lived out his life as a free man.

Immediately after assassination Lincoln became a martyr, but the same Radicals Lincoln fought throughout his entire tenure began claiming the assassinated President as the savior of their Radical agenda. After Lincoln's death the Radicals replaced his original Reconstruction policy with their own plan, ignoring the fact that theirs was the exact opposite of the postwar policy Lincoln had envisioned. His original policy was not implemented only because Lincoln was so violently removed from office. Ironically, their investigation to bring impeachment charges against Johnson was because he was advocating an even less lenient version of Lincoln's old Amnesty and Reconstruction policy that the Radicals had so violently opposed.[13]

The Judiciary Committee's Massachusetts Congressman, Benjamin But-ler, was beside himself to know how Booth thought he could *clear his name* by returning to Washington. Butler asserted that President Johnson must have been the one who persuaded Booth to change his plot from capture to assas-sination, posing the logical question: who would profit "if the knife made a vacancy?"[14] If not Johnson, then who else in Washington would benefit by removing Lincoln from office, and could also promise Booth immunity?

Benjamin Butler was appointed to be the head of a five-man Congressio-nal commission to investigate the possibility that President Johnson had been a Confederate spy, the mastermind behind Lincoln's assassination, and the one who had promised to clear Booth's name. Butler set out to find those "many persons holding high positions of power and authority … who were acting through inferior persons as their tools and instruments."[15] Stanton and Holt headed the investigation into Baker's claim that Johnson was a Confederate spy, but the wartime correspondence they had all anxiously sought could not be produced. Butler's committee, after conducting a thorough investigation, had nothing to report. Butler stated, "There was no reliable evidence at all … [or] ground for suspicions entertained against Johnson."[16] Baker was such a notorious liar that Benjamin Butler's commissioners stated, "it is doubtful whether [Baker] has in any one thing told the truth, even by accident."[17]

Butler's investigation into the architect of Lincoln's assassination began to take a different direction after Baker's promise fell through, and the hope-ful guilt of President Johnson became nothing other than an embarrassment to the committee. The recently discovered diary raised the question: why was the diary suppressed by the War Department? Judge Advocate General Joseph Holt explained to Congress, "There was nothing in the diary which I could conceive would be testimony against anyone except Booth, and he was dead." However, he was not asked to explain why the diary wasn't exhibited along with all the other items found on Booth after his capture. Judge John Bing-ham told the House of Representatives on March 26, 1867, "if one of several conspirators can thus make his declarations, made after the fact … either for himself or for his co-conspirators, how impotent is justice itself!"[18]

Holt and Bingham gave testimony to the fact that they knowingly with-held evidence that could shed light on the truth, but that truth would chal-lenge their preconcluded guilty verdicts for their chosen conspirators. They claimed that justice would be made impotent if they didn't conceal the diary. However, once the diary was made public, it revealed previously unknown facts and showed that it was due to *their* actions that justice was rendered impotent.

Immediately after the diary was exposed Congress realized that the plot to kidnap and the plot to assassinate were two separate conspiracies. The withheld evidence in the diary would have proven that the assassination was a last-minute decision. This would have, in turn, proven that Mary Surratt and Jefferson Davis were uninvolved in any plan of assassination. The vindication for Holt, Bingham and Stanton for not publicizing the book (resulting in a deliberate miscarriage of justice) was that they were justified in believing the diary may glorify Booth. Their reasoning was that the diary would inspire sympathy if they allowed Booth

JOHN ARMOR BINGHAM, Judge Advocate and Radical Congressman, admitted to Congress that he suppressed crucial evidence in the 1865 conspirators' trial.

to appeal to the many who felt Lincoln had been a tyrant who caused so many to suffer.[19]

Andrew Johnson had been thoroughly investigated, tried and found not guilty. Jefferson Davis had been cleared of any involvement in Lincoln's assassination, and released from his two-year incarceration. John Surratt had been captured, tried by a civilian court, and found uninvolved in Lincoln's assassination. The entire Confederate administration had been captured and released, with the exception of Judah Benjamin and John Breckenridge, who escaped to England, but were never extradited. It was quickly realized by the Radicals that if there was no Confederate plot, the conspirators behind Lincoln's assassination might be better left an unsolvable mystery, and the matter was wisely dropped.

Almost three quarters of a century passed before others would again try to solve the mystery of the missing pages in Booth's diary, but it can be safely said, whoever tore the pages out of the dairy will never be resolved. In 1937, the question of why the diary was suppressed by the War Department was once again brought up, but no definitive answer was concluded. However, the question led to an examination of the diary by the FBI forensics department in 1977. In their report the FBI concluded, among other things, that a total of 86 pages had been either, cut out, torn out, or removed from the diary, and that the four sheets containing the text of Booth's recorded deed (at some unknown point) was once removed, then rebound back into the book by lamination. The last two stubs of the twenty-seven consecutive sheets cut out before Booth's first entry are not visible because the third and fourth sheets of Booth's confession (dated June 23 and June 29) are laminated to them.

But it doesn't matter that those missing pages are gone forever, or that the diary has been altered and tampered with, because the evidence found in Booth's diary about conspiracy is not lost. That evidence, that many others have so earnestly sought, is plainly among the surviving scribble by Lincoln's assassin, who felt betrayed by the only man in Washington who could have promised Booth that he would be granted immunity. That same man had gained control over the conspiracy investigation, its trial, and he even captured the authority of the Executive branch with blackmail and the aid of Congressional legislation.[20]

Edwin Stanton was the man in Washington who *did* profit from Lincoln's vacancy (not Andrew Johnson, whom Butler presumed). Edwin Stanton was the only man in Washington who had the means to assure Booth access to the President, a means of escape, and the guarantee of immunity.

The diary is just one small part of the immense volume of evidence revealing the motive, opportunity and ability of the conspirators behind John Wilkes Booth. To understand who committed and concealed the crime is to realize the true reason Lincoln had to die.

Epilogue

The military trial by the War Department ended with nothing resolved establishing who actually conspired to remove Lincoln from serving a second term. Popular history has been saying that, to this day, the conspirators behind John Wilkes Booth remain an unsolved mystery. Meanwhile those convicted or accused by the War Department have been proven to be *not* guilty of conspiracy to assassinate Lincoln. Despite evidence presented after the trial, which found no one in the Confederacy was guilty, the conspiracy theorists still contend that the Confederates are the only possible suspects.

During the years following the tragedy of the Civil War, which ended with the equally tragic assassination of Abraham Lincoln, the mysterious deaths and suspicious accusations continued, also to this day unresolved.

Mary & Robert Lincoln

Mary Todd Lincoln was convinced that John Wilkes Booth was part of a government conspiracy, and she was not alone in that belief. Many people did not accept the official explanation that the assassination was merely a plot by a mentally disturbed actor aided by a tiny band of angry Maryland citizens. Mary Lincoln felt her husband's murder was an inside job. She wrote afterwards in a letter:

> Even if he had remained in the White House on that night of darkness, he would have been horribly cut to pieces—those fiends had too long contemplated his inhumane murder to have allowed him to escape.[1]

However, any skeptics suggesting a government cover-up were discredited in the newspapers, and Mrs. Lincoln was accused of insanity in the *Chicago Journal*. The *Morning Tribune* said she was deranged and predicted she would end up in a lunatic asylum.

Robert Lincoln had his mother committed to an asylum and had hired a private detective to follow her (Mary suspected that he was trying to kill her). Judge Robert David Davis and attorney Leonard Swett had Mary arrested and tried for insanity. Mary's attorney, Isaac Arnold, secretly agreed to cooperate with Robert. After spending ten months involuntarily committed to an insane asylum, her female attorney, Myra Bradwell, appealed and won her release.[2]

When Mary was 56, she severed all ties with Robert, saying: "You have tried your game of robbery long enough!"[3]

The Killing of Mary Surratt

Mary Surratt was sentenced to death by hanging, but with the death sentence was attached a petition for mercy, which was to be sent to President Andrew Johnson (the only authority who could prevent her execution). But Johnson later said he never received any such petition. Senators Preston King and James Henry Lane of Kansas blocked Mary Surratt's daughter, Anna, on the steps of the White House as she desperately tried to reach President Johnson prior to the execution. King and Lane were from the Missouri delegation that previously pressured Lincoln in 1863 to adjust his policies in favor of the Radical agenda (*see* Appendix E).

Four months after Mary Surratt was executed Preston King jumped off a ferryboat and drowned, with weights tied around his neck. Four months after that Senator James Lane was said to have committed suicide by shooting himself.

Jefferson Davis

After Jefferson Davis spent his first year in a Fort Monroe dungeon, Congress began a debate over what should be done with him. By May 1866, Davis was the last Confederate administrator who still remained in captivity. Stanton insisted that Davis should be tried and executed, but the War Department could not come up with a plausible charge against him.

Davis's inhumane treatment while being a War Department prisoner caused an outrage, inflaming even deeper hatred over the military occupation of the South. In the North empathy for the former Confederate President began to spread, from both the public and professional sectors, condemning the deplorable conditions Davis was forced to endure. A New York attorney, Charles O'Connor, offered his legal services to defend Davis, and soon afterwards his living conditions at the prison moderately improved. But the sadistic Stanton knew that Davis was his last piece of evidence that needed to be destroyed in order to hide his own involvement in Lincoln's assassination. Stanton was well aware that if Davis was found uninvolved in the conspiracy, then any objective investigation would undoubtedly determine that only Stanton could have helped Booth prevent Lincoln from serving his second term. Everyone who had participated in the cover-up knew that suspicions of conspiracy would never be put to rest until Jefferson Davis had been executed. However, a Congressional committee ordered an examination of the War Department's case against Davis, and the designated chief investigator, Francis Lieber, reported, "Davis will not be found guilty and we shall stand there completely beaten."[4]

Despite that report, an indictment of treason was issued for Jefferson Davis in May of 1866 by the Circuit Court of the United States in Virginia. Davis's attorney petitioned for an immediate trial, but the Federal court sidestepped the request by claiming that Davis was being held prisoner under the jurisdiction of a presidential order. However, the order was not signed by the President, but by the Secretary of War, Edwin Stanton. Varina Davis pleaded to President Johnson for help, but Johnson told her he was in a fight of his own against the Radicals, and if he released Davis, it would give them another reason to impeach him.[5]

Davis' defense attorneys continued to pressure the Federal courts to set a trial date, and in response the court appointed Chief Justice Salmon P. Chase to preside over the proceedings. Chief Justice Chase would also preside over President Johnson's impeachment. Meanwhile, the court continued to delay and postpone Davis' trial in the hope that Davis would die in his subterranean tomb sometime during the winter of 1867. But, as the winter months passed, Davis remained alive and continued to gather widespread support for his release.

While Chase was the Secretary of the Treasury, he often threatened Lincoln with his resignation, implying that the economy—at its most desperate state in history—would only worsen without his guidance. It was in June of 1864 when Lincoln accepted his resignation, dismissing the Radical Secretary from his Cabinet; then, on July 5, he appointed a moderate Republican Senator, William Fessenden from Maine, to replace Chase as head of the Treasury Department. Fessenden only served eight months at his new post, and very successfully reversed the financial decline that befell the Nation while under the leadership of the former Secretary Chase. Fessenden introduced a series of innovative, interest-bearing, government-issued bonds and other measures

JEFFERSON DAVIS **lived his final twenty-two years as a free man (photo ca. 1885, eighteen years after being acquitted of the charges of conspiring to assassinate Abraham Lincoln).**

that quickly stabilized the economic outlook and restored the value of the paper dollar. By March of 1865, William Fessenden felt the economy was once again secure and he resigned as Treasury Secretary to return to the Senate.[6]

The impeachment trail ran from March to May of 1868, and the decision to convict or acquit President Johnson (which required a 2/3 majority) hinged on the vote from the Republican Senators. Just before the vote was taken, William Fessenden and six other Republicans announced their intent to break ranks with the Radicals over removing Johnson from office. These rogue senators received letters and telegrams pressuring them to support the Radicals, and one seriously threatening telegram warned: "Any Republican Senator who votes against impeachment need never to expect to get home alive."[7]

Joseph S. Flower, James W. Grimes, John B. Henderson, Lyman Trumbull, Peter G. Winkle and Edwin G. Ross joined with William Fessenden to acquit President Johnson of all charges. A 35 to 19 decision defeated the Radicals by a single vote, and had Johnson been impeached, from that day on, the President of the United States would be little more than a powerless figurehead, much like the British Royal family of England is today. Johnson survived to serve out his term, but the major Northeastern newspapers attacked his character and reputation, and he could not even win a nomination for a second term.

But a big break came for Jefferson Davis during Johnson's impeachment proceedings. The diary that had been found on Booth after he was captured was never presented as evidence during the conspiracy trial, and was soon forgotten. Booth's little red book remained hidden away for the next two years deep inside the War Department. After Baker wrote his book, the diary came to the attention of Congress for the first time, and a subpoena was issued for the War Department to produce the book. A Congressional judiciary committee examined the diary, and astonishing new information was revealed about the conspiracy to kill Abraham Lincoln. The diary showed that Davis played no role in the assassination, and that Mary Surratt was unaware of Lincoln's assassination plot until after the murder had been committed.

The Secretary of War, Edwin Stanton, and the Supreme Court Chief Justice Salmon P. Chase had no choice but to relent from their conspiracy to get rid of the last of three Presidents (Lincoln, Johnson, and Davis) who had been the subjects of their attacks. If it had not been for Lafayette Baker's mention of the diary, the Radicals could have crossed out the last President, Davis, from their hit list, and then, perhaps, no one might ever realize who actually conspired to kill Abraham Lincoln.

The Demise of Lafayette Baker

Lafayette Baker suddenly fell ill and died in July of 1868, not even 18 months after implicating Stanton before Congress. His mysterious and untimely death has inspired a great deal of conjecture.

Gone Missing: Sarah Antoinette Slater

On May 1, the same day George Atzerodt gave his confession to Marshal James McPhail, another previous guest from the Surratt House, Sarah Antoinette Slater, was arrested and also interrogated by McPhail. Mrs. Slater was a very attractive, petite young woman from North Carolina who also had French citizenship. Based on McPhail's interrogation notes, she disclosed very little, but confessed to the Marshal that she first came to Baltimore with a Mr. Sharpe, a close friend and business associate of her husband, Rowan Slater (LAE, p. 1323). At the time she relocated, her husband was a Confederate soldier, eventually captured by the Union. When asked about her personal life, she reported that she was happily married. Mrs. Slater did not deny that she knew Mr. Sharpe had been a Confederate courier.

The next day, McPhail assigned detective William Parker to deliver Mrs. Slater to the office of Stanton's chief investigator at the War Department, Colonel Burnett, for further investigation into her possible involvement in the conspiracy plot. After this there is no further trace of Sarah Slater. It appears that both her family and the Pinkerton agency searched for her to no avail (the Pinkertons conducted no search for a Kate Thompson, of course). Sarah Slater, who, like George Atzerodt, was able to identify many persons of interest and the roles they played, was last known to be in Stanton's custody. The very few people to inquire about Booth's kidnapping accomplice Kate Thompson often conclude she was the same person as Sarah Slater.

Sarah's husband appeared in the 1880s census records as living alone in Albemarle, Virginia.

What Happened to George Emerson?

In the diary of John Wilkes Booth, a confession of his deeds occupied four consecutive sheets, though when the diary was presented to Congress in 1867, the second sheet was not only conspicuously blank, but had been cut out, then laminated back onto its stub. Booth's writing on the previous page ended mid-sentence, about to elaborate on his collaborators, apparently a person or party he believed could absolve him of his crime. Former Union General, Senator Benjamin Butler, was rightly convinced that the diary proved that Booth was persuaded to assassinate on the final day, that Mary Surratt was an innocent woman, and that Judge Advocates John Bingham and Joseph Holt were well aware of these facts, and suppressed the diary as evidence. In a Congressional investigation, Senator Butler and others interrogated numerous persons associated with the diary, including Colonel Everton J. Conger, who made a copy of the contents of Booth's diary before it entered Stanton's possession. The following is excerpted from the interrogation of Conger, which took place May 13–14, 1867 (IMPEACH, pp. 325–32).

Q. Were you present at the time [Booth] was shot?
A. I was.
Q. Who was the first person to examine his body after he was shot?
A. I was.
Q. What articles did you find upon his person?
A. I found a diary, bills of exchange, greenbacks, a compass, key, etc.
Q. Did you take possession of these articles?
A. Yes, sir. [...]
Q. To whom did you deliver them?
A. To Mr. Stanton.
Q. Did he retain possession of the diary?

A. Yes, sir. [...]

Q. Who was present when you delivered the diary to Mr. Stanton?

A. Colonel [Luther] C. Baker.

Q. Have you seen that diary since?

A. Yes, sir; I saw it to-day. [...]

Q. Are there any leaves cut or torn out?

A. Yes, sir. [...]

Q. Did you make any memorandum of the contents of the diary in writing at the time?

A. Yes, sir.

Q. Have you that memorandum?

A. No, sir.

Q. What did you do with it?

A. I gave it to Colonel L. C. Baker.

Q. Was that memorandum an abstract or a transcript of the diary?

A. So far as it went, it was a transcript of the diary. [... the proceeding interrogation took place on the following day]

Q. You stated in answer to a question by the Chairman, that your impression was that this memorandum book read differently from what it does now. ...

A. ... It is not worded exactly as I thought it was.

Q. Where were you when you copied what was written in the book?

A. On the steamer coming from Belle Plain to Washington. [...]

Q. Did you copy the first page?

A. Yes, I think so.

Q. Did you copy what was written on the loose sheet? [...]

A. I had read it; but I do not think I copied it. [...]

Q. Did you count the number of leaves cut out?

A. I did not. [...]

Q. Why did you give it to General Baker?

A. After having it in my possession I felt as if I had no right to retain it without permission. I told General Baker of it, and asked him to ascertain from Mr. Stanton if I might retain it. Subsequently he said that Mr. Stanton did not want that I should have it, and I gave it to him. I do not know what he did with it. [...]

Q. Did you read it to anyone?

A. I read it to one man.

Q. To whom?
A. To George Emerson.
Q. Where is he?
A. He is dead.

BIBLIOGRAPHY

WORKS REFERENCED IN THE CHAPTERS, AUTHOR'S NOTES AND APPENDICES

AHPH   Ketchum, Richard M., editor. *The American Heritage Picture History of the Civil War*. New York: American Heritage Publishing Company, Inc., 1961.

ALP   *Abraham Lincoln Papers at the Library of Congress*, Manuscript Division (Washington, D.C.: American Memory Project, [2000–02]), accessed 2010–12. http://memory.loc.gov/ammem/alhtml/alhome.html

Bak   Bak, Richard. *The Day Lincoln Was Shot: An Illustrated Chronicle*. Dallas: Taylor Trade Publishing, 2001.

Baker (L)   Baker, La Fayette C. *History of the United States Secret Service*. Philadelphia: L. C. Baker, 1867.

Baker (R)   Baker, Ray S. "The Capture, Death & Burial of J. Wilkes Booth." *McClure's Magazine, Volume 9*, pp. 574–585.

Barton   Barton, William E. *The Soul of Abraham Lincoln*. New York: George H. Doran Company, 1920.

Bates   Bates, David H. *Lincoln in the Telegraph Office: Recollections of the United States Military Telegraph Corps During the Civil War*. New York: The Century Co., 1907.

Bearss   Bearss, Edwin C. *Fields of Honor: Pivotal Battles of the Civil War*. Washington: National Geographic, 2006.

Blue   Blue, Frederick J. *Salmon P. Chase: A Life in Politics*. Boston & New York: Houghton-Mifflin & Company, 1899.

Booth   Booth, John Wilkes, edited by John Rhodehamel and Louise Taper. *"Right or Wrong, God Judge Me:" The Writings of John Wilkes Booth*. Chicago: University of Illinois Press, 2001.

Bowen & Neal   Bowen, Walter S. & Harry E. Neal. *The United States Secret Service*. Philadelphia: Chilton Co., 1960.

Brooks   Brooks, Noah. *Washington in Lincoln's Time*. New York: Century, 1896.

Burlingame   Burlingame, Michael. *Abraham Lincoln: A Life, Volume 1*. Baltimore: Johns Hopkins University Press, 2008.

Butler   Butler, Benjamin F. *Autobiography and Personal Reminiscences of Major-General Benjamin F Butler, Parts 1 & 2.* Boston: A. M. Thayer & Co., 1892.

Chamlee   Chamlee, Roy Z., Jr. *Lincoln's Assassins: A Complete Account of Their Capture, Trial, and Punishment.* Jefferson: McFarland & Company Publishers, 1990.

Chittenden   Chittenden, Lucius E. *Recollections of President Lincoln and His Administration.* New York: Harper & Brothers, 1891.

Clark   Clark, James C. *Last Train South: The Flight of the Confederate Government from Richmond.* Jefferson: McFarland & Company Publishers, 1984.

Cottrell   Cottrell, John. *Anatomy of an Assassination.* New York: Funk & Wagnalls, 1968.

Cox   Cox, Samuel S. *Eight Years in Congress, from 1857–1865: Memoir and Speeches* [of Samuel Cox]. New York: D. Appleton & Co., 1865.

Crook (F)   Crook, William H., Margarita Spalding Gerry, editor. *Through Five Administrations.* New York: Harper & Brothers, 1910.

Crook (M)   Crook, William H., Henry Rood, editor. *Memories of the White House.* Boston: Little, Brown & Co., 1911.

Cullen   Cullen, Joseph P. *The Siege of Petersburg.* Conshohocken: Eastern Acorn Press, 1970.

CW   Basler, Roy P., editor. *The Collected Works of Abraham Lincoln, Volumes VI, VII, VIII.* New Brunswick: Rutgers University Press, 1953.

DeWitt   DeWitt, David M. The Assassination of Abraham Lincoln and Its Expiation.

Doherty   Doherty, Ed. "John Wilkes Booth: A Talk with the Man that Captured Him," *McBride's Magazine, Vol. 40.* J.B. Lippincott and Company, 1887.

Fanny   Seward, Frances A., Patricia Carley Johnson, editor. *Sensitivity and Civil War: the Selected Diaries and Papers, 1858-1866, of Frances Adeline (Fanny) Seward.* University of Rochester, 1964.

Freeman (Lee)   Freeman, Douglas S. *R. E. Lee.* New York: Charles Scribner's Sons, 1936.

Freeman (LL)   Freeman, Douglas S. *Lee's Lieutenants: A Study in Command.* New York: Charles Scribner's Sons, 1944.

Fehrenbacher   Fehrenbacher, Don E. and Virginia Fehrenbacher. *Recollected words of Abraham Lincoln*. Stanford: Stanford University Press, 1996.

Fessenden   Fessenden, Francis. *Life and Public Services of William Pitt Fessenden, Volume 2*. Boston and New York: Houghton Mifflin & Company, 1907.

Flower   Flower, Frank. *Edwin McMasters Stanton: The Autocrat of Rebellion, Emancipation, and Reconstruction*. Boston: George M. Smith & Co., 1905.

GAC   "George Atzerodt's Confession" (via McPhail) School of Law, University of Missouri, Kansas City: Conspiracy Trial files. Accessed 2011–12 http://law2.umkc.edu/faculty/projects/ftrials/lincolnconspiracy/atzerodtconf.html

Gienapp   Gienapp, William E. *Abraham Lincoln and Civil War America: A Biography*. Oxford: Oxford University Press, 2002.

Gillette   Gillette, Abraham D. "The Last Days of Payne." New York: *World*, Sunday, April 3, 1892.

Goodrich   Goodrich, Thomas. *The Darkest Dawn: Lincoln, Booth, and the Great American Tragedy*. Bloomington: Indiana University Press, 2006.

Grant   Grant, Ulysses S. *Personal Memoirs*. New York: The Modern Library, 1999.

Hart   Hart, Albert Bushnell. *Salmon Portland Chase*. Boston & New York: Houghton-Mifflin & Company, 1899.

Hanchett   Hanchett, William. *The Lincoln Murder Conspiracies*. Chicago: University of Illinois Press, 1986.

Headley   Headley, John W. *Confederate Operations in Canada and New York*. New York & Washington: The Neale Publishing Co., 1906.

Humphreys   Humphreys, Andrew A. *The Virginia Campaign of 1864 and 1865: The Army of the Potomac and the Army of the James*. New York: Jack Brussel Publisher, 1903.

IMPEACH   *Impeachment Investigation: Testimony Taken before the Judiciary Committee of the House of Representatives in the Investigation of the Charges against Andrew Johnson*. House of Representatives, 2nd session, 39th Congress, First Session, and 40th Congress: Government Printing Office, 1867.

LAE Edwards, William C. and Edward Steers, Jr., editors. *The Lincoln Assassination: The Evidence*. Chicago, University of Illinois Press, 2009.

Katz Katz, D. M. *Witness to an Era: The Life and Photographs of Alexander Gardner*. Nashville: Rutledge Hill Press, 1991.

Kauffmann Kauffmann, Michael W. *American Brutus: John Wilkes Booth and the Lincoln Conspiracies*. New York: Random House, 2004.

Klement Klement, Frank L. *Dark Lanterns: Secret Political Societies, Conspiracies and Treason Trials in the Civil War*. Baton Rouge: Louisiana State University Press, 1984.

Korngold Korngold, Ralph. *Thaddeus Stevens: A Being Darkly Wise and Rudely Great*: New York, Harcourt Brace & Co., 1955.

Kunhardt Kunhardt, Philip B., III, Kunhardt, Peter W. & Peter W. Kunhardt, Jr. *Looking For Lincoln*. New York: Alfred A. Knopf, 2008.

Larson Larson, Kate C. *The Assassin's Accomplice*. New York: Basic Books, 2008.

Leech Leech, Margaret. Reveille in Washington: 1860–1865. New York: New York Review of Books, 2011.

Leonard Leonard, Elizabeth D. *Lincoln's Avengers*. New York: W. W. Norton & Co., 2005.

McClellan McClellan, George B. and William Cowper Prime. *McClellan's Own Story*. New York: C. L. Webster & Co., 1887.

McPherson McPherson, James M. *The Illustrated Battle Cry of Freedom: The Civil War Era*. New York: Oxford University Press, 2003.

Mogalever Mogalever, Jacob. *Death to Traitors: The Story of General Lafayette C. Baker, Lincoln's Forgotten Secret Service Chief*. New York: Doubleday & Company, 1960.

Nicolay (C) Nicolay, John and John Hay. *Complete Works of Abraham Lincoln*, 12 vols. New York: Francis D. Tandy, 1905.

Nicolay (H) Nicolay, John G. and John Hay. *Abraham Lincoln: A History*. New York: Century Co., 1890.

Niven Niven, John. *Gideon Welles: Lincoln's Secretary of the Navy*. New York, Oxford University Press, 1973.

Ownsbey Ownsbey, Betty J. *Alias 'Paine': Lewis Thornton Powell, the Mystery Man of the Lincoln Conspiracy*. Jefferson: McFarlane & Company, Inc., 1993.

Pinkerton (SR)   Pinkerton, Allan. *The Spy of the Rebellion; Being a True Story of the Spy System of the United States Army During the Late Rebellion, Revealing Many Secrets of the War hitherto Not Made Public.* New York: G. W. Dillingham Co., 1900.

Plum   Plum, William R. *The Military Telegraph.* Chicago: Donnelly Gassette & Loyd Publishers, 1892.

Pratt   Pratt, Fletcher. *Stanton: Lincoln's Secretary of War.* New York: Norton, 1953.

Randall   Randall, James G. *Constitutional Problems under Lincoln.* D. Appleton & Co., 1926.

Raymond   Henry J. and Francis Bicknell Carpenter. *The Life and Public Services of Abraham Lincoln: Together with His State Papers, Including His Speeches, Addresses, Messages, Letters, and Proclamations, and the Closing Scenes Connected with His Life and Death.* New York: Derby & Miller, Publishers, 1865.

Reck   Reck, Waldo E. *A. Lincoln His Last 24 Hours.* Columbia: University of South Carolina Press, 1994.

Robertson   Robertson, William G. *Back Door to Richmond: The Bermuda Hundred Campaign, April–June 1864.* Baton Rouge: Louisiana State University Press, 1991.

SAC   "Samuel Arnold's Confession," contained in Edwards, William C. and Edward Steers, Jr., editors. *The Lincoln Assassination: The Evidence.* Chicago, University of Illinois Press, 2009.

SAMRS   Dr. Samuel A. Mudd Research Site. Accessed 2011–12. http://www.samuelmudd.com

Scheips   Scheips, Paul J. *Union Signal Communications: Innovation and Conflict.* Iowa City: State University of Iowa, 1963.

Schroeder-Lein   Schroeder-Lein, Glenna R. and Richard Zuczek. *Andrew Johnson: A Biographical Companion.* Santa Barbara: ABC-CLIO, Inc., 2001.

Segal   Segal, Charles M., editor. *Conversations with Lincoln.* New York: G. P. Putnam's Sons, 1961.

Seitz   Seitz, Don C. *Lincoln the Politician.* New York: Coward and McCann Inc, 1931.

Seward   Seward, Frederick W. *Reminiscences of a War-Time Statesman and Diplomat.* New York: G. P. Putnam's Sons, 1916.

Sewell   Sewell, Richard H. *Ballots for Freedom: Anti-slavery politics in the United States, 1837–1860.* New York: W. W. Norton, 1980.

Sherman   Sherman, William T., M. A. DeWolfe Howe, editor. *Home letters of General Sherman.* New York: Charles Scribner's Sons, 1909.

Smith   Smith, William E. *The Francis Preston Blair Family in Politics.* New York: The McMillan Company, 1931.

Steers   Steers, Edward, Jr., editor. *The Trial: The Assassination of President Lincoln and the Trial of the Conspirators.* Lexington: University Press of Kentucky, 2003.

Steers, Swanson   Steers, Edward and James L. Swanson. *The Lincoln Assassination Encyclopedia.* New York: Harper Collins, 2010.

Stern   Stern, Philip V. D. *Secret Missions of the Civil War.* Chicago: Rand McNally, 1959.

Stevens   Stevens, Walter B., Michael Burlingame, editor. *A Reporter's Lincoln.* Lincoln and London: University of Nebraska Press, 1998.

Stewart   Stewart, David O. *Impeached: The Trial of President Andrew Johnson and the Fight for Lincoln's Legacy.* New York: Simon & Schuster, 2009.

Storey   Storey, Moorfield. *Charles Sumner.* New York: Houghton Mifflin Company, 1900.

Surratt   "John Surratt's 1870 Account of the Lincoln Assassination Conspiracy." School of Law, University of Missouri, Kansas City: Conspiracy Trial files. Accessed 2012 http://law2.umkc.edu/faculty/projects/ftrials/lincolnconspiracy/surrattspeech.html

Swanson   Swanson, James L. *Bloody Crimes: The Funeral of Abraham Lincoln and the Chase for Jefferson Davis.* New York: HarperCollins Publishers, 2010.

Tanner   Tanner, James. "The Assassination of President Lincoln, 1865," *The American Historical Review, 1924,* 29(3). American Historical Association.

Tidwell   Tidwell, William A. *Come Retribution: the Confederate Secret Service and the Assassination of Lincoln.* Jackson: University Press of Mississippi, 1988.

Trefousse   Trefousse, Hans L. *Benjamin Franklin Wade, Radical Republican from Ohio.* New York: Twayne Publishers, 1963.

TRIAL   Pitman, Benn, comp. *The Assassination of President Lincoln and the Trial of the Conspirators.* Cincinnati: Moore, Wilstach & Baldwin 1865. Facsimile edition with introduction by Philip Van Doren Stern. New York: Funk & Wagnalls, 1954.

Urwin   Urwin, Gregory J. W., editor. *Black Flag over Dixie: Racial Atrocities and Reprisals in the Civil War.* Carbondale: Southern Illinois University Press, 2004.

USC 1097   *United States Congressional Serial Set, Volume 1097.* U.S. Government Printing Office, 1861.

Waugh   Waugh, John C. *Reelecting Lincoln: The Battle For The 1864 Presidency.* Boston: De Capo Press, 1997.

Weichmann   Weichmann, Louis J. *A True History of the Assassination of Abraham Lincoln and of the Conspiracy of 1865*

Welles (G)   Welles, Gideon. "Lincoln and Johnson." *The Galaxy Magazine*, April, 1872.

Welles (D)   Welles, Gideon; Beale, Howard K., editor. *Diary, 3 vols.* New York: W. W. Norton & Co., 1960.

Williams   Williams, T. H. *Lincoln and the Radicals.* Madison: University of Wisconsin Press, 1972.

Winkler   Winkler, H. Donald. *Stealing Secrets: How a Few Daring Women Deceived Generals, Impacted Battles and Altered the Course of the Civil War.* Naperville: Sourcebooks, 2010.

OTHER WORKS INFORMING THIS BOOK

Alexander, Edward P. *Military Memoirs of a Confederate.* New York: Charles Scribner's Sons, 1907.

BoothieBarn: Discovering the Conspiracy
http://boothiebarn.com/picture-galleries/found-on-booth/
accessed 2013

Carman, Harry J. and Reinhardt H. Luthin. *Lincoln and the Patronage.* New York: Columbia University Press, 1943.

Clarke, Asia B., Terry Alford, editor. *Unlocked Book, John Wilkes Booth: A Sister's Memoir.* Jackson: C. P. Putnam's Sons, 1938.

Denson, John V. "The Hampton Roads Peace Conference During the War Between the States," January 10, 2006. http://LewRockwell.com Accessed 2011–12.

Executive Documents Printed by Order of the House of Representatives During the First Session of the Thirty-Ninth Congress, 1865–'66: Volumes II–III, Report of the Secretary of War. Washington: Government Printing Office, 1866.

Ford's Theare, National Parks Service, U.S. Department of the Interior. Web site accessed 2010–12. http://www.nps.gov/foth/index.htm

Forman, Major Robert J., et al. *Bermuda Hundred Campaign Tour Guide.* Chesterfield, Virginia: Chesterfield Historical Society, 2010.

Johnson, Robert U. and Clarence Clough Buel, editors. *Battles and Leaders of the Civil War, Vols. I–IV.* New York: The Century Company, 1887.

Longstreet, James. *From Manassas to Appomattox: Memoirs of the Civil War in America.* Philadelphia: J. B. Lippencott Company, 1908.

Nicolay, John. *Abraham Lincoln, A History.* New York: The Century Co., 1890.

Stephens, Alexander H. *A Constitutional View of the War Between the States: Its Causes, Character, Conduct and Results.* Philadelphia: The National Publishers Co., 1870.

Author's Notes

Introduction

1 MARYLAND ELECTION INTERFERENCE BY THE WAR DEPARTMENT

The motive for Lincoln's assassination was to control the majority vote in Congress, and the great deal of dissension in Maryland against the Lincoln administration was because of the War Department's efforts to maintain a Republican majority through military force. The Union men called John Boyle a "guerrilla desperado" because he was fighting against the War Department's interference in the polling districts over electing the Maryland administrators and representatives. He was a northern Democrat accused of killing a Captain Thomas H. Watkins. Watkins had arrested Boyle for horse theft, but Boyle escaped, then went to the home of Captain Watkins and shot him in the chest.

An example of this political infighting over free elections in Maryland was expressed to the President by one of his cabinet members from Maryland, the Postmaster General Montgomery Blair. At this time Blair was still a Maryland Republican. On November 11, 1863, Lincoln responded to Blair's note. Included with the note was a letter from the defeated Maryland Democrat Congressman, John M. Crisfield, informing the President of military interference in the election for Congress in the Districts of Maryland.

Under the direction from the Secretary of War, Stanton, General Robert C. Schenck had issued Order No. 53, which dispatched large bodies of troops to all voting places for the purpose of interfering with the free elections to Congress.

Blair informed Lincoln that it was in his own county of Somerset where hundreds of fully armed cavalry soldiers, equipped with pistols, swords, and carbines, gathered on Tuesday before the polls were to open, as a show of intimidation and threats to the voters. The cavalry then broke into squads of 5 to 30 soldiers in each voting place and took control of the elections. In the district of Tangier, an officer pulled from his pocket a yellow voting ticket that was for the Republican candidate, John A. J. Creswell, and announced that no other ticket would be allowed. The *Baltimore Clipper* reported: "The purse and the sword, the Treasury of the United States and all patrons of the War Department, elected [Creswell]." The authors of *Lincoln and the Patronage*, Harry J. Carman and Reinhardt H. Luthin, said, "No person ever wished [Creswell] to be a candidate but Henry Winter Davis and his friends" (pp. 232–33). In the County of Hungry Neck, every ticket was examined by the military before it was put into the ballot box, and in

Princess Anne County dismounted cavalry soldiers surrounded the polling place and required each voter to file past the commanding officer, Captain Charles C. Moore of the 3rd Maryland cavalry. Captain Moore then challenged the son of the defeated Democrat Congressman, John M. Crisfield, as he approached the polling box and questioned his loyalty to the Union. Captain Moore then ordered the Judges of the elections to administer an oath of loyalty to the congressman's son.

The Judges complained of this conduct at a free election and they themselves were then arrested and sent under armed guard to answer in person to General Schenck at his headquarters. The Judges were put in the guard house, awaiting transport to Baltimore, when General Lockwood intervened and had them released.

The elections for that entire district had been broken up after only one vote had been cast. Blair complained that these proceedings occurred in every county, and witnesses had been prepared and sent to the Governor, and copies would be published in every County paper. (CW, Vol. VII, pp. 9–10)

Lincoln responded to General Schenck's Order No. 53, instructing Judge Advocate Joseph Holt to have Captain Charles C. Moore tried by a military commission. However, Captain Moore was acquitted of all charges by the War Department, and a great deal more dissension further separated the Union. Unfortunately, Lincoln was viewed in Maryland as a tyrant, responsible for this violation of free elections. (*See also* note 7 for Chapter 4: "The Radicals' Campaign to Replace Lincoln and His Supporters")

2 Kunhardt, p. 294. When Booth's diary was examined by Congress two years after the assassination it was ruled that Jefferson Davis had no role in the assassination, directly contradicting the ruling of the conspiracy trial, and the former Confederate President was released from prison (*see also* Chapter 19).

Chapter 1: The Condemned

1 SAC

2 Chamlee, p. 16: The "Sam Letter" from the trial evidence; relevant excerpts appear in Chapter 7, and are discussed in Appendix D.

3 TRIAL: Testimony of Jacob Smith concerning Samuel Arnold. Smith saw Samuel Arnold every day in Hookstown, Maryland, from March 20 through 30, 1865.

4 TRIAL: Testimony of William O'Laughlen concerning Michael O'Laughlen, referring to a telegram submitted as evidence, which he received from
   his brother William, describing a boxcar of hay they were trying to sell. In
   a separate telegram to O'Laughlen from John Wilkes Booth, dated March
   13, 1865, Booth stated, "do not fear to neglect your business, you had better
   come on at once [to Washington]." Booth was referring to the load of hay,
   not wanting Michael to come late on account of the hay. The prosecution
   attempted to construe "your business" as a reference to assassination. To the
   contrary, Booth was urging O'Laughlen to *neglect* his business in order to
   meet with him on the 15th regarding the *kidnapping* plot.

5 TRIAL: Testimony of Francis S. Walsh concerning David Herold. Walsh,
   the druggist who employed Herold during the eleven months prior to the
   assassination, stated that Herold was "more like a boy than a man."

6 TRIAL: Testimony of James Nokes concerning David Herold: "very little
   reliability was to be placed in him" and "never entered into any argument
   on any subject" and "light and trifling."

7 TRIAL: Testimony of William H. Kilotz concerning David Herold. Kilotz
   lived next door to Herold for thirteen years, and stated "I consider him very
   boyish [… he] never associated with men, only boys."

8 TRIAL: Testimony of Dr. Charles W. Davis concerning David Herold:
   Herold was "not endowed with much intellect" and "I considered him far
   more like a boy than a man."

9 TRIAL: Testimony of Dr. Samuel A. H. McKim concerning David Herold.
   McKim was Herold's family doctor and lifelong acquaintance, who stated,
   "known him always light, trivial and unreliable […] in my mind I consider
   him about eleven years of age."

10 Gillette, p. 17. Lewis Powell disclosed to Reverend Gillette: "Until the
   morning of the fatal day no crime more serious than the abduction had
   been contemplated."

11 TRIAL: Testimony of James W. Richards concerning Dr. Samuel Mudd

12 TRIAL: Testimonies of James W. Richards, John H. Baden, Joshua S.
   Naylor, John Waters, Daniel W. Hawkins and Frank Ward concerning Dr.
   Samuel Mudd

13 TRIAL: Testimony of William A. Evans concerning Dr. Samuel Mudd

14 TRIAL: Testimony of Milo Simms concerning Dr. Samuel Mudd

15 TRIAL: Testimony of Melvina Washington concerning Dr. Samuel Mudd

16 TRIAL: Testimony of Elzee Eglent concerning Dr. Samuel Mudd

17 TRIAL: Testimony of Mary Simms concerning Dr. Samuel Mudd

18 TRIAL: Testimony of Jeremiah Dyer concerning Dr. Samuel Mudd

19 National Archives, College Park, MD: Presidential Pardon of Dr. Samuel Mudd, February 8, 1869

20 TRIAL: Testimony of Jacob Ritterspaugh concerning Ed Spangler

21 TRIAL: Testimony of James Lamb concerning Ed Spangler

22 TRIAL: Testimony of Lewis J. Carland concerning Ed Spangler

23 TRIAL: Testimony and cross-examination of John Greenawalt concerning George Atzerodt; *See also* Testimony of James Walker

24 LAE, p. 616

25 "The Positions of the Prisoners Two Hours Before the Executions" and "How They Died," *New York Herald*, July 8, 1865.

At the conclusion of the latter article, the correspondent, who witnessed the agonizing deaths of the condemned, wrote: "If death must, for the safety of society, be inflicted on the assassin for the sake of civilization, let some more summary means of inflicting be devised."

Chapter 2: Two Conspiracies

1 Nicolay, p. 286–87

2 Raymond, p. 793

3 Ibid, p. 795; *see also* Appendix A: "Booth's Manifesto"

4 Ibid, p. 793; *see also* Appendix A: "Booth's Manifesto"

5 CW, Vol. VIII, p. 372: Telegram from Lincoln to General Grant

6 CW, Vol. VIII, pp. 220–21: Telegram from Lincoln to Francis Blair, Sr.

7 Bates, pp. 299–300

8 Williams, p. 355

9 CW, Vol. VIII, p. 274–75

10 United States House of Representatives, Executive Document No. 59, February 8, 1865.

11 Raymond, p. 782: Bigelow's second letter to Morse

12 Ibid, p. 781: Bigelow's first letter to Morse

13 ALP, Van Alen; *also*
Reck, pp. 10, 12

14 CW, Vol. VIII, p. 413; *also*
Nicolay & Hay, Vol. XI, p. 94

15 Cullen, p. 47

16 CW, Vol. VIII, p. 387: Telegram from Dana to Stanton

17 Ibid, p. 333: Lincoln's Second Inaugural Address, March 4, 1865

18 Raymond, p. 693: Seward shows Stanton the letters, which Stanton agrees are urgent, then telegraphs Lincoln less than two hours before Seward is incapacitated by an "accident." This time interval is established by telegrams to Lincoln from Seward and Stanton on April 5 and 6 (*see* notes 20 and 21, below).

19 Raymond, p. 781: Bigelow's first letter to Morse

20 CW, Vol. VIII, p. 387: Telegraph from Seward to Lincoln, April 5, 1865; Lincoln's immediate telegraph reply to Seward.

21 Ibid, p. 388: Stanton sent Lincoln multiple telegraphs on April 6, 1865, informing him of Seward's accident and condition, and of Mrs. Lincoln's travel arrangements, but does not disclose news of the assassins from France.

Chapter 3: Cause for Alarm

1 CW, Vol. VIII, p. 386

2 Ibid, p. 286–87: Letter from Lincoln to the Senate

3 Raymond, p. 779

4 Ibid

5 Ibid, p. 781

6 Ibid, p. 780

7   The dramatization of Seward's meeting with Stanton was constructed from
    the documents referenced in notes 16, 18–21 for Chapter 2, plus the source
    indicated below.

8   SEWARD INFORMED STANTON OF ASSASSINS BEFORE HIS CARRIAGE ACCIDENT

    "… Secretary Seward received from … secret agents in France …
    warnings so distinct and direct, that Mr. Seward consulted Secretary
    Stanton in regard to them, and it was agreed that he should lay the
    subject before the President the next day, and earnestly represent to
    him the expediency of avoiding, for a time, all public gatherings,
    and all needless exposure to possible assault." (Raymond, p. 693)

    Henry J. Raymond was personally well acquainted with Lincoln, Stanton
    and Seward, and founder of *The New York Times*, whose journalists were
    covering the travels of the President as well as Seward's accident. Raymond
    was eventually Chairman of the Republican National Committee and a
    member of the House of Representatives from 1865 to 1867. Above, Ray-
    mond insists Stanton indeed declared to Seward that Lincoln must be pro-
    tected and kept from public gatherings—such as Ford's Theatre, where, nine
    days later, Stanton would insist on minimizing Lincoln's security against the
    President's wishes, while sending General Grant away due to assassination
    threats (*see* note 4 for Chapter 9).

CHAPTER 4: THE DESPERATE CHOICE

1   CW, Vol. VIII, p. 388: Lincoln's telegram to Grant

2   Ibid, p. 386: Lincoln's telegram to Campbell stipulating his three "indis-
    pensable things."

3   Ibid, p. 387: Dana reports to Stanton about Lincoln

4   Ibid, p. 392: Lincoln to Grant "let the thing be pressed."

5   *National Republican*, April 11, 1865. Washington, D.C.: Murtagh & Co.,
    available via the Library of Congress, http://chroniclingamerica.loc.gov/

6   Urwin, p. 106.

7   THE RADICALS' CAMPAIGN TO REPLACE LINCOLN AND HIS SUPPORTERS

    It was the purpose of the Radicals to reduce the rebel states to territories,
    ending their ability to threaten the political and economic powers of the
    northeast. To do this, the Radicals advanced a thesis of "state abdication,"

that by rebelling, the Southern states lost
their Constitutional rights. Lincoln and
his supporters, on the other hand, maintained that the rebel states did not have the
authority to secede, and therefore were still
states within the Union, with all Constitutional rights. To prevail in their objectives,
the Radicals had to remove the Conservatives who stood in their way, chiefly Abraham Lincoln, William Seward and Montgomery Blair. This campaign to remove
Lincoln came from two Radical factions:
one led by Chase, Sumner and Stevens;
the other by Ohio Senator Benjamin Wade
and Maryland Representative Henry Winter Davis.

MONTGOMERY BLAIR, the outspoken
cabinet member who, along with his
brother, enraged the Radical Republicans to the point that Lincoln eventually asked for his resignation.

MONTGOMERY BLAIR. In early 1863, the
Radicals began their attack on Lincoln's
conservative ally, Postmaster General Montgomery Blair, and his politically
influential family (*see* Appendix E). "Montgomery's dislike for Stanton bor-
dered on hatred, his contempt for Chase ran dark and deep" (Niven, p.
471).

Frank Blair, the brother of Montgomery, exposed the corruption of
Salmon P. Chase and his Treasury agents in his famous speech, "The Jaco-
bins of Missouri" (http://archive.org/details/jacobinsofmissou00blai). The
Treasury agents were using the Union military to steal agricultural prod-
ucts grown in the occupied territories. Through the issuing of government
cotton permits Chase's agents ran rampant with fraud, theft and bribery.
Commissions were appointed to examine the many argued claims over confiscated property, taken mainly from the Union-controlled cotton belt of the
Red River Valley region.

President Lincoln told the chairman of the 1860 Republican National
Convention, George Ashmun of Massachusetts, less than one hour before
his assassination, "I have done with commissions. I believe they are contriv-
ances to cheat the government out of every pound of cotton they can lay
their hands on" (Reck, p. 57).

Frank Blair accused Salmon Chase of tolerating corruption, and creating a corrupt political machine to solicit patronage for himself and against
Lincoln (Blue, p. 227; *see also* letters from Lincoln to Chase: CW, Vol. VIII,
pp. 181, 182, 184, 195 regarding corruption, *also* pp. 200–01, 212–13

regarding Chase endorsing a smear campaign against Lincoln, then lying to Lincoln about it).

Montgomery Blair was a strong pro-Lincoln and anti-Radical politician. In October, 1863, Blair attacked Charles Sumner on his state suicide doctrine during his Rockville, Maryland speech (Waugh, p. 65). Thaddeus Stevens wrote Chase about Montgomery's speech: "If such men [the Blair Brothers] are to be retained in Mr. Lincoln's Cabinet, it is time we were consulting about his successor" (Korngold, pp. 219–20).

Thaddeus Stevens then had a heated, two-hour meeting with the President to demand the removal of Blair and outline how the Radicals wanted his administration to be run, to which Lincoln responded: "Has it come to this that the voters of this country are asked to elect a man to be President—to be the Executive—to administer the government, and yet this man is to have no will or direction of his own? Am I to be the mere puppet of power—to have my constitutional advisers select for me before hand—to be told I must do this or leave that undone? It would be degrading to my manhood to consent to any such bargain. I was about to say it would be equally degrading to your manhood to ask it." (Segal, p. 338)

On December 8, 1863, Lincoln set out his reconstruction plans in his Proclamation of Amnesty and Reconstruction (CW, Vol. VII, p. 53–56). After that proclamation was issued, the decision was made among the Radicals to replace Lincoln and his conservative supporters. This Proclamation required state lawmakers to support all Congressional acts and Presidential proclamations with regard to slavery. However, at the time no acts of Congress or Presidential proclamations called for complete abolition.

As the nominations for the Republican Presidential candidacy began in 1864, the Radicals divided into two factions, each promoting their own candidates to rival Abraham Lincoln. Lincoln's challengers were [then] Treasury Secretary Salmon P. Chase (backed by Sumner and Stevens) and John C. Frémont (backed by Benjamin Wade and Henry Winter Davis). In an effort to eliminate the Radical Frémont from the race, Lincoln yielded to pressure from Michigan Senator Zachariah Chandler, and dismissed Montgomery Blair from his Cabinet (Gienapp, p. 163). The President sacrificed Blair in exchange for Frémont's withdrawal from the Republican nomination, and with that the Radicals eliminated their first enemy in Lincoln's Cabinet.

In February 1864, Charles Sumner addressed Congress: "Congress must provide for the termination of slavery." Several resolutions were laid upon the table, but never taken up. Sumner's idea of reconstruction was that Congress, not the President, should formulate reconstruction policy (Storey, pp. 218–19). Sumner offered a series of resolutions to prohibit slavery everywhere by amending the Constitution. Senator Benjamin Wade voiced the fear among the Radicals that if antebellum conditions were restored, the Northern Democrats would be reinforced by returning Southern politicians and the Republican Party might then lose its control and influence over Congress (Trefousse, p. 220).

Though Lincoln had replaced Montgomery Blair, Blair continued his support for the President. In late 1864, Blair wrote Lincoln a long letter challenging Salmon Chase for a Supreme Court appointment. Mr. Blair tried to impress upon the President that he would be a better Supreme Court justice than the Radical Chase. He pleaded to Lincoln that Sumner's doctrine of "state suicide" (also known as "state forfeiture" and "state abdication") which in his mind Chase co-authored, was to turn the whole rebel region into a *tabula rasa* (clean slate), to be essentially annihilated and rebuilt: "Mr. Sumner ... seems to confine his purpose of reducing the States to territories to the object of [removing the adoption of slavery from the Constitutional rights of individual states and] bringing Slavery within the grasp of Congress." He also harangued Chase for striving to deprive the Southern states of determining their own electoral processes: "There is a purpose, and one the accomplishment of which depends on Mr. Chase's idea of disfranchising the states, turning them into territories, and giving to Congress the power of making their local laws. It is the purpose of depriving the States of their hitherto unquestioned right of regulating suffrage." (ALP, Montgomery Blair to Abraham Lincoln, December 6, 1864)

William Seward was a major source of power in the Lincoln administration. He had been a founding member of the Republican party, and without his support Lincoln would have had little chance to secure the Presidency for either term. Seward had once voted in step with the Radicals, but had become essentially a traitor to their cause. Seward also posed a threat to the Secretary of War. The Secretary of State had his own network of spies for international deployment. It was Seward who had established some of America's first counter-espionage forces, including the presence of agents in Canada. Lafayette Baker had distinguished himself as a spy for Seward before coming under the direction of Edwin Stanton in the War Department. If anyone could uncover Stanton's abuses of the War Department, it was William H. Seward.

Abraham Lincoln. Lincoln was elected in 1860 with support from Radicals who thought their candidate, who had very little political experience on the national level, would be easy to control. One of the first Radical Congressmen to learn otherwise was Henry T. Blow, who then warned the independent-minded President, "your troubles in the future will far exceed those of the past" (CW, Vol VI, p. 234). In 1863, when Lincoln announced his intentions for amnesty for the Confederates, and his intention to restore "the Union as it was," the campaign to prevent his second term began. They wished to immediately deny the President the executive authority to readmit states, to write reconstruction policy, and to grant amnesty to the promoters of rebellion. The Radical Congressman Henry Winter Davis attacked Lincoln in the House of Representatives, while Benjamin Wade rallied opposition to the President in the Senate. Wade and Davis put together their own Radical reconstruction plan, which was approved by both houses of Congress on July 2, 1864. Lincoln was determined not to yield his Constitutional authority to the Radical Congress and effected a "pocket veto" by refusing to sign the Wade-Davis bill (Seitz, p. 404).

In a desperate fury, Wade and Davis turned to the newspapers and published a rant against Lincoln, in which they deemed his rejection of their bill "a rash and fatal act of the President," portraying his protection of executive powers as a "usurpation" of Congressional authority (*New York Tribune*, August 5, 1864). With the exception of this media attack on Lincoln, the Radical coalition of Sumner, Stevens, and Chase along with Wade, Davis and Frémont, regressed their attack against the President in order to beat back the threat from Democrat George B. McClellan taking the White House way from the Republicans (Allan Nevins, "War for the Union": *The Organized War to Victory, 1864-1865*, p. 126).

Lincoln's reelection ended the truce, and the Radical attack on the President was resumed (T. Harry Williams, *Lincoln and the Radicals*, pp. 352–53). In February, 1865, The Radicals were distrusting about Lincoln's possible concessions offered at the Hampton Roads peace conference. Sumner and Stevens called for the President to give a report to Congress on what was discussed. This resolution touched off a heated debate in Congress between Lincoln's Conservative allies and the Radicals. James Doolittle came to the President's defense and accused Benjamin Wade of a plot to sabotage the administration's program for peace and reconstruction (Williams, p. 355).

The Radicals wanted the President to not allow the return of Southern congressmen, and they believed public opinion (in the Union) would support instituting a Northeastern voter base in the South by mandating southern Negro suffrage (Williams, p. 357). On April 11 and 12, 1865, Salmon Chase gave the President his last warning to amend his reconstruction policy (CW, Vol. VIII, pp. 399–401). Lincoln did slightly revise his position on suffrage, but remained firm on amnesty and restoring the authority of the former Confederate states. Two days later Abraham Lincoln was assassinated.

8 **THERE WILL BE NO ONE WHO CAN FACILITATE AN OBJECTION.** Following Lincoln's assassination, only a handful of Republicans (Edward Bates, Oliver H. Browning, Henry McCulloch and Gideon Wells) opposed the use of a military tribunal to investigate and try the alleged assassins. The two justices (Porter and Comstock) who disapproved of the conduct of the military commission were dismissed. When Mary Lincoln alleged her husband's murder was orchestrated by insiders, she found herself accused in the press and courts of insanity. The widow Lincoln wrote: "Even if he had remained in the White House on that night of darkness he would have been horribly cut to pieces—those fiends had too long contemplated this inhuman murder to have allowed him to escape." (Kunhardt, p. 139)

9 CW, Vol. VIII, p. 405–06: Telegram from Dana to Stanton

10 Ibid, p. 406

11 Ibid: Telegram from Stanton to Weitzel

12 Ibid: Weitzel's reply to Stanton

13 Ibid: Telegram from James A. Hardie [for Stanton] to Weitzel

14 Ibid, p. 407: Telegram from Campbell to Weitzel

15 Ibid, p. 406: Telegram from Weitzel to Lincoln

16 CW, Vol. VI, pp. 33–34: Telegram from Lincoln to Curtis

17 CW, Vol. VIII, p. 405: Telegram from Lincoln to Weitzel

18 Ibid, pp. 406–07: Telegram from Lincoln to Weitzel

CHAPTER 5: LAST CHANCE

1 Pratt, p. 411

2 Smith, p. 232–33

3 Pratt, p. 141

4 **STANTON PROLONGED THE WAR** by eleven months in order to give Chase a chance to win the 1864 Republican nomination, and to give the military time to destroy the infrastructure (railroads, bridges, crops, homes and businesses) in the Southern states (Robertson, p. 120).

During Benjamin Butler's Bermuda Hundred campaign, Stanton and Thomas Eckert sent three deliberately misleading dispatches to pull Butler away from taking Petersburg only hours before he and Major General Edward Hincks could take the city virtually unopposed. Grant's situation at Spottsylvania Courthouse, 50 miles north of Richmond, was completely contrary to the description in the communiqués from Stanton to Butler.

The Situation. On May 8th, General Grant, in combat against Lee's forces, disclosed that he was hopeful to merge his forces with those of General Butler's to the south, between Richmond and Petersburg. However, Lee's army held off his advance (ending his hope to merge with Butler). Grant hoped he could crack Lee's line with a major attack by the 10th of May (Bearss, p. 307). Grant even sent a messenger to Washington (Illinois Congressman Elihu Washburne) to inform the War Department he would hold the line and fight Lee at that spot all summer if necessary (Lee was well situated to defend Richmond from the north).

The Deception. Butler received a dispatch from Stanton, sent May 9 at 3:20 PM, falsely stating that Lee was in full retreat for Richmond, with General Grant in pursuit (Butler, Part 2, Appendix 35). At 4:00 PM Stanton sent Butler a second dispatch: "Grant … is on the march with his whole force; army to form a junction with you" (Butler, Part 2, Appendix 36). At no time did Grant ever have Lee in retreat.

The last dispatch Butler received was falsely dated 10:00 AM, May 9, to look as if it were the first dispatch. Butler specifies it was actually received last, at a later hour in the day (Butler, p. 646), after Butler had called off his attack on Petersburg. The dispatch was deliberately misdated to cover the false information in the previous dispatches. It read: "Advices from the front give reason to believe that General Grant's operation will prove a great success and complete victory. On Saturday night [May 7th], the enemy had been driven at all points, and [Grant's II Corps Commander] Hancock was pushing forward rapidly…" (in reality Early had blocked Hancock at Todd's Tavern). Stanton concluded the dispatch offering a flimsy source for his chain of deceptive messages: "It was reported yesterday by a deserter, that the enemy's only hope was in heavy reinforcements from Beauregard." (Butler, Part 2, Appendix 37)

The Result. Butler, with 40,000 men, had been positioned to take the strategically vital city of Petersburg, just south of Richmond, which was guarded by approximately 5,000 Confederate soldiers. Historians have often criticized Butler for failing to make this move, which would have drastically altered the course of the war, perhaps ending it and preventing Sherman's destructive "march to the sea." It was Stanton's misinformation that diverted

Butler from Petersburg. In short order Petersburg was bolstered, and thus defended until April of 1865.

Stanton's deception was not only a series of lies, but a series of *bad* lies, and with disastrous consequences. Butler, in his memoirs, understanding the true situation and what Stanton clearly would have known, called Stanton's May 9th telegrams what they were: "It will be observed that one movement to take Petersburg was thus frustrated by information from headquarters ... which was in every substantial particular *misleading and untrue*" (Butler, p. 648, Italics by Butler). Butler even spelled them out (original parentheses changed to dashes): "'Lee's army was in full retreat toward Richmond,' 'Grant pursuing with his army on Friday night'—the 6th—not true, ... 'Hancock had passed Spottsylvania Court-House on Sunday morning, the 8th'—not true, ... 'Grant, on that day, was on the march to join me...' —not true, ... "General Grant's operations had proved a great success and a complete victory'—not true, and 'the only hope of Lee was in heavy reinforcements from Beauregard'—which I knew was futile ..." (Butler, p. 646).

The sequence of events in the field for Generals Butler, Lee and Grant, May 6–9, 1864, can be further illuminated in the following sources: Freeman, pp. 306–08; Grant, pp. 411, 423–25, 432–33; Freeman (LL), Vol. III, pp. 378, 387 and chapter 3: "Spottsylvania Courthouse"; Humphreys, pp. 57, 138; Robertson, pp. 109, 119; Bearss, p. 313.

Major General George McClellan was thoroughly persuaded that Edwin Stanton wished to prolong the war to further the Radical agenda, specifically that the war must continue until the Northern public was willing to abolish slavery nationwide (McClellan, pp. 149–51).

5   ALP: Letter from Blair to Lincoln, December 6, 1864.

6   *See* note 7 for Chapter 4: "The Radicals' Campaign to Replace Lincoln and His Supporters"

7   CW, Vol. VIII, p. 399–401 (footnotes): Letter from Chase to Lincoln, April 11, 1865

8   Ibid

9   Ibid, pp. 399–405

10 Ibid, p. 399

CHAPTER 6: AGENTS & SECRETS

1   Raymond, p. 795

2   Ibid, p. 794

3   Ibid, p. 794–95

4   James Donaldson and his role in Booth's gang is repeatedly described in the confessions of George Atzerodt and Samuel Arnold, yet is conspicuously absent from all trial transcripts and media reports following the assassination. *See* Appendices C and D.

5   James Hall, described by George Atzerodt, was also not investigated, prosecuted or reported in the media. Some historians have asserted that James Hall was one of Lewis Powell's many aliases; however, Atzerodt described Hall as being *with* James Wood [Lewis Powell] on an errand. Hall was another Booth associate protected by the War Department. Baker relied on agents within the Post Office for much of his information gathering, and Booth's associates—Harbin, Slater, Surratt, Weichmann, Hall—were either known postal employees or described as being at or on errands to and from post offices. Of the postal employees identified, *only* John Surratt was ever prosecuted. *See* Appendix C.

6   Larson, p. 30

7   Weichmann, p. 30

8   BAKER'S INFILTRATORS. Baker had a detective force of former cavalrymen and informants, numbering up to an estimate of 2,000 at one time, beyond the reach of judicial scrutiny (Stern, pp. 73–74). Even before Baker's post with Stanton, it was the War Department's policy to monitor suspected and known Confederate spies for as long as they were useful. One notable example would be that of Mrs. Rose Greenhow, an educated widow and legitimate spy who lived only blocks from the alleged spy Mary Surratt. At the order of the Secretary of War, Greenhow's home was thoroughly surveilled and infiltrated, by male and female agents, and her doings were documented for months before she was finally shut down (Stern, pp. 54–64).

9   Larson, Chapter 3

10   Scheips, p. 402

11   Bowen & Neal, p. 13

12   GAC

13   TRIAL: Testimony of Augustus Howell concerning Mary Surratt

14   Clark, pp. 6–9

15   Chamlee, p. 171

16   TRIAL: Testimony of Augustus Howell concerning Mary Surratt

17   Pinkerton, pp. 74–75

18   GAC

19   Kate Warne has been erroneously named as the Pinkerton agent in the photograph below (gripping the tent pole) by some recent Civil War enthusiasts (Allan Pinkerton is the bearded, seated gentleman).

The individual in this photograph is *not* a cross-dressing Kate Warne, but Pinkerton's documented agent John Babcock, who was also photographed that very same day (in the exact same outfit) in the image below.

CHAPTER 7: A BAND OF IDIOTS

1 John Surratt's Lecture in Rockville, Maryland, Dec. 6, 1870

2 TRIAL: Testimony by Louis J. Weichmann relevant concerning Dr. Mudd

3 GAC; *See also* Appendix C

4 CW, Vol. VII, p. 164

5 SAC; *See also* Appendix D

6 TRIAL: Testimony by McPhail concerning Michael O'Laughlen

7 Booth departed on business trips related to oil speculation in New York, Pennsylvania, Boston and Canada. A month into his travels, Booth was laid up with an ailment at the house of his brother Edwin. He wasn't seen again by his coconspirators from Baltimore until January, 1865. (SAC) Booth's months-long absence from Maryland was punctuated by one brief visit (Bryantown and Baltimore, November 13–14, 1864).

8 John Surratt's Lecture in Rockville, Maryland, Dec. 6, 1870

9 SAC

10 Ibid

11 Chamlee, p. 171

12 SAC

13 Yates as the oarsman comes from Atzerodt: GAC

14 SAC

15 *New York Herald*, March 18, 1865; *also* CW, Vol. VIII, p. 362

16 TRIAL: Testimony by Mrs. Van Tine concerning Michael O'Laughlen

17 TRIAL: Testimony by Louis J. Weichmann concerning Lewis Powell

18 TRIAL: Testimony by Louis J. Weichmann concerning Mary E. Surratt

19 TRIAL: Testimony by Louis J. Weichmann concerning Lewis Powell

20 SAC

21 Chamlee, p. 16

22 Ibid

23 Ibid

24 GAC

25 Steers, p. lxii

26 Hanchett, p. 52

27 Burlingame, p. 653

28 Hanchett, p. 52

29 GAC

30 Hanchett, p. 53

31 Gillette, p. 17

32 USC 1097, p. 2

33 Fanny, pp. 183, 191

CHAPTER 8: WEAPON & MOTIVE

1 CW, Vol. VIII, pp. 399–405: Lincoln's last public address.

2 WE, THE LOYAL PEOPLE, DIFFER ... AS TO THE MODE, MANNER, AND MEANS OF RECONSTRUCTION. Lincoln referred specifically to the fierce struggle between the Radicals and Lincoln's conservative supporters, which had culminated in both houses of Congress passing the Wade-Davis Bill (the Radical agenda for reconstruction), which Lincoln had just vetoed. *See* note 8 for Chapter 4: § "Abraham Lincoln."

3 Lincoln's unnamed critic is Salmon P. Chase, who agreed with Sumner's "suicide doctrine," that states whose politicians led them into rebellion had forfeited their right to self-government, and thus must re-enter the Union as territories. Lincoln's position was denial that the Confederate states had actually legally seceded. By yielding to Congress the authority to readmit Confederate states, it would be the "fatal admission" that those states had indeed left the Union (McPherson, p. 713). Chase argued that the Confederate states ought to remain, for some time to come, under martial law.

4 NO EXCLUSIVE AND INFLEXIBLE PLAN. The Wade-Davis Bill was a singular prescription for the fate of all Confederate states. While Lincoln rejected the concept of an inflexible plan, he insisted on *inflexible principles*, chief among which was the insistence that the rebel states had always been part of a "common nation" (CW, Vol. VIII, pp. 220–21), had never seceded (see previous note), and would retain the Constitutional rights of self-governance.

Rather than rely on a singular plan, Lincoln intended for reconstruction to deal with each state's issues on an individual basis. Part of Chase's singular prescription was a recurring theme in his letter was for immediate voting suffrage for all black males. This item was crucial to Chase in order that 1.6 million Northern-friendly [colored] voters be allowed to participate. Though Lincoln supported the eventual emergence of black suffrage, he felt it unconstitutional to mandate it under martial law.

5   CW, Vol. VIII, p. 401

6   Reck, pp. 34–35

7   Seward, p. 256–57

8   Welles (G), "Lincoln & Johnson," p. 526

9   Ibid

10 CW, Vol. VIII, p. 332–33: Lincoln's second inaugural address

11 AHPH, p. 160

12 GAC; *See also* Appendix C

13 Ibid

CHAPTER 9: REASSURANCE

1   On February 21, 1864, the Radicals openly and publicly attacked the President with a circular posted in two Washington newspapers, the *Constitutional Union* and the *Intelligencer*. The posted letter opposed Lincoln's renomination and advocated Treasury Secretary Salmon P. Chase in his place. The next day Chase responded to Lincoln's reaction, lavishly praising the President, while admitting having differences of opinion. Chase stated, "For yourself I cherish sincere respect and esteem; and, permit me to add, affection." The Treasury Secretary flatly denied having any knowledge of the circular, though he admitted consulting with the nominating committee about the inclusion of his name for consideration for the party's nomination, but with the insistence that he "could render them no help," and that his full attention was on running the Treasury. He went on to explain to Lincoln that the committee presumed, after his conversation with them, mistaking his intentions for using his name, claiming "I was not consulted about it; nor have I been consulted as to its action; nor do I even know who compose [the committee]."

However, it was later proven in 1874 that Chase lied to Lincoln about his knowledge of the circular, and that he himself had fully approved it, the publication of his name, and an arraignment of Lincoln's administration (CW, Vol. VII, pp. 200–01).

Two months after Chase lied to Lincoln, and only two weeks before the Republican Convention, Lincoln's Secretary of War, Edwin Stanton, took deliberate actions to prolong the war to aid in the promotion of a Radical candidate for President (*see* note 4 for Chapter 5: "Stanton Prolongs the War").

2 Salmon Chase had threatened the President on many occasions with his resignation if Lincoln would not agree to the customs house collectors the Treasury Secretary preferred, and Lincoln was well aware of the game Chase was playing. Any judicial claims concerning government property fell under the jurisdiction of the Treasury Secretary and his department agents. Salmon Chase was taking full advantage of his power and position by overlooking customs house corruption in exchange for their patronage to him (and against Lincoln).

Customs house patronage was rewarded with appointments and promotions and the collector for the Port of New York was one of the most prestigious appointments awarded by the Treasury Department. The New York Customs House controlled the most congressional votes of any state in the Union, and corrupt practices of theft and bribery had caused Congress to investigate their affairs (Hart, pp. 217–18). Lincoln had learned from, Moses H. Grinnell, a New York businessman, that a special agent for Salmon Chase, John Bailey, had called on the Congressional Committee Chairman in advance of the inquiry to smother the investigation (CW, Vol. VII, p. 181).

This competition over votes became the beginning of the end between President Lincoln and the Treasury Secretary. Chase was secretly trying to rob Lincoln of the 1864 Republican nomination for president, and when he was publicly discovered he lied to the President about his secret campaign committee (CW Vol. VII p. 201).

This situation finally ended in June after Lincoln accepted the resignation Chase had previously offered, thus dismissing him from his Cabinet post (CW, Vol. VII p. 419), replacing him with Senator William P. Fessenden.

3 Crook, William H. "The Home Life of Abraham Lincoln." *The Saturday Evening Post*, June 4, 1910.

4 Ibid, pp. 365–66 states: "On the day of the illumination, Mrs. Lincoln made plans for a small theater-party on the following evening, Friday, April 14, to see ... 'Our American Cousin.' Lincoln reluctantly acceded to Mrs.

Lincoln's request that he should be present, and suggested that General and Mrs. Grant be invited to join the party.

"The invitation was given and accepted, but when Stanton heard of it he made a vigorous protest, having in mind the numerous threats of assassination which had come to his notice through secret service agents and otherwise."

5   Brooks, p. 257

6   Reck, p. 54

7   Crook (F), p. 66

8   Reck, p. 54

9   Crook (M), p. 40

10   Bates, p. 367

11   Ibid

12   Ibid, pp. 367–68; *see also* note 4, in which Stanton diverts the Grants from Ford's Theatre.

CHAPTER 10: "I SAW JOHN WILKES BOOTH!"

1   Reck, p. 96

2   Chamlee, p. 118

3   Ibid, p. 53

4   Ibid

5   Kunhardt, p. 11

6   Ibid, p. 12

7   Reck, p. 98

8   Ibid

9   Ibid, p. 100

10   Ibid. Ferguson, two years later at the trial of John Surratt, Jr., omitted Booth using his knee to force the door open, simply stating that Booth "pushed open the door to the passage leading to the private boxes."

11   Parker arrived the next morning with a woman named Lizzie, whom Parker
     alleged was a prostitute. She was released without charges (National Ar-
     chives: Records of the Metropolitan Police Department, April 15, 1865).

12   Charge sheet against John Parker, dated May 1, 1865, an image of which
     was printed in the *Washington Sunday Star*, February 9, 1936.

13   Reck, p. 162

CHAPTER 11: THE CHAMBER MAID

1   All dialogue and events described in this chapter, unless noted otherwise, are
     taken directly from the transcripts of eyewitnesses (TRIAL: Testimonies of
     William Bell, Maj. Augustus Seward, Sgt. George F. Robinson, Emerick W.
     Hansell, and Surgeon General Joseph K. Barnes concerning Lewis Powell).

2   GAC

3   Gillette, p. 17. Reverend Gillette, who interviewed Lewis Powell, reported:
     "It was early in that day [of the assassination] that he [Powell] was instructed
     as to what was expected of him. A bottle of medicine was given to him and
     the pretext ... by which he would gain access to the Secretary's apartment."

4   Fanny, p. 183

5   TRIAL: Weichmann's testimony May 25

6   Baker (L), p. 486: Lafayette Baker stated that "Payne" had been identified
     by an informant lodging at the Surratt House, and that Payne had visited
     the house on two occasions using the name "Wood."

7   Fanny, p. 183

8   GAC

9   IMPEACH, p. 488

10   Fanny, p. 191

CHAPTER 12: OBSTRUCTION OF JUSTICE

1   The fourth dispatch of April 27th, 1865, to the *New York Tribune* from their
     reporter present at the autopsy of Booth quoted David Herold as saying:
     "Booth broke his leg on the stage."

2   John Wilkes Booth's autopsy reports: Mutter Medical Museum of the Col-
    lege of Physicians of Philadelphia, National Museum of Health and Medi-
    cine at the Walter Reed Army Medical Center.

3   Chamlee, p. 290

4   After the trail, when investigators approached Major Thomas Eckert regard-
    ing Atzerodt's withheld confession, Eckert stated that they were on file in
    the War Department, where they ought to be. The records of the prosecu-
    tion were also duplicated at the National Archives. Subsequent searches of
    the War Department and the National Archives failed to locate Atzerodt's
    suppressed confessions (Tidwell, pp. 417–18).

5   Steers, p. 27

6   SAC

7   The fourth dispatch of April 27th, 1865, to the *New York Tribune* from their
    reporter present at the autopsy of Booth recorded that the assassin was car-
    rying about $105 in greenbacks and sundry Canadian bills.

8   THE MUSIC STAND. James Ford, John T. Ford's eldest son, hurriedly wrote
    newspaper articles and handbills for the 2:00 PM press time, announcing
    that Lincoln and Grant would appear together at Ford's Theatre. This was
    the first public notice that the presidential party would be at Ford's and not
    Grover's Theatre.
        Clay Ford, the younger brother of James, supervised the accommoda-
    tions being prepared for the state box. Booth's friend, Ed Spangler, was one
    of seven employees that helped with the decorations. Theater boxes 7 and 8
    were divided by a heavy, wooden partition that was removed to make them
    into a larger, single box. A velvet covered sofa, along with velvet covered
    chairs and a rocking chair from the reception room, were added to provide
    the theater's most comfortable seating.
        The day clerk at the National Hotel discovered in Booth's trunk, after
    the assassination, a small hole-boring tool with a screw point and handles.
        It was 97 years after the assassination when the Ford's theater historian,
    Dr. George J. Olszeoski, was provided a requested response from Clay Ford's
    elderly son, Frank Ford, to questions he had about the preparations made
    in the theater's state box. Frank Ford argued in his reply that Booth was not
    the one who bored the hole in the state box door, but instead it was made by
    one of the theater employees. He claimed a hole was made for John Parker
    to look into the box to check on the Presidential party, rather than having
    to open the door. The notch in the floor to secure the music stand against
    the door, according to Frank Ford, could not have been created by Booth.

Whoever bored the hole through the door and carved a mortise to secure the music stand can never be known for sure. Of course, the Ford family would not want their ancestors to appear complicit in the assassination of Lincoln. It is *evidence*, and not testimony, that can be trusted to determine the logical truths, and in truth the state box was prepared for the murder. Booth's whereabouts for the day of April 14 can be accounted for, except for the time between 5:00 and 6:30 PM. This would provide a window of opportunity for cutting the peephole and notching the floor of the state box to accommodate the music stand, but this can't be known for certain. However, the fact that the notch and music stand were used *only* by Booth to bar the door shows that he, or an accomplice, altered the box for that intention. As the occupants of Lincoln's state box cried out that the President had been shot, doctors and officers present in the theater tried in vain to access the theater box. Major Rathbone stated in an affidavit that when he reached the vestibule's outer door he found it jammed by a music stand, which he had to pull from its notch with some effort before tossing it aside (Reck, p. 118). A music stand is an improvised device for obstructing a door, and for Booth to know it was there, along with a notch in the floor made to fit the stand, reveals that these were present that day for Booth's purpose.

It is too remote a coincidence to even consider that Booth only discovered the music stand, there in the dark, after entering the state box with his single-minded intention to shoot the President. What's more, he discovers a freshly-carved notch at a perfect angle and location to brace the large stand against the door. Booth had to know beforehand that the music stand would be there.

Chapter 13: Lie or Die!

1   Chamlee, p. 76

2   Ibid, p. 62

3   Ibid, p. 67

4   Ibid, p. 76

5   Ibid

6   Ibid, p. 23

7   TRIAL: Testimony by Louis J. Weichmann concerning Mary Surratt, May 13, 1865

8 FRAMING O'LAUGHLEN. Interestingly, Stanton's son, David, and two companions (John C. Hatter and Maj. Kilburn Knox), testified that Michael O'Laughlen showed up at the Stanton residence on the night of April 13th (a day before the attacks on Lincoln and Seward) asking for Edwin Stanton and General Grant, allegedly to assassinate them both. They described O'Laughlen as with a black moustache and dressed entirely in black.

MICHAEL O'LAUGHLEN died serving his life-sentence as a conspirator. On the night of the assassination he was elsewhere, dressed in the plaid vest and pants shown in above, in the company of multiple witnesses, including the tailor who made the outfit.

On that night, at the time specified by the Stanton house's witnesses, Michael O'Laughlen was dressed in a Scottish plaid vest and pants, socializing with numerous people (several of note) at Ruhlman's Hotel, who corroborated his alibi: Bernard S. Early (the tailor who made O'Laughlen's vest), Edward Murphy, Lieut. James B. Henderson (U.S. Navy, who invited Michael), Daniel Loughran (owner of a boardinghouse in D.C.), George Grillet (a salesman from New York), Henry E. Purdy (superintendent of Ruhlman's Hotel), John H. Fuller (a local businessman), John E. Giles (the hotel's bartender), F. H. Maulsby (O'Laughlen's brother-in-law, a Baltimore businessman). (TRIAL: Testimonies concerning Michael O'Laughlen)

On the night of the 14th, when Lincoln was fatally shot, O'Laughlen was still in the company of several of these men, including Daniel Loughran, John Fuller, and Lieutenant Henderson.

O'Laughlen was convicted as a conspirator to assassination on the testimonies of Louis J. Weichmann and the witnesses from Stanton's house and sentenced to life in prison. He was sent to Fort Jefferson penitentiary in Florida, where he died two years later of yellow fever.

9 TRIAL: Weichmann's testimony concerning Mary Surratt, cross-examination on May 18th, 1865

10 GAC

11   TRIAL: Testimony of Colonel W. R. Nevins concerning George Atzerodt

12   TRIAL: Testimony of John Lee concerning George Atzerodt

13   GAC

14   TRIAL: Testimony of Marshal James L. McPhail concerning George Atzerodt

15   TRIAL: Testimony of John Lee concerning George Atzerodt

16   TRIAL: Testimony of John Greenawalt concerning George Atzerodt

17   TRIAL: Testimony of James Walker concerning George Atzerodt

18   TRIAL: Testimony of Robert R. Jones concerning George Atzerodt

19   TRIAL: Testimony of Lyman S. Sprague concerning George Atzerodt

20   TRIAL: Testimony of John Lee concerning George Atzerodt

21   LAE, pp. 1323–24

22   LAE, p. 1327

23   LAE, p. 1328

24   TRIAL: Testimony of Louis J. Weichmann concerning Mary E. Surratt

25   TRIAL: Testimony of R. C. Morgan concerning Mary E. Surratt

26   TRIAL: Testimony of Captain W. M. Wermerskirch concerning Mary E. Surratt

27   TRIAL: Testimony of George B. Wood concerning Mary E. Surratt

28   TRIAL: Testimony of Miss Anna E. Surratt concerning Mary E. Surratt

29   TRIAL: Affidavit of Louis J. Weichmann

30   Chamlee, p. 151

CHAPTER 14: FOLLOWING THE SCRIPT

1   Steers, p. lxii

2   Leonard, p. 114

3   TRIAL: Testimony of Dr. Samuel A. H. McKim concerning David Herold

4   TRIAL: Testimony of Dr. Charles W. Davis concerning David Herold; *See also* notes 5–9 for Chapter 1.

5　*The New York Times*, April 26, 1864

6　*The Richmond Times*, April 24, 1864

7　TRIAL:　Comments of W. E. Doster (Atzerodt's attorney) during the testimony of James L. McPhail concerning George A. Atzerodt.

> **DISMISSAL OF ATZERODT'S CONFESSION.** George Atzerodt, upon his arrest and under extreme duress, confessed that he was to assassinate Vice President Andrew Johnson. That admission was accepted by the court, and for it Atzerodt would be put to death. The confession to which Doster is questioning Marshall McPhail was taken eleven days later, after Atzerodt had been sequestered in the belly of a ship, in irons with a bag over his head. Atzerodt's confession to McPhail was given away from guards, and in the company of his brother and brother-in-law under no duress. This confession said nothing of assassination plans, and in it Atzerodt named everyone he knew to be associated with the kidnapping plot (*see* Appendix C). Doster asked the court to ignore the confession on the grounds that it was rendered under duress, which was absolutely not the case.

8　Pitman, p. 70

9　GAC

10　TRIAL:　Testimony of Colonel W. R. Nevins concerning George Atzerodt

> **ATZERODT AT THE KIRKWOOD.** Though the clerk testified Atzerodt had checked into the Kirkwood on the 14th, the testimony of Nevins placed him at the hotel on the 12th. Atzerodt, in his confession, stated he was there at least two days, though he spent only one night there, and left with David Herold on the 14th at 7:30 PM. Investigators reported searching the room on the 15th where they found Herold's coat and personal belongings, agreeing with Atzerodt's statement.

11　Atzerodt was residing at the Kirkwood since the 12th "to try and get papers to Richmond from Mr. Johnson. ... He would get them out of the Theatre" (GAC). Booth had rented a box to attend Grover's Theatre the evening of April 14th. That morning Booth stopped at Grover's Theatre, and afterward went to the Kirkwood to inquire of Johnson (Reck, pp. 67–68).

12　CW, Vol. VIII, p. 410

13　Booth, p. 146

14　TRIAL:　Testimony of Mary Jane Anderson concerning John Wilkes Booth

15　TRIAL:　Testimony of John Miles concerning John Wilkes Booth

16   TRIAL: Testimony of Louis J. Weichmann concerning Mary E. Surratt

17   GAC: At no time does Atzerodt say the name "Payne" (or Paine), but iden- tifies Lewis Powell only as Wood or his nickname Mosby.

18   Ibid

19   TRIAL: Testimony of Honora Fitzpatrick concerning Mary E. Surratt. "I do not know him by any other name."

20   TRIAL: Testimony of Anna E. Surratt concerning Mary E. Surratt. "I do not know him by the name of Payne at all."

21   TRIAL: Testimony of John T. Holohan concerning Mary E. Surratt. "The name by which I knew him was Wood."

22   TRIAL: Testimony of Mrs. Eliza Holohan concerning Mary E. Surratt. "I asked Miss Anna Surratt who he was, and she said he was a Mr. Wood, a Baptist minister."

23   Baker, p. 486

24   TRIAL: Testimony of Captain W. H. Wermerskirch concerning Mary E. Surratt

25   TRIAL: Testimony of Thomas Price concerning Lewis Payne

26   TRIAL: Testimony of Sergeant George F. Robinson concerning Lewis Payne

27   TRIAL: Testimony of Dr. T. S. Verdi concerning Lewis Payne

28   TRIAL: Testimony of H. H. Wells concerning Lewis Payne

29   TRIAL: Testimony of William H. Bell concerning Lewis Payne

30   TRIAL: Testimony of Major Augustus Seward concerning Lewis Payne

31   GAC: Atzerodt stated Booth had an appointment to see James Donaldson on Friday evening (Donaldson's name was censored from Samuel Arnold's confession; Donaldson was never pursued by investigators or mentioned during the trial; and Booth and Powell had no assassination plans until less than a day before the deed).

CHAPTER 15: ONE MAN

1   Mogalever, p. 111

2   Bowen & Neal, p. 13

3   Chamlee, p. 117

4   Ibid

5   Winkler, Chapter 2: "Vanished without a Trace: Sarah Slater"

6   Leech, p. 158. Stanton personally ordered that the horses and even the groceries obtained by the party be confiscated. The minister, Buck Bailey, was held longest in prison.

7   The transcript of Booth's diary can be found in multiple locations, including photographs available online (http://boothiebarn.com/picture-galleries/found-on-booth/), and during President Andrew Johnson's impeachment investigation the diary was read aloud by Judge Advocate General Joseph Holt before Congress and retranscripted (IMPEACH, pp. 286–87).

8   Ibid

9   Ibid

10 Ibid

11 Louis Weichmann's affidavit

CHAPTER 16: MEANS OF ESCAPE

1   Tanner, p. 516

2   Fehrenbacher, p. 93

3   Stanton's "original gorilla" comment is a reference to the recently published *The Origin of Species* by Charles Darwin (1859), thus calling Lincoln a backwards, unevolved creature.

4   Flower, p. 109

5   Bates, p. 161

6   Scheips, p. 402

7   SAC

8   Baker, p. 485

9   IMPEACH, p. 673

CHAPTER 17: THE STACKED DECK

1 http://civilwarsignals.org, accessed 2011–12
   Glen Burnie, Maryland: Signal Corps. Association (1860 to 1865)

2 Mogalever, pp. 86–88

3 **BAKER'S REIGN OF TERROR.** The following is excerpted from *Secret Missions of the Civil War* by Philip Van Doren Stern:

> Lucius E. Chittenden, Register of the Treasury, has a poor opinion of Lafayette C. Baker. In 1891, he said of him: "He took into his service ... men who claimed to have any aptitude for detective work, without recommendation, investigation, or any inquiry, beyond his own inspection, which he claimed immediately disclosed to him the character and abilities of the applicant. How large his regiment ultimately grew is uncertain, but at one time he asserted that it exceeded two thousand men.
>
> With this force at his command, protected against interference from the judicial authorities, Baker became a law unto himself. He instituted a veritable Reign of Terror. He dealt with every accused person in the same manner; with a reputable citizen as with a deserter or petty thief. He did not require the formality of a written charge; it was quite sufficient for any person to suggest to Baker that a citizen might be doing something that was against the law. He was immediately arrested, handcuffed, and brought to Baker's office, at that time in the basement of the Treasury. There he was subjected to a browbeating examination, in which Baker was said to rival in impudence some heads of the criminal bar. This examination was repeated as often as he chose. Men were kept in his rooms for weeks, without warrant, affidavit, or other semblance of authority. If the accused took any measures for his own protection, he was hurried into the Old Capitol Prison, where he was beyond the reach of the civil authorities. ... [Baker] seemed to control the Old Capitol Prison, and one of his deputies [William P. Wood] was its keeper. He always lived at the finest hotels, hand an abundance of money, and I am sure did more to disgust good citizens and bring the government into disrepute than the strongest opponents of the [detective] system had ever predicted.

4 Goodwin (J), p. 240

5 Baker, p. 525

6 Ibid, p. 531

7   Chamlee, p. 151

8   Ibid, p. 152

9   Baker, Ray, p. 581

10 Goodrich, p. 227

11 The entire photographic process was carefully guarded so that nobody except Stanton and Baker at War Department would ever see them. The following account was given by Baker's detective James A. Wardell:

> "Under no circumstances was I to allow [Gardner] or his assistant out of my sight until they had taken a picture and made the print, and then I was to bring the print and the [negative] back to the War Department and give it only to Col. Baker or Secretary of War Stanton. … [The photographer] was told that only one plate was to be made and it was to have only one print made and both were to be given to me when finished. […]
>
> "Gardner took the plate and then gave it to the assistant and told him to take it and develop it and to make one print. I went with him and even went into the dark room. About 4:00 in the afternoon I got the plate and the print from the assistant and took it to the War Department. I went in to the outer office and Col. Baker was just coming out of the War Office. I gave him the plate and print and he stepped to one side and pulled it from the envelope. He looked at it and then dismissed me." (Katz, pp. 161–62)

12 The Military Commission received Boston Corbett's testimony with amusement, but obvious disbelief, they still gave him credit for killing Booth. Conger testified that he heard a pistol shot and thought that Booth had shot himself. Corbett carried only a rifle. Conger said Booth was holding a pistol in his hand after the shot. (Chamlee, p. 289)

13 When Luther Baker testified to the Committee on Claims regarding the death of Booth, he stated that his "first impression was that Conger shot him; his second, that if Conger shot him, 'it had better not be known.'" (DeWitt, p. 278)

14 FOLLOW THE MONEY. The Committee on Claims initially awarded Lafayette Baker and Conger $17,500 each from the $75,000 reward for the capture of John Wilkes Booth. However, after public protest by Conger (where Luther Baker asserted he thought Conger shot Booth) the Committee revised the award as follows (DeWitt, p. 277):

$15,000.00   Everton Conger (Booth's assassin)
  5,250.00   Edward P. Doherty (head of the detachment)
  3,750.00   Lafayette Baker "to his unutterable disgust"
  3,000.00   Luther Baker (witness to the shooting of Booth)
  1,653.65   Boston Corbett (the same as the rest of the detachment)

15   Chamlee, p. 290

16   *Washington Evening Star*, April 15, 1890.

17   Chamlee, p. 147

18   Klement, p. 138

19   Mogalever, pp. 278–92

20   Baker, pp. 452–76

21   Headley, pp. 211–382

22   John Wilkes Booth had been arrested by the provost marshal of St. Louis in 1862 for publicly making anti-government remarks (Hanchett, p. 41), and was at that time under surveillance. While under arrest Booth took an oath of allegiance (LAE, p. 852).

23   The very definition of "stacked deck," and "conflict of interest," and "miscarriage of justice," is that Joseph Holt, the Chief Prosecutor (Radical Republican, War Department insider) was the legal advisor to the military tribunal which decided the fates of the accused (Linder, Doug. UMKC Law Library, "The Trial of the Lincoln Assassination Conspirators." http://law2.umkc.edu/faculty/projects/ftrials/lincolnconspiracy/lincolnaccount.html, accessed April, 2013).

CHAPTER 18: TESTIMONY VS. EVIDENCE

1   Chamlee, p. 212

2   *Congressional Globe*, 40th Congress, 1st Session, March 26, 1867, p. 363.

3   Chamlee, p. 216

4   Cyrus B. Comstock Papers, Box 8

5   Cottrell, p. 166

6   Steers, Edward and James L. Swanson. *The Lincoln Assassination Encyclopedia*. New York: Harper Collins, 2010.

7   TRIAL: Testimony of Godfrey Hyams

8   Chamlee, p. 39

9   Schroeder-Lein, p. 275

10 Stewart, pp. 65–66

11 Chamlee, p. 362

12 Kauffmann, pp. 363–64

CHAPTER 19: "HOW IMPOTENT IS JUSTICE!"

1   Raymond, p. 795

2   Swanson, pp. 333–58

3   Kunhardt, p. 123

4   In addition to the efforts of Congressmen and spies (such as Baker) to build
    a case against Johnson, Stanton used his own Cabinet-level access to leak
    information about the executive to his Radical collaborators (Schroeder-
    Lein, p. 275).

5   Fessenden, p. 186

6   Hanchett, p. 85

7   Swanson, pp. 333–58

8   IMPEACH, p. 32

9   Ibid

10 Chamlee, p. 292

11 IMPEACH, pp. 2–12

12 Hanchett, p. 83

13 Lincoln described his own reconstruction policy (in his Proclamation of
    Amnesty and Reconstruction, plus his final public addresses, letters and
    cabinet meeting) as consisting of: [1] recognizing the Southern states as
    never having seceded, thus maintaining their rights of self-governance and
    Congressional representation; [2] amnesty for rebel leaders; [3] return of
    Southern assets; [4] asserting the Executive (not Congressional) right to de-
    termine reconstruction policy; and [5] an avoidance of using martial law or
    executive orders to govern reconstruction or alter the institution of slavery.

Andrew Johnson's position on reconstruction was less liberal than Lincoln's, yet he was nevertheless impeached by Congress for defending Executive powers, and specifically for using them to curtail the Radical reconstruction agenda in Congress. Many of the charges against Johnson were related to his attempts to remove Edwin Stanton, which the Radicals attempted to interpret as a crime. During Johnson's tenure many of the conditions of the Radical's Wade-Davis bill, which Lincoln had vetoed by deliberate neglect, were included in the 14th Amendment, and (by compromise) included also in Johnson's reconstruction policy.

14   *Congressional Globe*, March 26, 1867, p. 363

15   *Congressional Globe*, July 8, 1867, pp. 515–22

16   IMPEACH, pp. 29, 282

17   IMPEACH, p. 111

18   *Congressional Globe*, March 26, 1867, p. 364

19   Ibid, p. 363

20   The Tenure of Office Act was designed to deny the Executive branch the authority to dismiss certain officers without Senate approval. When passed Johnson vetoed the bill. Congress then overrode Johnson's veto. The Act was for the express purpose to keep Radicals like Edwin Stanton in power, and to keep the President from interfering with the Radical reconstruction plan (which Lincoln had also opposed). The Tenure of Office Act had no other purpose than to serve the Radical agenda, and was repealed in 1887.

EPILOGUE

1   Kunhardt, p. 139

2   Cottrell, inside front cover

3   Ibid

4   Clark, p. 138

5   Ibid, p. 139

6   McPherson, pp. 374–76

7   Fessenden, p. 186

APPENDIX A

Booth's 1864 Manifesto

Below is a reproduction of what was published in the *Philadelphia Inquirer*, April 21, 1865:

(Begin editorial comments of the newspaper)

THE MURDERER OF MR. LINCOLN — Extraordinary Letter of John Wilkes Booth — Proof that He Meditated His Crime Months Ago — His Excuses for the Contemplated Act — His Participation in the Execution of John Brown.

The following verbatim copy of a letter, in writing which is the hand-writing of JOHN WILKES BOOTH, the murderer of President LINCOLN, has been furnished us by the Hon. WM. MILLWARD, United States Marshal of the Eastern District of Pennsylvania. It was handed over to that officer by JOHN S. CLARKE, who is a brother-in-law of Mr. BOOTH. The history connected with it is somewhat peculiar. In November, 1864, the paper was deposited with Mr. CLARKE by BOOTH, in a sealed envelope, "for safe keeping," Mr. CLARKE being ignorant of the contents. In January last BOOTH called at Mr. CLARKE's house, asked for the package and it was given up to him. It is now supposed that at that time he took out the paper and added to it his signature, which appears to be in a different ink from that used in the body of the letter, and also from the language employed could not have been put to it originally. Afterward he returned the package to Mr. CLARKE again for safe keeping, sealed and bearing the superscription, "J. WILKES BOOTH."

The inclosure was preserved by the family without suspicion of its nature. After the afflicting information of the assassination of the President, which came upon the family of Mr. CLARKE with crushing force, it was considered proper to open the envelope. There was found in it the following paper, with some 7–30 United States bonds, and a certificate of shares in oil companies. Mr. CLARKE promptly handed over the paper to Marshal MILLWARD, in whose custody it now remains. From a perusal of this paper it seems to have been prepared by BOOTH as a vindication of some desperate act which he had in contemplation; and, from the language used, it is probable that it was a plot to abduct the President and carry him off to Virginia. If this was meditated it failed, and from making a prisoner of the President to his assassination was an easy step for a man of perverted principles. It also appears that BOOTH was one of the party who was engaged in the capture and execution of JOHN BROWN, of Ossawattomie, at which time he doubtless imbibed from WISE and his associates those detestable sentiments of cruelty which have culminated in an infamous crime. The letter is as follows:

(Begin Booth's "manifesto" as published)

_____, _____, 1864

MY DEAR SIR, — You may use this as you think best. But as some may wish to know when, who and why, and as I know not how to direct it, I give it (in the words of your master): "TO WHOM IT MAY CONCERN."

Right or wrong, God judge me, not man. For be my motive good or bad, of one thing I am sure, the lasting condemnation of the North.

I love peace more than life. Have loved the Union beyond expression. For four years have I waited, hoped and prayed for the dark clouds to break, and for a restoration of our former sunshine. To wait longer would be a crime. All hope for peace is dead. My prayers have proved as idle as my hopes. God's will be done. I go to see and share the bitter end.

I have ever held the South were right. The very nomination of ABRAHAM LINCOLN, four years ago, spoke plainly, war — war upon Southern rights and institutions. His election proved it. "Await an overt act." Yes, till you are bound and plundered. What folly! The South were wise. Who thinks of argument or patience when the finger of his enemy presses on the trigger? In a foreign war I, too, could say, "country, right or wrong." But in a struggle such as ours, (where the brother tries to pierce the brother's heart,) for God's sake, choose the right. When a country like this spurns justice from her side she forfeits the allegiance of every honest freeman, and should leave him, untrameled by any fealty soever, to act as his conscience may approve.

People of the North, to hate tyranny, to love liberty and justice, to strike at wrong and oppression, was the teaching of our fathers. The study of our early history will not let me forget it, and may it never.

This country was formed for the white, not for the black man. And looking upon African Slavery from the same stand-point held by the noble framers of our constitution, I, for one, have ever considered it one of the greatest blessings (both for themselves and us,) that God has ever bestowed upon a favored nation. Witness heretofore our wealth and power; witness their elevation and enlightenment above their race elsewhere. I have lived among it most of my life, and have seen less harsh treatment from master to man than I have beheld in the North from father to son. Yet, Heaven knows, no one would be more willing to do more for the negro race than I, could I but see a way to still better their condition.

But LINCOLN's policy is only preparing the way for their total annihilation. The South are not, nor have they been, fighting for the continuance of slavery. The first battle of Bull Run did away with that idea. Their causes since for war have been as noble and greater far than those that urged our fathers on. Even should we allow they were wrong at the beginning of this contest, cruelty and injustice have made the wrong become the right, and they stand now (before the wonder and admiration of the world) as a noble band of patriotic heroes. Hereafter, reading of their deeds, Thermopylae will be forgotten.

When I aided in the capture and execution of JOHN BROWN (who was a murderer on our Western border, and who was fairly tried and convicted, before an impartial judge and jury, of treason, and who, by the way, has since been made a god), I was proud of my little share in the transaction, for I deemed it my duty, and that I was helping our common country to perform an act of justice. But what was a crime in poor JOHN BROWN is now considered (by themselves) as the greatest and only virtue of the whole Republican party. Strange transmigration! Vice to become a virtue, simply because more indulge in it!

I thought then, as now, that the Abolitionists were the only traitors in the land, and that the entire party deserved the same fate as poor old BROWN, not because they wish to abolish slavery, but on account of the means they have ever endeavored to use to effect that abolition. If BROWN were living I doubt whether he himself would set slavery against the Union. Most or many in the North do, and openly curse the Union, if the South are to return and retain a single right guarantied to them by every tie which we once revered as sacred. The South can make no choice. It is either extermination or slavery for themselves (worse than death) to draw from. I know my choice.

I have also studied hard to discover upon what grounds the right of a State to secede has been denied, when our very name, United States, and the Declaration of Independence, both provide for secession. But there is no time for words. I write in haste. I know how foolish I shall be deemed for undertaking such a step as this, where, on the one side, I have many friends, and everything to make me happy, where my profession alone has gained me an income of more than twenty thousand dollars a year, and where my great personal ambition in my profession has such a great field for labor. On the other hand, the South have never bestowed upon me one kind word; a place now where I have no friends, except beneath the sod; a place where I must either become a private soldier or a beggar. To give up all of the former for the latter, besides my mother and sisters whom I love so dearly, (although they so widely differ with me in opinion,) seems insane; but God is my judge. I love justice more than I do a country that disowns it; more than fame and wealth; more (Heaven pardon me if wrong,) more than a happy home. I have never been upon a battle-field; but O! my countrymen, could you all but see the reality or effects of this horrid war, as I have seen them, (in every State save Virginia.) I know you would think like me, and would pray the Almighty to create in the Northern mind a sense of right and justice, (even should it possess no seasoning of mercy,) and that he would dry up this sea of blood between us, which is daily growing wider. Alas! poor country, is she to meet her threatened doom? Four years ago I would have given a thousand lives to see her remain (as I had always known her) powerful and unbroken. And even now, I would hold my life as naught to see her what she was. O! my friends, if the fearful scenes of the past four years had never been enacted, or if what has been had been but a frightful dream, from which we could now awake, with what overflowing hearts could we bless our God and pray for his continued favor! How I have loved the old flag, can never now be known. A few years since and the entire world could boast of none so pure and spotless. But I have of late been seeing and hearing of the bloody deeds of which she has been made the emblem, and would shudder to think how changed she had grown. O! how I have longed to see her break from the mist of blood and death that circles round her folds, spoiling her beauty and tarnishing her honor. But no, day by day has she been dragged deeper and deeper into cruelty and oppression, till now (in my eyes) her once bright red stripes look like bloody gashes on the face of Heaven. I look now upon my early admiration of her glories as a dream. My love (as things stand to-day) is for the South alone. Nor do I deem it a dishonor in attempting to make for her a prisoner of this man, to whom she owes so much of misery. If success attends me, I go penniless to her side. They say she has found that "last ditch" which the North have so long derided, and been endeavoring to force her in, forgetting they are our brothers, and that it is impolitic to goad an enemy to madness. Should I reach her in safety and find it true, I will proudly beg permission to triumph or die in that same "ditch" by her side.

A Confederate doing duty upon his own responsibility.

J. WILKES BOOTH.

APPENDIX B

Booth's Diary

Below is the "confession" of John Wilkes Booth as recorded in his pocket diary. The diary was a mass-produced, leather-bound, 1864 edition by James M. Crawford of St. Louis, Missouri (other copies of this product have survived). Since Booth's flight and recorded confession were in 1865, it is important to note that his entries *do not* correspond with the dates printed on each page. Each sheet was preprinted with three calendar days per page (six days per sheet). Booth's account spans four sheets, beginning on the sheet labeled "Saturday, June 11, 1864," but the entry began (most likely) on the 17th of April or later (Booth apparently back-dated the first entry to the night of the deed).

In the entries below, Booth was reacting to the newspaper reports of his deed, and his disappointment that his "article" was not published, nor that some expected outcome had not taken place. The preprinted dates at the top of each page are indicated in bold, gray type to aid the reader in visualizing the pagination of this account.

[SHEET 1, FRONT]
SATURDAY, JUNE 11, 1864

Ti Amo [written toward the top of the page, apparently unrelated to the account that follows]

April 14th, the Ides.

Until today nothing was ever thought of sacrificing to our country's wrongs. For six months we had worked to capture, but our cause being almost lost, something decisive and great must be done. But its failure was owing to others, who did not strike for their country with a heart. I struck boldly, and not as the papers say. I walked with a firm step through a thousand of his friends, was stopped, but pushed on. A colonel was at his side. I shouted *Sic semper* before I fired. In jumping broke my leg. I passed all his pickets, rode sixty miles that night with the bone of my leg tearing the flesh at every jump. I can never repent it, though we hated to kill. Our country owed all her troubles to him, and God simply made me the instrument of his punishment. The country is not

[SHEET 1, BACK]
TUESDAY 14

what it was. This forced Union is not what I have loved. I care not what becomes of me. I have no desire to outlive my country. The night before the deed I wrote a long article and left it for one of the editors of the *National Intelligencer*, in which I fully set forth our reasons for our proceedings. He or the gov'mt [The bottom half of this page contains a calendar drawn supposedly by Booth.]

[SHEET 2, FRONT]
FRIDAY, JUNE 17, 1864
[apparently blank]

[SHEET 2, BACK]
MONDAY, JUNE 20, 1864
[apparently blank]

[SHEET 3, FRONT]
THUSDAY, JUNE 23, 1864

After being hunted like a dog through swamps, woods, and last night being chased by gunboats till I was forced to return wet, cold, and starving, with every man's hand against me, I am here in despair. And why? For doing what Brutus was honored for. What made Tell a hero. And yet I, for striking down a greater tyrant than they ever knew, am looked upon as a common cutthroat. My action was purer than either of theirs. One hoped to be great himself. The other had not only his country's, but his own, wrongs to avenge. I hoped for no gain. I knew no private wrong. I struck for my country and that alone. A country that groaned beneath this tyranny, and prayed for this end, and yet, now, behold the cold hands they extend to me. God cannot pardon me if I have done wrong. Yet I cannot see my wrong, except in serving a degenerate people. The little,

[SHEET 3, BACK]

SUNDAY, JUNE 26, 1864

the very little, I left behind to clear my name, the Government will not allow to be printed. So ends all. For my country I have given up all that makes life sweet and holy, brought misery upon my family, and am sure there is no pardon in the Heaven for me, since man condemns me so. I have only heard of what has been done (except what I did myself), and it fills me with horror.

God, try and forgive me, and bless my mother. Tonight I will once more try the river with the intent to cross, though I have a greater desire and almost a mind to return to Washington, and in a measure clear my name—which I feel I can do. I do not repent the blow I struck. I may before my God, but not to man.

[SHEET 4, FRONT]

WEDNESDAY, JUNE 29, 1864

I think I have done well. Though I am abandoned, with the curse of Cain upon me, when, if the world knew my heart, that one blow would have made me great, though I did desire no greatness. Tonight I try to escape these bloodhounds once more. Who, who can read his fate? God's will be done. I have too great a soul to die like a criminal. Oh, may He, may He spare me that, and let me die bravely. I bless the entire world. Have never hated or wronged anyone. This last was not a wrong, unless God deems it so, and it's with Him to damn or bless me. As for this brave boy with me, who often prays (yes, before and since) with a true and sincere heart—was it crime in him? If so, why can he pray the same?

I do not wish to shed a drop of blood, but "I must fight the course." 'Tis all that's left to me.

APPENDIX C

Atzerodt's Confession

Passages in *Italics* are quotations from the confession transcript.

An important fact about this evidence is that detective John L. Smith, who took George Atzerodt's confession in note form, was also his brother-in-law. Detective Smith worked for James McPhail, and he recorded the confession. Some historians assert that the confession is rambling and hard to understand. The confession is only jumbled and confusing if the people who are mentioned in the text are not identified.

The information below identifies the people whom George Atzerodt was telling about, and explains the reasons behind the questions MacPhail was asking him. The confession was actually an interrogation, but the questions were not recorded. It is evident from the transcript, where Atzerodt jumped from topic to topic in the form of answers, that he was being questioned. Each time Atzerodt named a conspirator who was not being charged with any crime—James Hall, James Donaldson, Charles Yates, Thomas Harbin and Louis Weichmann—the interrogators abruptly changed the subject before he could elaborate. James McPhail gave a false testimony when he claimed there were no questions asked.

The confession is most noteworthy for the fact that it can prove just how many people in the Baltimore and Washington area knew about Booth's kidnapping plot prior to the assassination. Booth and his kidnapping gang were also very well known to the National Police Force and the War Department, but despite that fact Booth was never arrested. George Atzerodt's brother, John Atzerodt, was also a Maryland detective who had worked for James McPhail, lending more evidence to substantiate just how many people were aware of Booth's plans for the President.

Atzerodt begins by identifying Lewis Powell, but Atzerodt knew Powell only as, *James Wood sometimes called Mosby.* Powell also later used the alias *Lewis Paine* but not until after he was arrested in Baltimore, and he wasn't known as "Paine" by anyone in Washington until three days after the assassination. Lewis Powell was charged for the assassination attempt on Secretary of State William Seward.

9 & F St. three story house was the Herndon House, where Lewis Powell stayed while he was in Washington from March 27 until 5:00 PM April 14, 1865. The Herndon House was owned by Mrs. Martha Murray.

James Hall was one of Colonel Baker's paid informants posing as a Southern sympathizer, and he too was just one of many who monitored the mail for Baker before it was delivered.

Atzerodt answered McPhail's question about where Lewis Powell (alias James Wood) came from. *He was brought up from New York. He was arrested.* Lewis Powell stayed at the Revere House while he was in New York. Atzerodt was saying that Lewis Powell had been arrested in Baltimore [by Provost Marshal H. B. Smith], but Atzerodt only knew Powell as James Wood or Mosby. Atzerodt answered McPhail's next question, "What other names did Wood go by?" *Did not know him by any other name than mentioned.*

Marshall McPhail asked Atzerodt, "Who is Powell?" And Atzerodt answered: *Gust. Powell, also Gustavus Spencer.* Atzerodt was trying to say Augustus Howell, a blockade-runner and smuggler who had been arrested prior to the assassination. Howell was in jail before the assassination, but he was still called to be a witness in order to implicate Mary Surratt as an assassination conspirator. James McPhail knew Augustus Howell, but he was trying to find out who Lewis Powell was, because James Wood used so many aliases. On May 1, McPhail was still not sure that James Wood, Mosby, Lewis Paine and Lewis Powell were all the same man.

James Donaldson was a Stanton double agent who had been assigned to infiltrate Booth's kidnapping gang, but he was never arrested or called to testify because that would prove Stanton knew all about Booth and his kidnapping plot. He was also the same man Samuel Arnold talked about in his confession, however, Arnold's transcript was not allowed to contain his name, and referred to him only as "unknown."

James Donaldson maintained the low profile of a shadowy figure even among Booth's gang members. He discreetly participated in the conspiracy to kidnap Lincoln, and kept his identity from the other conspirators a mystery (as one might expect a professional agent would do).

Atzerodt claimed he only met Donaldson one time. That was not a deliberate lie but an honest mistake. Atzerodt's role as a conspirator was to be the labor of dirty jobs and he had no direct association or dealings with the elusive Donaldson. During the saloon meeting, when Samuel Arnold first met Donaldson, George Atzerodt was there also, but was enjoying the free drinks, and paid no attention to Donaldson, who was moving quietly among the other patrons in the noisy, crowded saloon. That explains why Samuel Arnold remembered Donaldson at the saloon meeting, but Atzerodt did not.

Saloon or restaurant on the Aven. bet 13 &14 St. was Gautier's Saloon where the meeting was held (*see* Appendix D: Samuel Arnold's Confession) to learn the mystery of March 31.

Saml. Thomas was Samuel Thomas, very likely a detective for Colonel Baker. He shared room 53 at the Pennsylvania House with Atzerodt on the night of the assassination (*see* John Greenawalt's testimony in Chapter 1).

Atzerodt told McPhail where he was after the assassination, saying, *A Lieut. will prove this.* Lieutenant W. R. Keim had often shared room No. 51 at the Pennsylvania House with Atzerodt. Keim knew George Atzerodt, and he substantiated the confession during his trial testimony. However, Atzerodt did, in fact, deliberately leave out that he was also with Herold when the guns were carried to John Lloyd at Surrattsville Tavern. Herold first delivered the guns to Donaldson, and Donaldson carried them to the Tee Bee post office five miles south of Surrattsville. Five or six weeks before the assassination, John Surratt, George Atzerodt, and David Herold picked the guns up at the Tee Bee post office and took them to John Lloyd (*see* Appendix D: Samuel Arnold's confession).

Weightman … at Post Office was Louis Weichmann, the prosecution's prime witness and one of Colonel Baker's civilian informants. He was provided a job at the War Department to spy on John Surratt Jr., and he reported directly to Captain Gleason. Colonel Baker made Weichmann a clerk in the Commissary General of Prisoners under General Hoffman, and before the assassination he reported all his undercover investigations about John Surratt directly to the War Department.

Charles Yates was a conspirator in Booth's kidnapping plot, assigned to row everyone across the Potomac River after they kidnapped the President. He too was never arrested or called to testify—another obviously planted Baker informant.

Thos. Holborn was Thomas Harbin, another of many civilian informants for Colonel Baker, a double agent, and an active member in Booth's gang. He worked at the Allen's Fresh Post Office with Sarah Slater in Charles County, Maryland. Harbin secretly monitored the mail (and Mrs. Slater) for Baker.

McPhail asked Atzerodt about "Bailey and Barnes." Marcellus H. Bailey had been a bartender in Port Tobacco, and therefore was very well acquainted with George Atzerodt. He had lost his job and was living on a farm with relatives, ten miles south of town. Walter C. Barnes, a friend and drinking companion of Baily and Atzerodt, was arrested April 19th by Brigadier General James A. Hardie. (LAE, p. 868–69) George answered, *Bailey & Barnes knew nothing of the affair, unless Booth told Bailey & he told Barnes. Booth had met Bailey on C Street with me.*

Atzerodt was answering a question pertaining to John Boyle, and he told the Marshal that, *Boyle also killed Capt. Watkins.* John Boyle was known by the Union supporters in the village of Bryantown, Maryland, as a guerrilla and desperado who was fighting against the Republican candidates during the Maryland state elections. John H. Boyle was wanted for the killing Captain Thomas Watkins of Ann Arundel County, Maryland, after clashing over the army's interference in local elections (*see* "Election Interference by the War Department," the first note in the Author's Notes section). Boyle was originally a prime suspect as Booth's accomplice who attempted to assassinate William Seward.

Provost Marshal James McPhail was asking George Atzerodt if he knew anything about a secret meeting that took place on March 31. Part of this confession is incomplete and has obviously been edited from the text (*See* "The Mystery of March 31," ahead).

Atzerodt proved he did not believe Booth's April 14th claim that he was going to assassinate the President when he said, *I had the horse out to help take the President. I did not believe he was going to be killed, although Booth had said so.* The stable foreman, John Fletcher, corroborated this when he testified that: "At 10 PM: Atzerodt came for the dark gray mare, and headed towards Ford's Theater." Atzerodt actually believed Lincoln was going to be abducted (not killed), because the dark gray mare was to carry Lincoln to the Potomac River.

The knife I threw away just above Mrs. Canby's boarding house the night of the murder ... when I took my horse to stable. When Atzerodt found out Lincoln was assassinated, he hurried back to the stables to return the horse, throwing his knife away along the road. The knife was found the next morning at the spot where he said he threw it away. What Atzerodt described about his pistol was verified by John Caldwick's testimony.

Atzerodt had made no preparations to escape Washington after the assassination, because he did not believe Lincoln would be killed. And when he found out Lincoln had been shot he had no place to run or hide. Atzerodt's claim, *I run around the city like a crazy man,* was substantiated by the witness Washington Briscoe (Atzerodt wanted to stay the night with him in the store down at the Navy Yard). Atzerodt had no idea what he should do after he found out Lincoln had been shot.

Wood went with Booth last February to New York. ... I know nothing about Canada. This is an obvious answer to McPhail's question concerning something about Canada.

I overheard Booth when in conversation with Wood say, that he visited a chambermaid at Seward's house and that she was pretty. He said he had a great mind to give her his diamond pin. When Booth was killed, among the items on his body that were inventoried was this diamond pin (IMPEACH, pp. 452, 482, 488, 672). Secretary of State William Seward's chambermaid was Margaret Coleman, and she gave Booth inside information about Seward's home, and she helped plant a pistol at the crime scene. She was never arrested or called to testify, and this information is one reason why Atzerodt's confession was withheld from the court evidence.

Kate Thompson or Brown was Kate Warne, America's first woman detective. She was a prominent member in Booth's kidnapping gang, but she was never arrested or called to testify (her story is in Chapter 6). After describing Kate to his interviewer, Atzerodt added, *Young Weightman* [Weichmann] *ought to know about this woman.* Of course, Louis Weichmann could never (and didn't) mention her name without implicating himself as a spy.

Booth met a party in New York that would get the President certain. They were going to mine the President's house near the War Department. They knew an entrance to accomplish it through, spoke about getting friends of the President to get up an entertainment and they would mix it in and have a serenade and thus get at the President and party. The "friends of the President" could only be people within the Federal government. Atzerodt would not refer to anyone in the Confederate government as friends of the President (*see* section "Tracing the Weapon" in Chapter 8).

The "party in New York" that George Atzerodt was referring to is the evidence of an assassination plot already in progress long before Booth had any idea to kill Lincoln.

Appendix D

Arnold's Confession

Passages in *Italics* are quotations from the confession transcript.

Samuel Arnold's confession was given in the back room of Provost Marshall James McPhail's office to his brother William McPhail at No. 4 Fayette Street, Baltimore. An unnamed detective wrote down Arnold's answers, making occasional errors ("Peedee" instead of "Tee Bee"; "Heard" instead of "Herold").

The Unknown Conspirator. One conspicuous discrepancy in the transcript is the use of *unknown* in place of the name James Donaldson, a key member of Booth's gang. The transcript attributes this omission to Arnold's faulty memory, though that is unlikely, or perhaps Arnold knew better than to say his name. Donaldson was already familiar with Arnold's best friend, Michael O'Laughlen, and Michael introduced them at Gautier's Saloon.

Though the detective never recorded Donaldson's name, he recorded Arnold's description of him: *young, five-foot-five or -six inches high, thick set, long nose, sharp chin, wide cheek, small eye—I think grey, dark hair and well-dressed.* This matches George Atzerodt's less eloquent description of James Donaldson: "a low, chunky man, about 23 or 24 years of age, small-potted, dark complexion, not very … plain black suit." Donaldson was a name not to be known: omitted from Arnold's confession, and Atzerodt's entire confession was destroyed (except for a fortuitous copy by his attorney that resurfaced in 1977). Donaldson was described in both confessions as having a significant role in the kidnapping plot, and Atzerodt stipulated that Donaldson had a meeting with John Wilkes Booth the evening Lincoln was assassinated. Though named and described by two of Booth's coconspirators, James Donaldson was never pursued by the War Department, nor mentioned in the trail, nor has he been mentioned by any historians after these transcripts were made public.

Samuel Arnold spoke of Lincoln's unguarded trips to the Old Soldiers' Home. This was the same confidential information William Seward had passed on to his foreign agent, Freeman M. Morris in London, on July 15, 1864.

Months rolled around, he [Booth] *did not make his appearance until some-time in January.* Booth could not have attempted to kidnap Lincoln until after he got back together with his gang in early January, 1865.

John Surratt … Most of Booth's time was spent with him. Booth did not collaborate with John Surratt until after he returned to Washington, also in early January 1865 (Louis Weichmann's testimony, May 13, 1865).

March 12, 1865, Lewis Powell (alias James Wood or Mosby) was arrested in Baltimore by Provost Marshal H. B. Smith. March 14, Mosby was released from jail and he signed the name "Lewis Paine" to his oath of allegiance. Powell then returned to Washington as James Wood or Mosby, and no one knew him as Lewis Paine until three days after the assassination. The civilian informant, Louis Weichmann, gave false testimony when he said that James Wood used the name Lewis "Payne" before the assassination.

March 13, Booth sent a telegram to Michael O'Laughlen (John Hapman was the dispatcher at No. 57 North Exeter Street, Baltimore):

Don't fear to neglect your business. You had better come at once.

—J. Booth

John Wilkes Booth's mother owned the property the O'Laughlen family lived on, and Booth had a personal interest in Michael's business affairs. Michael and his brother William had owned a produce and feed business, but William sold the business. Michael, however, stayed on and received orders for shipments and was in charge of distributing the feed and produce, up until the end of March, 1865. During early March, Michael was dealing with a boxcar load of hay, but Booth wanted him to neglect his business and come instead to his meeting at Gautier's Saloon, planned for the night of March 15 (that was what Booth was saying in the March 14, telegram). The telegram was about planning a kidnapping and it had nothing to do with an assassination plot.

In the late evening of March 15, around 11:00 or 12:00 PM, James Donaldson contacted Michael about the saloon meeting and he met Samuel Arnold that night for the first time.

March 16, Arnold did not go to bed until 6:00 or 7:00 AM Thursday morning, he slept until noon. Booth was still mad at Arnold that afternoon and he called on Michael only at 2:00 or 3:00 PM Thursday afternoon. Arnold told Booth he would drop out if they did not kidnap Lincoln that week, and he went to bed about 7:30 PM Thursday night.

March 17, the kidnapping ambush at Campbell Hospital failed, and on March 20 Michael moved back to Baltimore and stayed with his brother-in-law, P. H. Maulsby at 57 North Exeter St., Baltimore, and remained there until April 13.

On Saturday night, March 18, Booth played the leading role in a play at Ford's Theatre.

Louis Weichmann testified that on Monday, March 19, John Surratt inquired about a room at the Herndon House for a "delicate gentleman," referring to Lewis Powell (alias James Wood), and if he could have meals sent up to his room. The room was made ready on March 27 for James Wood (Mrs. Murray never knew James Wood as Lewis Paine). She testified, "He (James Wood) was two weeks in our house, and left the day of the assassination about 5:00 PM" (*see* Mrs. Martha Murray's testimony concerning Mary Surratt).

Atzerodt said in his confession, *This was the meeting place because Wood could not go out for fear of arrest.* Lewis Powell had to keep out of sight for fear of being arrested. He was told by Provost Marshall Smith to stay north of Philadelphia for the duration of the war. He could not risk being seen in the daytime; if he were recognized south of Philadelphia he would be rearrested (*see* Chapter 11, p. 88, where Powell exclaimed, "I'm made, I'm made!" Powell lost his hat and realized he could be identified).

March 20, Samuel Arnold and Michael O'Laughlen checked out of Mrs. Mary Van Tine's boarding house in Washington at No. 420 D Street and both returned to Baltimore.

March 21, Arnold moved back to Hookstown (in the country), and Booth left for New York, stopping in Baltimore. Billy Williams testified that he delivered two letters for Booth from the hotel in Baltimore, and said Booth told him he was leaving for New York at 3:30 PM (proving that Booth left Washington on March 21).

March 23, Booth sent Louis Weichmann a coded telegram from New York to pass on to John Surratt. That physical evidence proves Booth was still in New York on the 23rd.

March 25, Booth returned to Baltimore from New York and sent a message to Arnold in Hookstown to come to the city for a meeting, but Booth did not wait for Arnold and left for Washington with only Michael O'Laughlen.

March 27, Samuel Arnold wrote his infamous "Sam" letter. Booth also sent Michael another telegram (Edward C. Stewart at the Metropolitan Hotel sent the dispatch) and it read:

Get word to Sam. Come on with or without him. Wednesday morning we sell that day sure. Don't fail.

J. Wilkes Booth

Michael O'Laughlen asked Samuel Arnold to go to Washington with him to finally arrange his affairs (selling the boxcar load of hay). On Friday, March 31, Arnold went to Washington with Michael on business, then returned alone to Hookstown that same evening. There Arnold's brother Frank gave Samuel a letter of employment from J. H. Wharton at Fortress Monroe, Virginia.

THE MYSTERY OF MARCH 31 IN ATZERODT'S CONFESSION. During George Atzerodt's confession, Marshal James McPhail had the telegram Booth sent to Michael O'Laughlen from the Metropolitan Hotel ("… we sell that day sure. Don't fail."), but the Marshal didn't know what it meant. McPhail knew there was a meeting on or about March 31, and this is what he was asking Atzerodt about during his confession (interrogation) on May 1, 1865. The telegram was speaking of selling a boxcar of hay, and had nothing at all to do with President Lincoln. Booth's dairy, in 1867, convinced Congress that Booth had no assassination plot before Lincoln's final day. One reason the War Department needed to conceal Booth's diary was so the prosecution could claim the Metropolitan Hotel telegram was pertaining to an assassination plot.

On April 1, Arnold left for his new job at Fort Monroe, and he never saw or heard from Booth again.

The painted black box with the kidnapping supplies—guns (two carbines), rope (to lower Lincoln to the stage), handcuffs (for Lincoln) and monkey wrench (to turn off the theater's gas lights)—was transferred in a wagon to David Herold's house in Georgetown by Michael O'Laughlen. From there James Donaldson carried them to his house, then later delivered the box to the Tee Bee post office, five miles south of Surrattsville.

John Lloyd testified on May 13, 1865, that: "Some five or six weeks before the assassination (very early March) John Surratt, David Herold and George Atzerodt came from Tee Bee to my tavern at Surrattsville with a box." John Surratt showed Lloyd where to hide the guns, rope, and monkey wrench that were in the box that Donaldson had left for them at the Tee Bee post office.

Colonel Ingraham and Lieutenant William H. Terry gathered the papers found in Booth's hotel room by William Eaton at the National Hotel on the morning after the assassination. Colonel Taylor marked the envelope containing the Sam letter "Important."

Jacob Smith was a witness who testified he saw Samuel Arnold every day from March 20 to March 30 at Hookstown. Both of Samuel Arnold's brothers, Frank and William, testified Samuel was in Maryland throughout late March. Despite all these witnesses and evidence, Samuel Arnold was still given life in prison for his part in the assassination plot.

Appendix E

The Radicals in Missouri

The President' s troubles with the Radicals first began soon after General Benjamin Butler, then later Generals John Fremont and David Hunter, took it upon themselves to proclaim freedom to the slaves in the Union occupied slave states.

General William T. Sherman wrote his foster father, Thomas Ewing, from St. Louis in May 1861:

> I am satisfied with Mr. Lincoln's policy, but I do not like that of the Blairs. I know Frank Blair openly declares war on slavery. I see him daily and yesterday had a long talk with him. I say the time is not yet come to destroy slavery, but it may be time to circumscribe it. We have not in America the number of inhabitants to replace the slaves. Nor have we the national wealth to transport them to other lands. (Sherman, p. 197)

During the first year of the war, the welfare, protection and maintenance for the refugee slave population fell upon the Government. Able-bodied, liberated slaves could serve as labor for the Union war effort, but the many incapable children, elderly, and sick presented a serious burden upon the Army's resources and supervision.

In his first Annual Message to Congress, Lincoln announced a plan to give compensation for abolition with a hope to bring about total emancipation. He later stated that nothing would contribute to that end better than a well-considered scheme of colonization. Lincoln strongly urged Congress to appropriate money for the acquisition of territory for that objective. Congress responded with three enactments. The first appropriation of $100,000 was to empty the refugee camps around the District of Columbia by financing a colonization program. An additional $500,000 was approved by Congress to colonize refugees freed by the First Confiscation Act. The third clause of the Second Confiscation Act was to authorize the president to make provisions for the transportation of slave refugees to a tropical country beyond the limits of the United States. Those tropical countries would have to consent to the same protection for the refugees as they afforded to their other free citizens. Panama, Île-à-Vache, Haiti, Liberia, British Honduras, British Guiana and Suriname were pressured by the Lincoln administration to receive liberated American slave refugees. (John G. Nicolay and John Hay, *Abraham Lincoln: A History, Vol. VI*, pp. 355–57)

Secretary of State William Seward received many heated complaints from the countries pressured to accept slave refugees, and he himself opposed colonization.

General Frank Blair of Missouri and Senator James R. Doolittle of Wisconsin endorsed the colonization plan into their party platform. Senators Preston King, Lyman Trumbull, Henry Wilson and Benjamin Wade joined the cause. Governors from Ohio, Illinois, Iowa and Wisconsin as well as the editors of the *Albany Evening Journal, The New York Times*, the New York *Evening Post*, the *National Era* and the *Chicago Tribune* also supported a colonization program. However it was soon realized (as General Sherman had stated) colonization was completely impractical and unaffordable. (Sewell, pp. 324–25)

After the war broke out, the Union slave state of Missouri held a convention to vacate all the state elected representatives, including the Democrat Governor, Claiborne Fox Jackson (a former "border ruffian" who was rejecting Lincoln's request for troops). However, the convention had no legal authority to set up a new state government. (Barton, p. 380)

Loyalists in the state of Missouri (a Union slave state) broke into two political factions: the conservatives (called "Claybanks"), who supported Lincoln; and the Radicals (referred to as "Charcoals"). In 1862, General John Schofield had been given command of St. Louis and four months later given command of an entire district of Missouri. In early 1863, General Schofield became commander of all of Missouri. Schofield opposed the confiscation legislation and the Radicals campaigned successfully to replace him with their man General Samuel Curtis, an accused cotton speculator (ALP: Gamble to Blair, September 24, 1862). The Radicals also wanted to replace Lincoln's stubbornly conservative Governor, Hamilton R. Gamble, while Lincoln's ally and Governor Gamble's brother-in-law, Attorney General Edward Bates (from Missouri), argued to keep him and remove General Curtis. On May 5, 1863, the President apologetically relieved Curtis and reappointed General Schofield because of his close alliance with Governor Gamble, Lincoln's conservative choice. (CW: Vol.VI, p. 253)

The Radical agenda advocated rapid emancipation without compensating the former slave owners. Attorney General Edward Bates wrote in his diary on May 30, 1863:

> The Radicals came to the conclusion that Mr. Lincoln's plan of emancipation was all wrong, too slow and too costly. In their view the best way is violence and fraud, and if the state were thrown into anarchy all the better. The issue could all be settled anew, and in the process the Radicals could get improved lands for nothing.

The Radical Missouri Congressman Henry T. Blow was just one of many who criticized the President over his conservative policy toward slavery in the state of Missouri. On May 15, 1863, President Lincoln began to run out of patience with the Radicals, and he wrote to Congressman Blow, Charles D. Drake and others, "I have been tormented … beyond endurance." (CW, Vol. VI, p. 218)

The Congressman arrogantly responded:

> My opinion is … that if you cannot rely upon the representative men elected by your own friends, and advocates of your own policy, your troubles in the future will far exceed those of the past. (ALP, Henry T. Blow to Abraham Lincoln, Monday, May 18, 1863)

The political rivalry in Missouri was between the Conservatives like General Frank Blair and Governor Gamble, who supported the President's emphasis on saving the Union, versus the Radicals, who gave priority to abolishing slavery. (CW: Vol.VII, p. 85–86)

When the slave refugees flooded St. Louis, General Henry W. Halleck utilized martial law and labeled any Missouri citizens found to be conservatives "Secesh" (successionists) and confiscated their property to pay the costs of providing for the homeless slave refugees. (CW: Vol. VI, p. 36–37)

The Radicals of Missouri met in Jefferson City on September 1, 1863, and decided to send a delegation to Washington to pressure the President into imposing the Emancipation Proclamation in Missouri (a Union state, not covered by the Proclamation), and to allow the Negroes to be enlisted as

Union troops. The delegation's platform was to forcefully wipe out the legal ownership of slaves of the "Claybank" Missouri loyalists, and without any compensation. (Stevens, p. 237)

When the Missouri delegation arrived in Washington they first met for three days with the Radical faction in Washington, led by Salmon P. Chase, Charles Sumner and Thaddeus Stevens, to discuss their presentation before meeting with Lincoln. Charles D. Drake of St. Louis and Kansas Senator James Lane led the Radical delegation presenting their argument to the President about replacing General Schofield. Kansas Senator James Lane pressed the argument to Lincoln saying: "The massacre of Lawrence is, in the opinion of the people of Kansas, solely due to the imbecile General Schofield." (CW: Vol. VII, p. 10)

The President responded:

> As to that, it seems to me that it is a thing which could be done by anyone making up his mind to the consequences, and could no more be guarded against than assassination. If I make up my mind to kill you, for instance, I can do it and [300 men] could not prevent it. They could avenge but could not save you. (ALP: John M. Schofield to Lincoln, November 10, 1863)

Ironically this quote by Lincoln would turn out to be a chilling foreshadowing. Lincoln told the Missouri Radicals he had no intention of withdrawing his support from Governor Gamble. Lincoln ordered General Schofield:

> Allow no part of the Military under your command, to be engaged in either returning fugitive slaves, or in forcing, or enticing slaves from their homes; and, so far as practicable, enforce the same forbearance upon the people. [...] Allow no one to assume the functions of confiscation of property ... except upon orders from here. (CW, Vol. VI, pp. 492–93)

INDEX

The following is a simple, single-level index of significant names and terms appearing in this book. Ubiquitous terms are not listed (such as *assassination* or *Confederate*), and ubiquitous proper nouns are listed in small capitals case without page references (such as WASHINGTON, D.C., JOHN WILKES BOOTH, ABRAHAM LINCOLN, EDWIN M. STANTON).

A

accident(s): 27, 34, 35, 41, 76, 89, 156, 179, 180

Anderson, Mary Jane: 116

Arnold, Frank: 65, 224, 225

Arnold, Isaac: 77, 159

Arnold, Samuel: 7, 60–67, 96, 98, 103, 104, 113, 117, 133, 152, 155, 176, 188, 201, 217, 218, 221–25

assassin(s) from France: 25, 27, 29–34, 73, 76, 179

Atkins (defense attorney).: 105

ATZERODT, GEORGE

Atzerodt, John: 56, 65, 216

Augur, Christopher: 90, 98

B

Babcock, John C.: 5, 189

Bailey, Marcellus H.: 219

BAKER, LAFAYETTE

Baker, Luther: 138, 154, 165, 204–06

Baltimore: 8, 51, 55, 57, 58, 60, 62–67, 101, 102, 113, 119, 121, 163, 176, 190, 216, 217, 221–23

Barnes, Joseph K.: 91, 93, 195

Barnes, Walter C.: 219

Bates, David Homer: 79, 167

Bates, Edward: 146, 185, 227, 228

Beauregard, P. T. G.: 109, 186, 187

Bell, William: 87, 88, 90, 91, 118, 195

Belle Plain: 20, 21, 165

Benjamin, Judah P.: 66, 157

Bigelow, John: 31, 32

Bingham, John A.: 105, 108, 110, 128, 148, 155–57, 164

Blackburn, Luke P.: 148

Blair, Frank: 181, 182, 226–28

Blair, Montgomery: 46, 123, 175, 176, 181, 226

BOOTH, JOHN WILKES

Bradwell, Myra: 160

Breckenridge, John: 46, 157

Brooks, Noah: 76, 77, 79

Brown, John: 208–10

Brown, Kate: 53, 56–58, 107, 220; *See also* Thompson, Kate

Browning, Oliver: 185

Browning, William: 115

Buchanan, James: 45, 131, 142

Buckner, Louisa: 123, 124

Burnett, H. L.: 99–101, 108, 128, 163

Butler, Benjamin: 46, 156, 158, 164, 185–87, 226

C

Calhoun, John C.: 30

Campbell Hospital: 63, 66, 223

Campbell, John: 22, 26, 33, 35, 36, 40–44

carbine: 94, 144, 145, 175, 224

Carland, Louis J.: 13

carpetbaggers: 48

City Point: 23, 26, 29, 32, 35, 36 64, 67

Clark (assassin): 31, 32

Clarke, John Sleeper: 19, 20, 208

Clay, Clement C.: 66, 148, 149

Clendenin, David R.: 98, 102

Coleman, Margaret: 56, 58, 69, 88, 89, 116, 122, 143, 150, 220

Colfax, Schuyler, Jr.: 24

Comstock, Cyrus B.: 147, 185

Conger, Everton J.: 122, 128, 138–40, 143, 145, 164, 204, 205

Conover, Stanford: 148

conservatives: 2, 46, 181, 182, 184, 191, 227, 228

Constitutional Union, The: 192

Cooper (European agent): 32

Copperheads: 2, 3, 142

Corbett, Boston: 94, 121, 122, 138, 139, 142, 145, 204, 205

Crawford, Alexander M. S.: 83, 84

Crook, William H.: 85, 86, 77–79

D

dagger: 81, 84

Dana, Charles: 33, 34, 36, 40, 41

Davis, Charles W.: 114, 177

Davis, David: 77, 159

Davis, Henry Winter: 175, 181, 182, 184; See also Wade-Davis Bill

Davis, Jefferson: 1, 5, 22, 23, 26, 28, 35, 41, 54, 59, 75, 80, 108, 109, 113, 119, 130, 145, 148, 152, 154, 157, 160–63, 176

Dean, Miss: 116

Dempsey (investigator): 110

Derringer (firearm): 4, 95, 96, 109, 123, 124, 150

Doherty, Edward P.: 138, 205

Donaldson, James: 1–3, 51–58, 61, 62, 66, 69, 89–91, 119, 130, 145, 148, 152, 154, 157, 160–63, 176

Dorsey, Ann: 153

Doster, W. E.: 94, 95, 114, 200

Douglas, Stephen: 76

Durham, Charles: 148

Dyer, Jeremiah: 10

E

Eckert, Thomas: 23, 24, 33, 34, 57, 79, 100, 119, 131, 132, 133, 134, 137, 140, 143, 185, 196

Eglent, Elzee: 9

Emancipation Proclamation: 9, 228

emancipation: 29, 74, 76, 226, 228

Evans, William A.: 9

F

Ferguson, James P.: 84, 85, 194

Fitzpatrick, Honora: 116, 201

Forbes, Charles: 84–86, 96, 97, 121, 122, 140, 142, 152

Ford, Clay: 97, 196

Ford, Frank: 196

Ford, Harry: 81

Ford, James: 196

Ford, John T.: 12, 97, 115, 121, 141

Ford's Theatre: 12, 27, 28, 62, 63, 66, 77, 79, 81, 82, 84, 87, 95, 96, 97, 116, 121, 124, 125, 132, 135, 180, 194, 197, 219

Fort Monroe: 24, 29, 67, 104, 113, 152, 153, 160, 224

Frémont, John C.: 46, 182, 184, 226

G

Gardner, Alexander: 139, 204

Garrett's farm: 7, 138

Gettysburg: 62

Gifford, James: 12

Gleason, D. H.: 64, 89, 117, 218

Gourlay, Jeannie: 81

Grant, Julia: 77, 194

Grant, Ulysses S.: 32, 35–37, 44, 59, 67, 71, 77, 79, 130, 140, 146–50, 152, 155, 186, 187, 194–97

Greeley, Horace: 17

Greenawalt, John: 14

Greenhow, Rose: 118

Grover's Theatre: 196, 200

H

Hall, James: 52, 53, 56, 58, 69, 122, 150, 188, 216, 217

Hansell, Emerick W.: 89, 195

Hapman, John: 222

Harbin, Thomas: 53, 150, 188, 216, 218

Harris, Clara: 77

Hawk, Harry: 83

Hay, John: 18, 77

Herndon House: 117, 217, 223

Herold, David: 7, 8, 15, 16, 57, 62, 92, 94, 105, 106, 114, 125, 137–39, 144, 150, 152, 155, 177, 195, 200, 218, 221, 224

Holland, John C.: 9

Holohan, Eliza: 116, 201

Holohan, John: 99, 201

Holt, Joseph: 56, 57, 100, 104, 108, 124, 128, 142, 143, 147, 153, 154, 156, 157, 164, 176, 202, 205

Hookstown: 64, 67, 176, 223–25

Hoover, J. Edgar: 121

Horner, Eaton G.: 104

horse(s): 8, 13, 62, 90, 150, 202, 219

Howell, Augustus: 53, 54, 57, 59, 108, 217

Hunter, Robert M. T.: 22, 226

Hyams, Godfrey: 148

J

Jackson, Andrew: 30

Jackson, Claiborne Fox: 227

Johnson, Andrew: 2, 3, 19, 95, 99, 105, 114, 115, 123, 145–50, 152–58, 160–63, 200, 202, 206, 207

Johnston (assassin): 31, 32, 73

K

Kennedy, John F.: 1

Kirkwood Hotel: 105, 106, 114, 115, 146, 200

knife or knives: 4, 11, 12, 61, 81, 82, 84, 88–91, 96, 97, 105, 106, 108, 109, 124, 133, 141, 156, 219; *See also* dagger

L

Lamb, James: 13

Lawrence, Richard: 30

Leale, Charles A.: 84

Lee, Edwin G.: 66, 67

Lee, John (detective): 105, 106

Lee, Robert E.: 35–37, 41, 45, 49, 60, 64, 66, 67, 77, 108, 149, 186, 187

Lewis, Pryce: 5

Lichau House: 61, 63

LINCOLN, ABRAHAM
Lincoln, Mary Todd: 26, 35, 77, 92, 159, 160, 179, 185, 193
Lincoln, Robert: 77, 159, 160
Lincoln, Tad: 36, 37, 76
Lloyd, John: 144, 145, 150, 218, 224
Lohmann, F. W. E.: 5
Lomax, Virginia B.: 5
loyalists, loyal, disloyal (citizens or states): 9–11, 27, 29, 41–46, 48, 49, 52, 60, 70, 110, 144, 147, 176, 191, 227, 229

M

Matthews, John: 126, 127
Maulsby, P. H.: 198, 223
McClellan, George: 109, 110, 184, 187
McDevitt, James: 99
McGowan, Theodore: 84
McKim, Samuel A. H.: 114, 117
McPhail, James: 55, 56, 58, 65, 94, 98, 104, 107, 122, 143, 163, 200, 216–21, 224
McPhail, William: 221
Miles, John: 116
Millward, William: 208
Montgomery, Richard: 150
Morgan, Richard: 101, 109
Morse, Freeman Harlow: 30–33, 61
Mosby (nickname): 62, 66, 89, 103, 116, 117, 201, 216, 217, 222; *See also* Powell, Lewis
Mosby, John: 8
Mudd, Dr. Samuel: 9–11, 82, 122, 150, 152, 155
Murray, Martha: 116, 217, 223
Myer, Albert James: 132

Mystery Man, the: 103, 113, 120; *See also* Powell, Lewis; Paine, Lewis; Payne, Lewis; *also* Wood, James

N

National Hotel: 53, 57, 63, 68, 104, 106, 196, 225
National Intelligencer, The: 126, 127, 192, 214
New York Times, The: 114, 180, 227
Newcomb (captain): 110
Nicolay, John: 18, 19
Northeastern industrialists: 3, 18, 38, 39, 48, 49, 74
Nothe, Mr.: 116

O

O'Beirne, James: 98, 105, 138
O'Laughlen, Michael: 7, 60–67, 103, 104, 113, 152, 155, 177, 197, 198, 221–24
O'Laughlen, William: 222
O'Sullivan, Timothy H.: 139
Old Soldiers' Home: 30, 31, 61, 221
Oswald, Lee Harvey: 1

P

Paine, Lewis: 62, 66, 101–03, 117, 119, 201, 216, 217, 222, 223; *See also* Payne, Lewis; *also* Powell, Lewis; *also* James Wood
Parker, John: 79, 85, 86, 96, 97, 121, 140–42, 152, 195, 196
Parker, William: 163
Payne, Lewis: 102, 103, 105, 108, 113, 116, 117, 119, 201, 222; *See also* Powell, Lewis; *also* Paine, Lewis; *also* James Wood
Peace Democrats: 2, 142
Pendel, Thomas: 85

Petersburg: 26, 46, 186, 187

Peterson, William: 135

photograph(s): 84, 92, 93, 109, 110, 119, 122, 123, 139, 140, 150, 189, 202, 204

Pinkerton, Allan: 54, 55, 58, 136, 170, 189

Pinkerton (agency): 163–64

pistol(s): 30, 89–91, 93, 94, 106, 108, 139, 140, 144, 145, 175, 204, 219, 220; *See also* revolver(s)

Port Tobacco (nickname): *See* Atzerodt, George

Port Tobacco (town): 219

Porter, Horace: 147, 185

Potts (captain): 110

Powell, Lewis: 1, 8, 11, 15, 16, 57, 62, 66, 68, 87–91, 95, 101–08, 112, 113, 116–19, 152, 177, 188, 195, 201, 216, 217, 222, 223; *See also* Paine, Lewis; *also* Payne, Lewis; *also* Wood, James; *also* Mosby (nickname); *also* Mystery Man, the

Pumphrey, John: 82

R

Randall, Voltaire: 104

Rathbone, Henry R.: 77, 84, 92, 133, 197

Reeves, A. R.: 64

refugee(s): 226–29

revolver(s): 91, 106, 109; *See also* pistol

Richards, Almarin C.: 82, 99

Richer, Hartman: 105

RICHMOND (city)

Ritterspaugh, Jacob "Jake": 12, 13

Robinson, George F.: 88, 90, 118, 195

Ruhlman's Hotel: 61, 198

S

Sam Letter, the: 64, 65, 67, 104, 106, 223, 225

Scott, Winfield: 136

Scully, John: 5

SEWARD, WILLIAM

Seward, Augustus: 88–90, 118

Seward, Frederick: 71, 87, 88, 90, 91

Shepley, George F.: 41

Sherman, William T.: 23, 27, 31–33, 46, 132, 186, 226, 227

Signal Corps: 8, 52, 57, 61, 132

Simms, Mary: 9

Simms, Milo: 9

Slater, Sarah Antoinette: 53, 57, 58, 69, 108, 122, 150, 163, 164, 188, 218

slave owner(s) or slaveholder(s): 10, 228

Smith, H. B.: 62, 217, 222, 223

Smith, Jacob: 176, 225

Smith, John L.: 56, 65, 216

Spangler, "Ed": 12–14, 142, 152, 155, 196

Speed, James: 145

Sprague, Lyman S.: 106

spur(s): 81, 82, 84, 106, 108, 109, 123, 124

Stager, Anson: 132

STANTON, EDWIN M.

Stephens, Alexander H.: 22, 109

Stewart, Edward C.: 223

Stewart, Joseph B.: 13

Surratt House: 13, 53, 54, 57, 89, 90, 101, 103, 107, 109, 110, 114, 117, 123, 163

Surratt, Anna: 110, 116, 160

Surratt, John, Jr.: 8, 11, 12, 52, 64, 57,
    59, 61, 62, 64, 66, 69, 89, 98, 101,
    104, 107, 108, 110, 112, 113, 150,
    153, 157, 188, 194, 218, 222–24
Surratt, John, Sr.: 110
Surratt, Mary: 11, 12, 15, 16, 53,
    54, 57, 66, 89, 98, 99, 101, 103,
    107–10, 113–17, 121, 123, 128,
    143, 152, 153, 157, 160, 163, 164,
    188, 217
Swett, Leonard: 77, 159

T

Tanner, James: 100
telegraph lines: 132–34, 137, 140
telegraph office: 23, 33, 131, 132, 140
Thomas, Daniel: 9, 11, 150
Thomas, Samuel: 14, 218
Thompson, Jacob: 66, 108, 148
Thompson, Kate: 53–59, 69, 107, 143,
    150, 164, 220; *See also* Brown,
    Kate; *also* Warne, Kate
Todd, George B.: 84

U

U.S.S. Montauk: 93, 139
U.S.S. Saugus: 55, 73

V

Vallandigham, Clement: 142, 146
Van Alen, James H.: 18, 25
Van Buren, Martin: 30
Van Lew, Elizabeth: 5
Van Steinacker, Henry: 149
Van Tine, Mary: 63, 67, 223
Verdi, Dr. T. S.: 87, 118
Von Winkiestein, Hans: 149

W

Wade-Davis Bill: 75, 184, 191, 207
WAR DEPARTMENT
Warne, Kate: 54–58, 189, 220; *See also*
    Thompson, Kate; *also* Brown, Kate
WASHINGTON, D.C.
Washington, Melvina: 9
Webster, Timothy: 5
Weichmann, Lewis: 11, 52, 53, 57,
    58, 63, 64, 67, 89, 98, 99–110,
    114–21, 128, 150, 188, 198, 216,
    218, 220, 222, 223
Weitzel, Godfrey: 35, 39–44
Wells, H. H.: 98, 101, 102, 118
Wermerskirch, W. M.: 117, 119
Wharton, J. H.: 65, 67, 224
White House: 5, 36, 37, 50, 51, 70, 73,
    74, 76, 79, 85, 131, 140, 154, 155,
    159, 160, 184, 185; Confederate:
    23, 26
Wood, Fernando: 142
Wood, George B.: 109
Wood, James: 8, 62, 66, 89, 91, 102–
    04, 113, 116–20, 188, 201, 216,
    217, 220, 222, 223; *See also* Powell,
    Lewis; *also* Mosby (nickname)
Wood, William P.: 53, 121, 203
Woodall, Theodore: 137, 138
Woodward, Dr. Joseph J.: 93

Y

Yates, Charles: 56, 58, 59, 62, 69, 122,
    143, 150, 190, 216, 218
yellow fever: 7, 11, 123, 148, 155, 198

Z

Zekiah Swamp: 21, 125

READER'S NOTES

READER'S NOTES

www.ReasonLincoln.com

Visit the web site above for the latest information about this and upcoming books by Don Thomas and Pumphouse Publishers, along with related articles and links.

Available also in large print
and e-book editions.

CPSIA information can be obtained
at www.ICGtesting.com
Printed in the USA
LVHW031722220119
604809LV00002B/301/P

9 780989 422529